The Bible Speaks Today
*Series Editors:* J. A. Motyer (OT)
John R. W. Stott (NT)

# The Message of Chronicles
One Church, one Faith, one Lord

*Kevin Roy*

# Titles in this series

# The Message of Chronicles

## One Church, one Faith, one Lord

**Michael Wilcock**
*Vicar of St Nicholas' Church,*
*Durham*

Inter-Varsity Press
Leicester, England
Downers Grove, Illinois, U.S.A.

InterVarsity Press
*38 De Montfort Street, Leicester LE1 7GP, England*
*P.O. Box 1400, Downers Grove, Illinois 60515, U.S.A.*

*InterVarsity Press®, USA, is the book-publishing division of InterVarsity Christian Fellowship®, a student movement active on campus at hundreds of universities, colleges and schools of nursing in the United States of America, and a member movement of the International Fellowship of Evangelical Students. For information about local and regional activities, write Public Relations Dept., InterVarsity Christian Fellowship, 6400 Schroeder Rd., P.O. Box 7895, Madison, WI 53707-7895.*

*Inter-Varsity Press, England, is the publishing division of the Universities and Colleges Christian Fellowship (formerly the Inter-Varsity Fellowship), a student movement linking Christian Unions in universities and colleges throughout the United Kingdom and the Republic of Ireland, and a member movement of the International Fellowship of Evangelical Students. For information about local and national activities in Great Britain write to UCCF, 38 De Montfort Street, Leicester LE1 7GP.*

*USA ISBN 0-87784-299-X*
*USA ISBN 0-87784-925-0 (set of The Bible Speaks Today)*
*UK ISBN 0-85110-769-9*

*Text set in 11 on 12 Garamond in Great Britain by Swanston Graphics Limited, Derby*
*Printed in the United States of America* ∞

**Library of Congress Cataloging-in-Publication Data**
*Wilcock, Michael*
  *The message of 1 & 2 Chronicles.*
  *(The Bible speaks today)*
  *1. Bible. O.T. Chronicles—Commentaries.*
*I. Title  II. Series.*
*BS1345.3.W43  1987      222'.607      86-27700*

**British Library Cataloguing in Publication Data**
*Wilcock, Michael*
  *The message of Chronicles: one church, one faith, one Lord.*
  *—(The Bible speaks today)*
  *1. Bible. O.T. Chronicles—Commentaries*
*I. Title      II. Series*

16   15   14   13   12   11   10   9   8   7   6   5   4   3   2
05   04   03   02   01   00   99   98   97   96   95   94

# General preface

*The Bible Speaks Today* describes a series of both Old Testament and New Testament expositions, which are characterized by a threefold ideal: to expound the biblical text with accuracy, to relate it to contemporary life, and to be readable.

These books are, therefore, not 'commentaries', for the commentary seeks rather to elucidate the text than to apply it, and tends to be a work rather of reference than of literature. Nor, on the other hand, do they contain the kind of 'sermons' which attempt to be contemporary and readable, without taking Scripture seriously enough.

The contributors to this series are all united in their convictions that God still speaks through what he has spoken, and that nothing is more necessary for the life, health and growth of Christians than that they should hear what the Spirit is saying to them through his ancient – yet ever modern – Word.

J. A. MOTYER
J. R. W. STOTT
*Series Editors*

*To the Atkinsons,*
*Adèle, David, Alan, Peter, and Joy,*
*in memory of John:*
*their husband and father,*
*my colleague and friend*

# Contents

# Contents

# Author's preface

When in 1977 I knew that I should soon be leaving the church I had served for some years past, and that it was likely to be without a full-time minister for an unusually long period, I preached a sermon-series which I hoped would be helpful to those who would be leading the church's life and work in that rather novel situation. The subject of the series was the responsibility of leadership, and for guidelines it looked to the experience of some of the great kings of Judah in Old Testament times, under the title 'The Weight of the Crown'. Since 1977 was, as it happened, the silver jubilee year of Queen Elizabeth II, and the pageantry of the British monarchy was much in evidence in this country, the phrase had an added aptness.

During the years that followed, my mind was increasingly captivated by the lessons God has to teach his people today through those great men of old. The study of Jehoshaphat, Uzziah, Hezekiah, and Josiah led to the study of the other rulers of their line, and then to the way the Books of Chronicles (unlike Samuel/Kings) place the whole Davidic monarchy in the setting of the history of the world and the covenant plan of God. I have tried to share with God's people in many different places some of the good things I have learned from the Chronicler's magnificent sermon. Since the publication of these studies was first mooted, I have much appreciated the patience of Alec Motyer and Frank Entwistle, the hospitality of Bill and Shirley Lees, and the encouragement of all four, as the gaps have been gradually filled in and the exposition written up. My prayer is that the Chronicler may be heard by yet another generation of the one church, as he preaches the one faith, to the glory of the one Lord.

MICHAEL WILCOCK

# Chief abbreviations

Ackroyd — *I & II Chronicles, Ezra, Nehemiah* by Peter R. Ackroyd (*Torch Bible Paperbacks*, SCM, 1973).

AV — *The Authorized* (King James') *Version* of the Bible (1611).

Coggins — *First and Second Books of Chronicles* by R. J. Coggins (*Cambridge Bible Commentary on the NEB*, CUP, 1976).

Curtis & Madsen — *Chronicles I and II* by E. L. Curtis and A. A. Madsen (*International Critical Commentary*, T. & T. Clark, 1910).

GNB — *The Good News Bible* (The Bible Societies and Collins; NT 1966, 4th edition 1976; OT 1976).

Goldingay — 'The Chronicler as a Theologian', *Biblical Theology Bulletin*, Vol. 2, June 1975, pp. 99–126.

*IBD* — *The Illustrated Bible Dictionary* (IVP, 1980).

JB — *The Jerusalem Bible* (Darton, Longman and Todd, 1966).

Keil — *The Books of the Chronicles* by C. F. Keil (*Biblical Commentary on the Old Testament*, Eng. tr. Edinburgh 1872).

McConville — *Chronicles* by J. G. McConville (*Daily Study Bible*, St Andrew Press, 1984).

Myers — *1 Chronicles* and *2 Chronicles* by J. M. Myers (*Anchor Bible*, Doubleday, New York, 1965).

NAS — *The New American Standard Bible* (1963).

NEB — *The New English Bible* (NT 1961, 2nd edition 1970; OT 1970).

NIV — *The New International Version* of the Bible (Hodder & Stoughton; NT 1973; OT 1979).

Payne — *Kingdoms of the Lord* by David F. Payne (Paternoster, 1981).

RSV — *The Revised Standard Version* of the Bible (NT 1946, 2nd edition 1971; OT 1952).

RV — *The Revised Version* of the Bible (1885).

Thiele — *The Mysterious Numbers of the Hebrew Kings* by Edwin R. Thiele (Eerdmans, Grand Rapids, revised edition 1965; originally published Chicago, 1951).

Williamson    *Chronicles I and II* by H. G. M. Williamson (*New Century Bible*, Marshall Morgan & Scott/Eerdmans, 1982).

Williamson,    *Israel in the Books of Chronicles* by H. G. M.
Israel         Williamson (CUP, 1977).

## A note on commentaries

Commentators and authors of related studies who have been quoted in the text are listed under 'Chief abbreviations' above. Two of the most recent works are also among the most useful. Hugh Williamson's must now be the standard English commentary on Chronicles; together with his earlier *Israel in the Books of Chronicles* it is a mine of good things, exegetically rich and theologically perceptive. Gordon McConville's contribution to the *Daily Study Bible* is, like the New Testament volumes with which William Barclay established that series, more of an exposition than a commentary. Reading it when my own manuscript was nearly complete, I found it so helpful that I almost began to wonder whether there was any point in the publication of a *Chronicles* volume in this series as well! But the interested reader who gets to know Williamson's and McConville's books will find, I hope, that mine builds on the one and complements the other.

11

# Introduction

First impressions can be misleading. In the case of Chronicles they usually are. But they may be pointers to the true nature of these books, if we consider them more closely. 'Is that *really* what Chronicles is?' we ask ourselves; and though the answer may be No, the enquiry will have proved productive.

## 1. A valley of dry bones

Hearing some while ago that I was engaged in this project, an old friend remarked that I could scarcely have chosen a drier subject, and that my book should be called 'Can these bones live?'! The long term lists of names which confront us especially in 1 Chronicles could deaden the enthusiasm of the keenest reader, and some are even repeated, as if once were not enough. Long descriptions of the temple and its worship are surely nowadays of antiquarian interest only. When the story-telling does get under way, events in the northern kingdom of Israel, where so much of the action was, are practically ignored, and even the colourful wickednesses of the Davidic kings in the south are tidied out of the way. Besides, that whole world is in any case long dead.

We should remember, though, that it was equally dead for the first readers of Chronicles. The book – two volumes in our Bibles, but a single one originally – was probably published in the fourth century BC.[1] We know nothing about the author beyond what we can deduce from his own writing,[2] and so we call him for

[1] See Williamson, pp. 15f.; Williamson, *Israel*, pp. 83–86.
[2] Against the old tradition that he was Ezra the scribe, and therefore wrote a century earlier, see Williamson, p. 17.

convenience the Chronicler. But we do know something about those for whom he wrote. They were subjects of the Persian empire, descendants of those Israelites who had been restored to their homeland in Judah after the deportations of the sixth century. Practically everything in the Chronicler's book was for them part of an age gone by. His stories belonged to a world separated from theirs by the gulf of the exile, and the people in those stories were all, by the time of writing, dry bones – as dry for his original readers as for us.

But he would say that that memorable picture in the prophecy of Ezekiel, the valley of dry bones,[3] should be understood the other way round. It is his present readers who need the breath of life, and his message from the past which will bring it to them.

In mentioning just now his omissions from the story of the Hebrew kingdoms, I have already taken for granted another view of his book. It can of course be read as an historical narrative running parallel to that of the books of Samuel and Kings. Hence our next heading.

## 2. Alternative history

What seems at a casual glance to be a re-telling of Samuel/Kings turns out to be something more than a mere repeat. Indeed there are considerable differences between the two histories. In Goldingay's words, the Chronicler writes history of an unprecedented sweep, going back to the very beginnings of mankind; and where he does cover the same ground as Samuel/Kings, he uses those books as a source, but with great freedom, adding quite as much as he omits.[4] So although he may seem in some ways an unattractive writer, with a number of bees in his bonnet, eccentric ideas as to what is important and interesting, and a tendency to exaggerate, he can at any rate be seen as a helpful provider of extra information about the history of the people of God.

But this neglected book deserves a better rehabilitation than that. It is more than an alternative history. It is, as I shall be emphasizing right from the outset of this exposition, a sermon. Its object is the fostering of a right relationship between God and his people. It sees in the records of Israel the 'great overall pattern … of failure and

---

[3] Ezk. 37.    [4] See below, pp. 25–26; Goldingay, pp. 99ff.

judgment, grace and restoration',[5] and with a perceptive eye to those events in the nation's history which highlight the pattern, it first selects and then proclaims.

Two of the words just quoted ('failure and judgment') can however indicate a third easy misunderstanding of the meaning and purpose of Chronicles. Granted that it is not just a narrative, but a sermon; not just history, but theology – granted these things, it does seem to the superficial reader to be preaching a God who, in the best traditions of folk-religion, looks down from heaven with alternate smiles and frowns, blessing good people and punishing bad ones. Can that simple view be right?

## 3. Popular morality

Forsaking for the moment the pulpit for the stage, one might almost call such a presentation of history a 'morality play'. It is highly dramatic (yes, there is drama in Chronicles, once you get beyond the dullness of the genealogies), with villains of the deepest dye and heroes who are paragons of virtue. It is all flamboyant gestures, thick black eyebrows, and ham acting. The curtain is not allowed to fall until evil has been confounded and good has triumphed.

Needless to say, this is a caricature of what the Chronicler has to proclaim. But we do need to consider what there is in his work that gives rise to such notions. We shall in due course look at his teaching about retribution,[6] but we may say at once that his God is a God of inflexible justice. We must not 'so expound one place of Scripture, that it be repugnant to another',[7] and we must not set up a contradiction between the simple view of moral consequences in Psalm 1:3, 6 ('In all that he does', the good man 'prospers ... but the way of the wicked will perish') and the difficult one in Psalm 73:12–14 ('The wicked ... at ease ... increase in riches', but 'I ... in innocence ... have been stricken').[8] But the Chronicler does more often than not choose to recount incidents of the first sort, as the clearest kind of demonstration that divine justice cannot fail.

Nor, on the other hand, can divine grace fail; that too is

---

[5] Ackroyd, p. 27.

[6] See below, p. 36, 182 n. 14, 258–259.

[7] Article XX of the Church of England.

[8] We might similarly contrast the simplicity of Proverbs (*e.g.* 12:21) and the complexity of Job (*passim*).

unchangeable. The very institution of kingship in Israel illustrates it. In the north, the hereditary principle never holds good for more than five generations in a row; crown and sceptre are for those who can take them. In the south, it persists almost throughout; crown and sceptre are for those to whom God gives them – David and his descendants are kings, not through their merit, but through God's grace. And by many examples besides this one the Chronicler shows how unfailing is God's *ḥesed*, his constant mercy and steadfast love. Even those dull name-lists are all about the binding together of the generations in the one gracious plan of the covenant-keeping God.

With the kingship we shall note also the priesthood. Together they form the double core of the life of Israel. There will be much to say on that subject later; we shall come back repeatedly to their inner meaning, the representation of God to man and of man to God, and to the application of such lessons to the life of God's people today. But kingship and priesthood too provide a clear, simplified picture of the constant principles by which God deals with man.

In a word, 'principles' is the Chronicler's theme. He finds them operating in history selects unmistakable, black-and-white instances of them, and applies them to his own times. 'It was his purpose to hold up to his contemporaries as a mirror the history of the past.'[9] And as he speaks to the people of his own time, so he speaks to us. The very objection that 'Our world is different from the world of the Israelite monarchy' makes us exactly the kind of audience he means to address.

We note at this point that it is the *facts* of history from which he is preaching. He has no need to distort them in order to get his message across. Indeed it would defeat his object were he to do so. But the thought points to another inaccurate notion of what his book is: the work of a spinner of tales.

## 4. Inventive story-telling

The Chronicler certainly makes additions and alterations in his re-writing of the Samuel/Kings narratives, and he certainly does heighten the effect thereby. It has been suggested, for instance, that in describing the events of a past era Chronicles may use the

[9] Keil, p. 19. On the 'mirror' of history, see below, p. 141 n. 25.

corresponding terms and figures of its own era ('He was *what we should call* commander-in-chief'; 'They paid *the equivalent of* a million pounds').[10] But to say that the Chronicler dresses his subjects in modern clothes, so to speak, by what translators call 'dynamic equivalence', is one thing; to say that he is less interested in objective facts than in creating an effect if necessary by fabrication, is quite another. I shall have a good deal to say on this in the course of the exposition; but it is worth pointing out here and now the unfortunate tendency, even among moderate writers, to regard the Chronicler's way of writing history as being somehow inferior to the way we try to do it today. For example: 'The Chronicler is not at all a writer of history in our sense of the term; he does not aim to relate what took place but what serves to edify.'[11] Or again: 'It is anachronistic to expect standards of historical accuracy such as are nowadays regarded as usual.'[12] The truth is that there is no such thing (in the writing of history or anywhere else) as unprejudiced study, an approach without presuppositions, an objective search for 'the facts' which does not select some data and reject others. There is, in brief, no such thing as an open mind. The very judgment that the Bible historians' standards were inferior to ours itself arises from a set of presuppositions. *Of course* the Chronicler adds here, omits there, highlights this, soft-pedals that; he is writing selectively. The modern 'objective' historian does exactly the same. *Of course* the modern historian is pursuing facts and accuracy. The Chronicler is doing exactly the same. It is a false dichotomy to set, as Benzinger did, 'what took place' in opposition to 'what serves to edify'. The Chronicler does not need to invent in order to edify. He lets the facts speak – some speak more plainly than others – and then tells us what they say; and it is 'what took place' that edifies.[13]

[10] See Goldingay, pp. 110f.

[11] I. Benzinger, *Die Bücher der Chronik* (1901), quoted by Myers, *1 Chronicles*, p. 59.

[12] Coggins, p. 5. The older liberal commentators went further: Chronicles is 'a tendency writing of little historical value' – such facts as it contains are 'few indeed compared with the products of the imagination, and must be sifted like kernels of wheat from a mass of chaff' (Curtis & Madsen, pp. 14f.).

[13] *Cf.* Barbara Tuchman, *Practising History* (Macmillan, 1983): 'The writer of history ... has a number of duties ... The first is to distil. He must ... assemble the information, make sense of it, select the essential, discard the irrelevant ... Selection is what determines the ultimate product' (p. 17). If the historian will 'submit himself *to* his material instead of trying to impose himself *on* his material, then the material will ultimately speak to him and supply the answers' (p. 23). *Cf.* also David Bebbington, *Patterns in History* (IVP, 1979), especially chapters 7 and 8.

## 5. The last book of the Bible

A reader new to Chronicles might see it (wrongly, in the event) as a valley of dry bones, as alternative history, as popular morality, or as inventive story-telling. It is unlikely that he would see it as the last book of the Bible! Unless, that is, he were reading in Hebrew – for then he would find it right at the end; it closes the canon of the Hebrew scriptures.

There is no agreement as to why it stands in that position; but it seems a fitting one. The Chronicler's selectivity, which we have just been considering, is not unlike that of the writer of the last of the Gospels, reflecting on innumerable memories of the earthly life of Christ, and making a new selection from them to teach afresh the old fundamental truths.[14] Similarly, the way the Chronicler summarizes such truths, teaching nothing which could not be found elsewhere in Scripture, yet teaching with a sense of vividness, contrast, and drama which are all his own, must recall the last book of the New Testament. Like John and Revelation, Chronicles rounds off an entire major section of Scripture by saying 'This is what it is really all about. This is what it has always been about, what it always will be about.' The countless people that our writer has named and chronicled for us are not dry bones; they are part of the one army of the living God. They are real, and by their continuity and solidarity with us they make real also for us the truth by which God's people in every generation are to live. Strikingly apt are the well-known lines by the Victorian hymn-writer Edward Hayes Plumptre:

> Thy hand, O God, has guided
> Thy flock from age to age;
> The wondrous tale is written
> Full clear on every page;
> Our fathers owned thy goodness,
> And we their deeds record;
> And both of this bear witness,
> 'One Church, one Faith, one Lord'.

[14] Jn. 20:30–31; 21:24–25.

# Part One
# THE TREE OF THE LORD'S PLANTING
# (1 Chronicles 1 – 9)

## 1 Chronicles 1 – 3

## 1. Roots

'The first book of the Chronicles. Adam, Seth, Enosh, Kenan, Mahalalel, Jared ...' What in the world is this? Turn the page quickly: in fact turn the next ten pages, and let us try to find something at least readable, if not actually interesting. For what is the use of a book, said Alice, without pictures or conversations? And what could be more stupendously dull than the first nine chapters of 1 Chronicles? Concerning its opening words, we may in due course revise that opinion. But the look of its opening pages as a whole! Nowadays a more modern turn of phrase has usually replaced the AV's 'begats', the crumbling mortar which once held all this together, but even with such a repointing the bricks remain their antiquated selves – hundreds of proper names (200 in chapter 1 alone), in a foreign, not to say a dead, language, most of them conveying little or nothing to the present-day reader.

But the Chronicler, the unknown writer of these histories, has great stories to tell and powerful lessons to teach. And it is in this way that he has chosen to introduce them. We may take it therefore that to grasp his message we need to come to grips with his introduction.

When we see that it consists almost entirely of genealogies, we are supplied with a key to the understanding of it. For what we have here is a series of family trees; and the 'tree' image is one of those universal pictures by which God so often in Scripture illustrates his greatest truths with such simplicity that anyone can understand them.

## 1.  The Tree

Sometimes the tree is an oak, sometimes a fig-tree, sometimes a vine.[1] In each case it represents the people of God. Since we speak of a table of descent, and usually trace a genealogy downwards, the idea of a 'river' might seem more apt. But that points to the greatness of the latest generation, and tends to belittle the streams that have contributed to it. The Chronicler's object is if anything the reverse. The nature and unity of the great stock from which the branches have grown upwards – these are his theme.

The details he puts together to make up the picture of his Tree are varied in origin. He may use some of the older biblical books that we also know, or similar histories that have since been lost. He is (and this is to be borne in mind throughout our reading of Chronicles) *reminding* his earliest readers of things which they, as Israelites steeped in Israelite history, already know well.

Let us see what goes to make up his first three chapters.

The trunk of the Tree rises straight for ten generations from Adam to Noah (1:1–4a). At that point it begins to divide, but still between the branches we can glimpse the vertical central stem, from Noah's son Shem to Abraham, Isaac, and Jacob (or Israel, as the Chronicler habitually calls him; 1:24–28, 34); then through Judah to Hezron, and on to Jesse and David (2:1, 3–5, 9–15); rising

---

[1] Is. 61:3; Lk. 13:6ff.; Ps. 80:8ff.; Is. 5:1–7; and Mt. 21:33–45. Compare also the mustard shrub of Mt. 13:31ff.

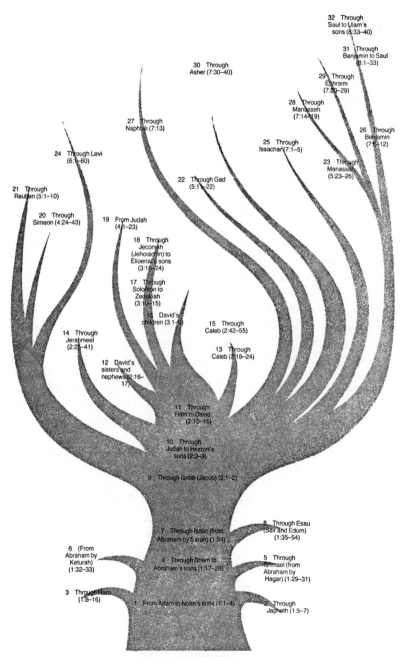

32 Through Saul to Ulam's sons (8:33–40)

31 Through Benjamin to Saul (8:1–33)

30 Through Asher (7:30–40)

29 Through Ephraim (7:20–29)

28 Through Manasseh (7:14–19)

27 Through Naphtali (7:13)

26 Through Benjamin (7:6–12)

25 Through Issachar (7:1–5)

24 Through Levi (6:1–80)

23 Through Manasseh (5:23–26)

22 Through Gad (5:11–22)

21 Through Reuben (5:1–10)

20 Through Simeon (4:24–43)

19 From Judah (4:1–23)

18 Through Jeconiah (Jehoiachin) to Elioenai's sons (3:16–24)

17 Through Solomon to Zedekiah (3:10–15)

16 David's children (3:1–9)

15 Through Caleb (2:42–55)

14 Through Jerahmeel (2:25–41)

13 Through Caleb (2:18–24)

12 David's sisters and nephews (2:16–17)

11 Through Ram to David (2:10–15)

10 Through Judah to Hezron's sons (2:3–9)

9 Through Israel (Jacob) (2:1–2)

8 Through Esau (Seir and Edom) (1:35–54)

7 Through Isaac (from Abraham by Sarah) (1:34)

6 (From Abraham by Keturah) (1:32–33)

5 Through Ishmael (from Abraham by Hagar) (1:29–31)

4 Through Shem to Abraham's sons (1:17–28)

3 Through Ham (1:8–16)

2 Through Japheth (1:5–7)

1 From Adam to Noah's sons (1:1–4)

**The growth of the Tree**

21

through the reigns of twenty kings up to Zedekiah (3:1, 5, 10–16), and finally, after the Babylonian conquest, reaching its most recent generation, presumably in the Chronicler's own time (3:17–24).

As much space if not more is devoted to the lateral branching of the Tree. At each of a dozen points we are shown a group of brothers, the immediate families, for example, of Noah, of Israel/Jacob, of Jesse and David, of Josiah and Jehoiakim (1:4; 2:1–2, 13–16; 3:1–9, 15–16). Where these branches fork, the first son to be mentioned may be the eldest, as with Noah's son Shem and Jacob's son Reuben (1:4; 2:1), or a younger but more important one, as with Abraham's sons Isaac and Ishmael (1:28). A noteworthy point here, however, concerns the order in which the sons are followed up in detail. In chapter 1, the side branches are dealt with first, and the son representing the main trunk is reserved till last. But from the beginning of chapter 2 the opposite method is used. The Chronicler lists the twelve sons of Israel, and then focuses at once on Judah, who is only fourth in order but will be of prime importance. The fact that this change in method comes in the time of Jacob is another hint (along with the fact noted above, that in these books he is almost always known as Israel) that he holds a special place in the Chronicler's scheme of things.

Included with these genealogies are lists, not of family relationships, but of rulers – the kings, and after them the chiefs, of Edom (1:43–54). Sometimes indeed the Tree includes names which from those of individual persons shade into those of whole peoples (e.g. 1:11–12, 14ff.), countries (1:5–8), and even towns (2:42, 50–51).

To complete the rich confusion, the Chronicler here and there weaves into his fabric various incidents and events, which are related to people he has mentioned. Unexpectedly, these are not great turning points of biblical history such as the flood and the exodus, but an odd scattering of curiosities (e.g. 1:19, 50; 2:7, 34–35).

The idea of the Tree serves us in two ways, as we try to see Israel's history through the Chronicler's eyes. From one point of view he is working *upwards* from ground level; the remotest past is the base of the trunk, and the Chronicler and his readers are the topmost branches. But from another, he and they (and we) are to be regarded as the Tree itself, and his delving into past history is a working *down* from ground level to discover and understand the roots of the people of God. We follow out this latter idea.

## 2. Why the roots are needed

Seven sons of a man named Elioenai (3:24) are the most recently-sprouted leaves at the top of the Tree, perhaps men residing in the very town in which the Chronicler himself is living and writing. The kingdoms of Israel and Judah have both long since ended in invasion, ruin, and exile. Years have gone by. Some of the exiles have returned, and their descendants are living quietly as subjects of the king of Persia in what is now merely a small province of his immense empire. The date is some time in the fourth century BC, and we are at the very end of Old Testament history. In fact we might see Chronicles in a new, and truer, light if it occupied in our English Bibles the position it holds in the Hebrew scriptures; for it is, as we have already noted, the last book of the Hebrew Bible, the conclusion, in more senses than one, of God's Old Testament message.

This is what makes it of peculiar interest today. The circumstances of the people for whom the Chronicler first wrote are scarcely unfamiliar to us. We have only to imagine those readers looking back over history. 'There were great days once', we hear them say, 'days when great things happened – so at least one is told – and when God was unmistakably at work in our world. He used to send prophets to teach men his ways; he appointed kings, and before kings, judges, to govern and protect them; before all that he had rescued his people from slavery, formed them into a nation, and given them a land. Earlier still, he had brought Abraham out of the city of Ur, and Noah out of the waters of the flood, and Adam out of the dust of the earth, and the earth itself out of nothing. But', they continue, 'those fabulous days are past. We live in a different world. The story of old Israel is just that – a tale in a story-book: we will not say fictional, but we will say irrelevant. We have moved out of that ancient Bible world into this secular modern world. We do not deny that there are links between the two; but we wonder very much how meaningful those links are. There is still a nation of Israel, but it comprises only a few of the twelve tribes and only remnants of any of them. There is still a land of Canaan, but we occupy only a small portion of it. There is still a house of David, but its royal glory has long departed. There is still a temple in Jerusalem, but it is a second-rate thing, far inferior to the one it replaces. Even if the people of God are not persecuted, they are (which is worse) ignored. They are a feeble minority in a world which in practice bears no relation to the world of their Bible. For them the future is unknown, and the past is meaningless.' So these fourth-century Israelites might complain.

It is precisely to this situation that the Chronicler addresses himself. It is, in modern jargon, an identity crisis. The people of God need to know what they are and what they are meant to be, in a society which, if it interests itself in them at all, will want only to use them for its own worldly ends. And when they question what they, the people of God, are, the Chronicler's answer is to remind them of what they *have been*. The 'changes and chances of this fleeting world' tend to disconcert the church of God; an understanding of the great continuities will reassure and inspire it. For at bottom the nature and calling of the church are no different now from what they always were. I say 'the church'; for that perpetual 'now' enables us to associate ourselves directly with the Chronicler's own generation. By the very terms of his argument, the principles he is going to set forth apply equally to all his readers, ancient and modern, and are in no way affected by the mere lapse of centuries.

Hence his prescription for those who, like a plant growing on rocky ground, are scorched and withered in the heat of circumstance:[2] 'What you need is roots.' Or rather, they *feel* rootless; and he wants them to be aware of, and to learn to draw up nourishment through, the roots which do in fact exist.

## 3. Where the roots take hold

It is into that very history which you think irrelevant (he tells them) that your roots must strike down to find nourishment. Today's Israel is to be encouraged and invigorated by the study of yesterday's Israel.

It is not hard to follow the Chronicler's reasoning. In a time of bewilderment we are glad of the guidance of one who says 'I know this path; I have been this way myself; come with me.' That is the voice of experience. Particularly do we appreciate it if the total testimony, from birth to death, of a leader in God's church is speaking to us in this manner: that is the voice of biography — 'consider the outcome of their life, and imitate their faith.'[3] When a series of biographies is put together, and they are integrated with one another and with as much social, political, and religious

---

[2] See Mt. 13:5–6.     [3] Heb. 13:7.

24

background material as will enable us to see the overall picture, that is more helpful still – the voice of history. And when the history is that which God himself has moved his servants to record as an authoritative account of his ways with men, and what we are listening to is the voice of *biblical* history, that is best of all. 'Whatever was written in former days was written for our instruction, that by steadfastness and *by encouragement of the scriptures* we might have hope.'[4]

So the soil in which the roots are to take hold is biblical history. The Chronicler prepares it well. The notion that his work is nothing but a slightly differing version of the books of Samuel and Kings, as if he and the earlier writer were a couple of rival newspaper reporters, is scotched at once by a look at the opening pages. This is something quite different from the work of that other great Old Testament historian. What exactly *is* our man doing, though?

We should in these chapters notice two characteristics of the way he writes history. One is that he is writing for people who are in any case very history-conscious, and who have been brought up to be keenly aware of their nation's past and well versed in the contents of their scriptures.[5] In other words (and this is something we shall need to recall frequently), his first readers, as I said earlier, know the facts already. We may even suppose them to possess histories like Samuel and Kings, and to be able therefore to check what this new book says both by reference to the older ones and by memory. The Chronicler is not informing them of things they do not know; he is interpreting for them and applying to them things they do know. He is, in a word, preaching.

He preaches the inner meaning, the spiritual message, of his people's history by a careful editing of the material which is available. This is what he is doing in his first three chapters, when he pieces together name-lists drawn from the entire time-span of the historical books of the Old Testament. This is what he will continue to do in his remaining sixty-two chapters, by means of a detailed treatment of the monarchy. In order to make his various points, he will for one thing add material which the other authors omit. Hence what may seem the more obvious differences between him and

---

[4] Rom. 15:4.

[5] Many Old Testament passages refer to the way the story of God's dealings with Israel was handed down from generation to generation. See Gn. 18:19; Ex. 12:26–27; Dt. 4:9; 6:7; Jos. 4:6–7; Pss. 44:1; 78:1–8; 102:18; Joel 1:3; *etc.*

them, when in the regular reading of the older books, for example in lectionaries for public worship, his work may be called on to fill the gaps; indeed the Greek name for it was actually *Ta Paraleipomena*, 'The Omissions'.[6] But he does not simply insert items elsewhere omitted. Sometimes he leaves out items elsewhere included. Sometimes, again, he uses the Samuel/Kings account practically as it stands; whereas sometimes he alters it drastically. The methods by which he gives his own slant on the story are, as we shall see, intensely interesting, and their object is always to re-present already-known facts so as to preach a sermon and teach a lesson.

But although he is *preaching* from facts, yet still he is preaching from *facts*. It is important to realize this. The two kinds of history-writing, the new and the old, may seem very different from each other. Modern history can indeed, on occasion, be a kind of 'preaching', with points to be applied and lessons to be learned by its readers. But its primary concern is *the facts*, objectively researched and accurately recorded, whether or not they have any present-day application. So it may be felt that the older kind of history (such as the Chronicler's), which regularly tried to 'make a point', must occasionally have sat rather loose to objective accuracy, and should be allowed its little exaggerations here and embroideries there, which were thought to make it more effective as preaching. As Goldingay makes clear, however, these ancient historians were not, as a matter of fact, given to inventing material.[7] On reflection, one can see why. If the lesson to be conveyed is that 'the Lord is the kind of God who deals with men in such-and-such a way', and if then the preacher can find no actual examples of the Lord's acting in this way, and is compelled to invent them, what sort of a lesson is that? Either God does act thus, in which case the preacher will be able to cite historical examples, or he does not, in which case there is no point in preaching the sermon anyway.

## 4.  How far the roots reach down

Which book of the Bible has the most arresting first verse? Genesis? John? Or perhaps Mark, or Revelation, or (in its famous AV translation) Hebrews? In that august company Chronicles holds a worthy place. The reading eye strays down the page, and is too soon

---

[6] See Ackroyd, pp. 21–22.    [7] Goldingay, pp. 109f.

dismayed by the genealogical labyrinth that lies ahead. But to the hearing ear the names come one at a time, and then (especially if the ear is Hebrew) with how majestic a roll of distant drums is this book heard to begin! 'Adam,' proclaims the Chronicler. 'Adam: the Man, founder of the race, father of humanity, first of the people of God ... Seth, Enosh; Kenan, Mahalalel, Jared; Enoch who never died, and Methuselah who lived so long; Lamech and his famous son Noah ...'

We remind ourselves that our writer's contemporaries are men like Elioenai (3:23–24), whose 'modern' generation has to face an uninspiring present and a bleak future, and sees little help in an alien past. That is why roots are needed. The Chronicler knows however that that past is actually the soil in which the roots must take hold, and he sketches a swift panorama of it from 1:1 to 3:24. So moving back towards his opening verses we now find how far the roots reach down.

As we have seen, the central question to which he addresses himself is: 'Who and what are the people of God?' His answer is: 'I will show you that the church, the community of those who know God, "the blessed company of all faithful people", can be traced back from our day through every generation of our ancestors to the very beginnings of history; and its essential nature is throughout unaffected by the revolutions of time.'

In his review of the past he fastens on three points in particular. We might think (and we should be right) that few events in the Old Testament story can equal in importance the creation of all things, the call of Abraham as the father of the chosen family, and the forming of that family into a nation under Moses at the time of the exodus. The Chronicler, however, far from stressing these three crucial acts of God, does not even mention them. Abraham and Moses themselves appear simply as names in the genealogies, the former three times, the latter only once (1:27, 28, 34; 6:3). Instead, we notice three other points of emphasis. First, there is the space devoted to David, his ancestors and descendants (2:3–12; 3:10–24), his immediate family (2:13–17; 3:1–9), and others of his relatives within the tribe of Judah (2:18–55).[8] Secondly, moving

---

[8] Note the careful structure of these paragraphs about David's family:

> 2:3–12 his ancestors
>   2:13–17 his brothers, sisters, and nephews
>     2:18–55 his 'cousins'
>   3:1–9 his wives and children
> 3:10–24 his descendants

back down the Tree, at an important juncture we find Jacob. The detailed genealogies of his twelve sons begin at 2:1, at a point where there is a change in the way the Chronicler's lists are set out;[9] our attention is also caught by his being called persistently by his second name Israel. Thirdly, we cannot miss, at the root of the whole mighty growth, the name of Adam, to which I have already referred.

Why Adam, Israel, and David, rather than Abraham and Moses, as key figures in this scheme of things? The choice is, I believe, not only deliberate, but highly significant. To Moses came one of the most spectacular initiatives of grace in the story of mankind, when God, having rescued his people from slavery in Egypt, 'came down upon Mount Sinai' to constitute them his own holy nation.[10] To Abraham had come an earlier revelation, which, although in the nature of the case given to an individual and not to a people, was even more extraordinary, as by it God appointed his servant to be the father not only of a great family, but of many nations.[11] God would in due course speak also to Jacob and to David; but it was his covenants with Abraham and Moses which were the great creative, constitutive, words of grace. Before David establishes the kingdom, God has through Moses created a nation which will become that kingdom. Before Israel fathers his twelve sons, God has in Abraham appointed the ancestor from whom will spring that entire family. Nor is it otherwise with the last – the first – of these great figures of antiquity: before Adam begets Seth, God has taken the most awe-inspiring of all the initiatives, and covenanted with himself to bring into being the one who will stand at the head of the whole human race, as well as the world he is to rule.

The framework of history is in this way seen to comprise three pairs of events. God creates all things; in due course Adam procreates the rest of mankind. God calls Abraham; in due course Israel sires the twelve patriarchs. God calls Moses; in due course David sets up the kingdom. In each of these three pairings, it is with the second member that the Chronicler is concerned. Not, of course, that he is uninterested in the prior workings of grace; very

This pattern of writing, known as 'chiasmus' (= 'crossing over', from the Greek letter *chi*, **X**), is not uncommon in the Old Testament; see Williamson, p. 49, the discussions in F. I. Andersen, *Job* (Inter-Varsity Press, 1976), pp. 110–111, and J. G. Baldwin, *Haggai, Zechariah, Malachi* (Inter-Varsity Press, 1972), pp. 74–81, and the headings for chapter 8 of this book.

[9] See above, p. 22.    [10] Ex. 19:20, 6.    [11] Gn. 12:1–3; 17:5.

far from it, as we shall see. But his great interest is to show how they 'surface', so to speak, at the level of human activity. What, as a practical response to the grace of God, are we, the people of God, to be like? As descendants of David, we are to be the twentieth-century version of his kingdom; as descendants of Israel, the modern equivalent of his family; as descendants of Adam, the true humanity. The model which Chronicles will develop in greatest detail is the kingdom. But the people of God are one continuous entity from root to topmost leaf, from Adam to the sons of Elioenai – that is, to us ourselves.

## 5. What the roots draw up

It remains to define (though it may already have been sufficiently suggested) what it is that the roots draw up – what, in a word, the sap of the Tree is.

Two particular features of chapters 1 to 3 should be noted. One is the Chronicler's insistence on the *connections* within his narrative. The father-to-son connection, plainly seen where the vertical trunk of the Tree is being depicted, as from Adam to Noah (1:1–4a) or from Solomon to Josiah (3:10–14), is only one of several kinds to be found here. We have seen also lists of brothers (2:1–2), of tribes and peoples (1:5–16), of unrelated but consecutive kings (1:43–51), and so forth. There is not always genealogical descent; but there is always some kind of sequence. Although several of the details may be obscure to us, and the links between the sequences may not always be obvious, and the Chronicler himself may occasionally have found them hard to reconcile or to complete, there is no escaping the impression that for him the thing is all of a piece. 'Only connect', pleads the title page of E. M. Forster's *Howard's End*, and this is a dominant theme in that novel: the tragedy of not seeing the necessary relations between people, and things, which may indeed seem to be remote from each other, but which nevertheless belong together and need each other.

The overall connection, binding the generations of antiquity to those of the Chronicler and ourselves, implies also that old and new are equally factual. We must not let ourselves be persuaded that at any point in Chronicles we have to do with mere legend or invention. The main characteristic of all stories which begin 'Once upon a time ...' is that their 'time' nowhere actually connects with any real historical time of ours. But that his records do all belong to the same continuum is the very point the Chronicler is labouring to make. The connection between these ancients and us means that they are as real as we are.

This leads directly to the second noteworthy feature of chapters 1 to 3. Scattered throughout them we find a variety of miniature portraits, bits of information, odd incidents which (if for a moment we desert our 'sap' metaphor) we may compare to knots in the weave of fabric or the grain of wood. For 1:10, the cameo of Nimrod 'who became the world's first great conqueror' (GNB), we have a parallel in Genesis 10:8, where verses 9 to 12 tell us more about this remarkable man. For the curious facts concerning Hadad king of Edom, in 1:50, no such cross-reference has survived. But for the Chronicler's original readers both items were no doubt meant as reminders, locating his references in an outline of history they already knew. So a list of the kings of England might include 'Henry VIII (the one who had six wives)', or a sketch of American history might mention 'Lincoln (who was president during the Civil War)'.

Other 'knots' may have the further purpose of illustrating theological points. The sins of Er (2:3) and of Achar (2:7) show that birth among the people of God does not in itself guarantee a good standing before God. On the other hand the inclusion of Bathshua (2:3) and Tamar (2:4) shows that neither a pagan background nor an incestuous relationship in itself precludes membership of that people. Racial descent is not ultimately the thing that decides who does and who does not belong to God. As Nimrod and Hadad are to be thought of as historical facts, so these are theological facts. Indeed they are themes destined for important development later in the book,[12] and they even point forward to our New Testament church, able to appropriate these teachings as its own because, being itself constituted by grace and not by race, it finds itself to be one with this church of Old Testament days.

That profound spiritual unity across centuries and across cultures may also be the reason for the 'knot' in 1:19, the comment on the meaning of Peleg's name ('Division'). In his days there began to be

---

[12] They are also points which tell against the widely-held view that Chronicles, Ezra, and Nehemiah are all by the same author, being distinctly unlike the emphasis of the two latter books. *E.g.* 'We note again', seeing Bathshua the Canaanitess followed by Jether the Ishmaelite (2:3, 17), 'that the Chronicler does not seem to have been troubled by the inclusion of non-Israelites' (Williamson, p. 52).

imposed on the map of mankind the territorial divisions which soon became, and have remained, one of the most troublesome of all the facts of human life. But 'from the beginning it was not so'.[13] Humanity is a stronger, because older, bond than nationality, and insofar as the Chronicler is describing not only the peoples of the earth but the people of God, faith is a stronger bond still. This too will be developed by him as an unchanging lesson for his readers in all ages.[14]

So his finger, tracing the connections and pointing out the knots, shows us that (to revert to our original image) the sap of the Tree, its strength, is continuity. All his narratives will illustrate the unchanging principles of God's dealings. The men of whom we shall read are real flesh-and-blood people, and our ancestors. Our fathers, the scripture would call them; and if we were to say how quaint it' seemed to call someone our father when he was 'really' a distant ancestor,[15] the Chronicler would I think retort that his idiom represented the truth better than ours. It is one of our modern heresies to hold that the great continuities can be stretched to breaking-point by the mere passage of time. It is no virtue for the twentieth century to regard itself as a period whose needs and problems are unique. Even if no-one else will do it, the church must put its roots down through a century of centuries, and find in every one of them the continuing people of God, and the continuing principles by which they prove his reality: 'one church, one faith, one Lord'.

[13] Mt. 19:8.
[14] The New Testament implications may be followed up in Acts 17:26–27; Rom. 3:22–23, 29–30; 1 Cor. 15:22; Gal. 3:28; Col. 3:11.
[15] See below, p. 178 n. 6.

# 1 Chronicles 4 – 7

## 2. Branches

The Chronicler brings together as his next four chapters a bewildering collection of name-lists. Here is the stock of God's people in all its ramifications – no, not all, for that would be impossible; but enough of its branching, up through those times and across those territories, to give an impression of the whole. In other words, chapters 4 to 7 portray the tribes of Israel.

To the modern mind the picture is no doubt a rather unsatisfying one. Some of its peculiarities – for example disproportion (Levi with more than eighty verses, Naphtali with only one) and repetition (Judah figuring in chapters 2 to 3, and Benjamin in chapter 8, as well as here in chapters 4 to 7) – we may in due course be able to account for.[1] Others, such as the variation in names for the same person[2] and the omission of certain important individuals,[3] we may just have to take on board as belonging to a method which was deliberate on the Chronicler's part, and acceptable to his readers. Yet others simply represent corruptions in the Hebrew text, where we can only guess at what was originally written.[4] But with all allowances made, these chapters still wear a formidable aspect, perhaps even more so than chapters 1 to 3.

We attempt then to explore them section by section, remembering that they are made up, as before, of a kaleidoscope of names, of lists genealogical, geographical, and military, and of (here and there) little incidents and historical references. Similarly, what will emerge from them is a display of the Chronicler's chief concerns, preparing us for the main themes of the sermon he will be preaching throughout the greater part of his book.

---

[1] See below, pp. 41ff.

[2] *E.g.* Gershon/Gershom, 6:1 RV, 16; Shomer/Shemer, 7:32, 34. Ethan (6:44) may be the Jeduthun of 25:1, and Izhar (6:2) the Amminadab of 6:22; but see the commentaries.

[3] *E.g.* the high priest Jehoiada. A key figure in 2 Ch. 23 – 24, his name might have been expected to appear here in 6:11–13.

[4] 4:17 AV, and still more 7:14–15 AV, show the old translation at its wits' end. The newer ones are not so much better informed as more imaginative.

## 1. The tribe of Judah (4:1–23)

That great branch of Israel's Tree which is the tribe of Judah has already been allotted a good deal of space in chapters 2 to 3, in connection with David, its most illustrious Old Testament scion. This present section is in some respects an amplification, in others a summary, of that one. Here three features may be noted.

First, there appear increasingly often among the names in the genealogies some which are surely place-names. One man is 'the father of Bethlehem', another 'the father of Tekoa' (4:4–5), and so forth. *Beth* (house), *Ir* (city), and *Ge* (valley) do normally, of course, refer to places; in fact Irnahash (4:12) takes us a step further, for it may mean not simply a town ('city of Nahash') but a town devoted to a particular industry ('city of bronze'), while Geharashim (4:14) is actually explained – it means, we are told, 'valley of craftsmen'. Not only did these ancient Israelites inhabit places which may well be known still to the Chronicler's readers, but they were real down-to-earth working people: smiths and craftsmen, 'linen workers' and 'potters' (4:21, 23).

Among these flesh-and-blood personalities, Jabez (4:9–10) is remarkable, though for a different reason. His immediate family links are not clear, but he takes his place with assurance both as a member of the tribe of Judah, among 'his brothers', and as an illustration of a second theme dear to the Chronicler. It is not at once obvious why he should be thought 'more honourable' than the rest of his family. The only indication of his character is the prayer of 4:10, which begins blamelessly enough, but seems in the end to be rather self-centred. The point would not however have been lost on Hebrew readers. Jabez' mother 'bore him in pain', and named him accordingly; in Hebrew 'Jabez' and 'pain' have the same letters (*ʿbṣ*, *ʿṣb*). It might not occur to a modern Mr Payne to want to change the surname he had inherited; but suppose he had been given the forename 'Misery'! In the world of the Bible, such a 'christening' would have been far more unfortunate, for there names were things of meaning and power, and Jabez had no mind to go through life oppressed by one of such ill omen. Hence his prayer: 'Keep me from harm so that I will be *free from pain*' (4:10 NIV). He proved that the threat of evil can be overcome by believing prayer and the power of a prayer-answering God.

So the Chronicler shows his concern both for practical facts

(Geharashim and Irnahash) and for spiritual truths (Jabez). To these concerns we must add a third, which emerges towards the end of this passage. Verses 17 to 18, puzzling in the older versions but made clear by the RSV's rearrangement, nonchalantly include Mered's Egyptian wife as well as his Israelite one. As has been noted before,[5] the Chronicler shows an openness to relationships between Israel and other nations which adds to his practicality and his piety an evangelistic breadth of vision. All these attitudes we shall find much developed in the histories he will go on to recount, and it is appropriate that we should find them clearly evinced here at the beginning of the story of the tribes of Israel, particularly in relation to the tribe of Judah, whose position, strength, and destiny are outstanding among the twelve (5:2).

## 2. The tribe of Simeon (4:24–43)

Two kinds of information mark the section on the Simeonites: places and numbers. There is more explicit geography here than in the case of Judah, with a list of their 'cities' and 'villages', or towns and hamlets (4:28–33), and a note of two military campaigns which enabled them to increase their land-holdings at the expense of earlier Hamite and Amalekite settlers (4:39–43). These expansions are related to an increase in numbers (4:38), and one man in particular, Shimei, is singled out as the father of many children (4:27).

But the mention of Shimei highlights the other side of the story. Such large numbers were exceptional in this tribe. 'His brothers had not many children, nor did all their family multiply like the men of Judah.' As with the Simeonites' numbers, so with their territory; although the campaign against the Hamites takes place 'in the days of Hezekiah' – that is, they are still (literally) on the map in the late eighth century BC, when the might of Assyria is threatening to bring the whole history of Israel to an end – their claims to land seem to be in some way limited already by the time of David (4:31b).

In a sense, the tribe of Simeon is a missing branch. It is missing not because of sudden destruction at the hands of Assyria or Babylon, but because of gradual disintegration long before the exile, as it merges with other Israelite groups and loses its distinctive identity. The towns and villages of 4:28–33 are listed, with slight variations, in the allocation made to Simeon when the promised land

[5] See above, p. 30.

was first occupied in the days of Joshua, and we are there told that 'its inheritance was in the midst of the inheritance of the tribe of Judah'.[6]

What then does the Chronicler have in mind? He is highlighting the tension between the ideal Israel and the actual Israel. On the one hand, he presents Simeon as a nonentity; that is by analogy how the kingdom will be again in the sixth century, and also how the men of his own day, 200 years later still, may in a mood of depression see themselves. On the other hand, he shows Simeon flourishing; he does so by means of a picture which is not imaginary (this must again be stressed)[7] but selective – he pieces together a mosaic of descriptions of times and places where the withered branch was growing strongly. That is by analogy how the kingdom will be in the age of David and Solomon, and also how it will be with the Chronicler's contemporaries when they grasp, even in the 'day of small things' in which they live, the real meaning of grace and covenant and blessing.


## 3. The Transjordan tribes (5:1–26)

'The Reubenites, the Gadites, and the half-tribe of Manasseh' (5:18) are grouped together because they all 'received their inheritance, which Moses gave them, beyond the Jordan eastward'.[8] Ten verses are devoted to Reuben, seven to Gad; Manasseh is given only a very brief mention here (5:23–24; the other half of the tribe is to be dealt with at greater length in 7:14–19). At the beginning of this chapter the Chronicler puts in parenthesis a comment worth bearing in mind with regard to one mistaken notion about his work. He is sometimes said to regard as the true people of God only the line of David and the kingdom of Judah, and to have no real interest in the 'Joseph' tribes and the northern kingdom. But in fact he is at pains to point out, here in his introductory chapters, that 'though Judah became strong among his brothers and a prince was from him, yet the birthright', taken away from the eldest brother Reuben, was

---

[6] Jos. 19:1–9.

[7] Not, that is, like T. H. White's *The Once and Future King*, as described by its *New York Times* reviewer: 'A glorious dream of the Middle Ages as they never were but as they should have been'! This resembles rather the way that Tennyson pictures, carved over the gate of Camelot, 'Arthur's wars in weird devices done, New things and old co-twisted, as if Time Were nothing' (*Gareth and Lynette*, in the *Idylls of the King*).

[8] Jos. 13:8.

transferred to and then always 'belonged to Joseph' (5:2).

An equally interesting passage forms the latter part of the chapter (5:18–26). This describes two experiences of opposite kinds which befell the Transjordan tribes, and which illustrate another of the Chronicler's principal themes.

By his time these tribes, like Simeon, no longer exist. But their fortunes have differed greatly from those of their brother-tribe. While Simeon has long since vanished as a separate entity, Reuben's line has continued intact until the Assyrian invasion of 732 BC (5:6), and it is in that cataclysm that he, with his fellow Transjordanians, disappears into exile (5:26). The genealogies mentioned in 5:17 date from the glorious days of the mid-eighth century; those days were to come to a fearful end within the space of a single generation.

Here for the first time the Chronicler lays down the spiritual laws which underlie the ebb and flow of history. He brings together references to two kings, one at either end of a three-century span in the life of Israel (5:6, 10). Neither he nor anyone else would pretend that the men of 700 BC were carbon copies of those of 1000 BC in the areas of life in which one age obviously differs from another. But it is equally obvious that there are other areas in which, as he insists, unchanging principles operate. The reason for the downfall of the Transjordan tribes in the days of Tiglath-pileser (5:6)[9] is spelt out in 5:25–26: 'they transgressed ... and he carried them away'. The reason for their victory over the Hagrites in the days of Saul (5:10) is spelt out in 5:20: 'they cried to God in the battle, and he granted their entreaty because they trusted in him'.

The Chronicler may be thought to have an oversimplified theology of spiritual cause and effect – faith results in blessing, sin results in trouble, and God is behind both processes – and to impose it on the facts of history, which are actually a lot more complicated than this. It would be more accurate to say that the theology is, *in the last analysis*, nothing but the truth. Unless those who constantly reject God do, in the end, lose him, and unless those who persistently seek him do, in the end, find him, then how can there be justice in God, and how can there be hope for man? The Chronicler's pattern of cause and effect is not an alien one imposed on the facts; rather, it is the underlying pattern, often obscured by

[9] Tiglath-pileser III (this spelling is closer to the original than the Chronicler's 'Tilgath-pilneser'; he was also known as Pul, 5:26) was the king of Assyria who invaded Israel and the neighbouring states in 734–732 BC.

the complications of the story, which is exposed by his selecting the facts which most clearly bring it out.

## 4. The tribe of Levi (6:1–81)

As much space is devoted to this tribe as to several of the others put together. The reason for the preoccupation with Levi will be considered later, when we deal with chapters 8 to 9.[10] Here we simply note the contents of chapter 6.

Verses 1 to 30 set out, by the Chronicler's usual method of name-lists, the *history* of the tribe. Of the three original sons of Levi the middle one, Kohath, is taken first; from him were descended Moses and Aaron (6:2–3). This is one of the few references in Chronicles to the former, in spite of his key role in the story of Israel; his brother Aaron, from whom sprang the line of the high priests, is of greater consequence for our author. The Aaronic line is twice anchored in history, in the times of the exodus (6:3) and of the exile (6:15).[11] The life of the nation is inseparable from it. From verse 16 onwards equal importance is given to all three of Levi's sons, Gershom and Merari as well as Kohath, with the horizontal line of the cousins of the first generation followed by a vertical line for each family.

Verses 31 to 53 deal with the *function* of Levi in the nation's life. The focus is on the reigns of David and Solomon (6:31–32), and on the function of the Levites as it was then established for the worship of first the tabernacle and later the temple. Three famous musicians, Heman the Kohathite, Asaph the Gershomite, and Ethan the Merarite (6:33, 39, 44), led the praises; the Kohathite line of Aaron (6:49–53) offered the sacrifices.

Verses 54 to 81, like the similar gazetteer in Joshua 21, indicate the *extent* of the tribe's settlement. It was given, not a territory like those of other tribes, but a large number of towns and villages distributed throughout the land. Every one of its members would thus be in a position analogous to that of Samuel's father Elkanah,

---

[10] See below, pp. 40ff.

[11] 6:10 too looks like an anchor; but where it has been dropped is not clear. This Azariah served in Solomon's temple, but not in Solomon's time. Perhaps the parenthesis in 6:10 refers to Zadok's grandson (6:9), and with its omissions (*cf.* p. 32; n. 3) the list is a scheme of 12 + 12 generations linking the times when the tabernacle, the first temple, and the second temple were constructed (1 Ki. 4:2; Hg. 1:1; and *cf.* Mt. 1:17; Williamson, pp. 70f.).

who was an Ephraimite by residence[12] but a Levite by birth.[13]

Levi thus provides a religious leadership which acts as a binding force through the length of Israel's history and the breadth of its territory. Again the picture is a selective one, showing things as they were at their best. But more of this supremely important tribe in due course.

## 5. The military tribes (7:1–12)

The paragraphs on Issachar and Benjamin hark back, as chapter 6 did, to the great days of David (7:2). A memorable time, of course, for all the tribes, it seems to have been so for these two particularly on account of their military prowess.

This is a feature we have not so far come across. 'Mighty warriors' (7:2; *etc.*) may to us have a story-book ring, but the Hebrew phrase probably means nothing more romantic than 'fighting men' (so NIV), and similarly, 'chief men' (7:3), 'units of the army for war' (7:4), and 'ready for service in war' (7:11) may simply be technical military terms.[14] These tribes, noted for their interest in soldiering, are thus portrayed by means of records which were probably, in the language of the day, perfectly straightforward army lists.

Yet again we have a picture of departed glories which must to the Chronicler's contemporaries have seemed ironic and unhelpful. Why show Simeon as a flourishing tribe, they might have said, when it has in fact now disintegrated? Or Levi as influential in every corner of the land, when most of that land no longer belongs to us anyway? Or Issachar and Benjamin as a military power, when today, in the fourth century BC, the weakness of God's people is a byword?

But the answer is as before, and as it will be throughout Chronicles. 'In changing circumstances, seek the unchanging principles. Look for the inner meanings. Look for equivalents. Blessing and influence and power (if not in that obvious, outward

---

[12] 1 Sa. 1:1.

[13] Samuel in 6:28 is clearly *the* Samuel; with slight variations in the names, in all the three lists — 6:26–28; 6:33–35; and 1 Sa. 1:1 with 8:1–2 — seven-generation sequences (from Zuph/Zophai to Joel) tally with one another.

[14] So also may the confusing words 'hundred' and 'thousand'. The Chronicler seems regularly to inflate his statistics in a way which has made many accuse him of gross exaggeration and therefore of unreliability. We should bear in mind, therefore, from this early stage, that 'hundred' (*mēʾāh*) may mean 'contingent', while 'thousand' (*ʾelep̄*) may mean 'family' or 'clan', or even, with the same consonants pointed differently (*ʾallup̄*), an individual 'officer' or 'captain'. See *IBD*, art. *Number*, II.

form, then in another) will always be found among God's people when he and they are rightly related.'

## 6. The rest of the tribes (7:13–40)

In the sections on Naphtali, the other half of Manasseh, Ephraim, and Asher, various items underline points made earlier. We take these paragraphs in the reverse order. The Asher list (7:30–40) has, appended to the usual genealogies, a note of the tribe's warriors, chiefs, and 'thousands', like those of the 'military' tribes Issachar and Benjamin. Ephraim (7:20–29) presents an extraordinary tangle of relationships,[15] but within it we find examples of the illustrative incident, the geographical and historical cross-reference, and the mention of flesh-and-blood people, which as we have seen are typical of the Chronicler's style in these chapters. The Ephraimite heiress Sheerah (7:24) has her counterparts in the western settlements of Manasseh (7:14–19) in the person of the daughters of Zelophehad, the central figures in a famous legal case described elsewhere in the Old Testament;[16] while in the same connection the Manasseh account also provides us with another instance of an almost unintelligible Hebrew sentence, of which any translation will be largely guesswork (7:15).

The paragraph about Naphtali (7:13) is remarkable only for its brevity, in contrast to the great length of Levi's section (6:1–81). It brings us to the final peculiarity of this whole survey of the branches of Israel. We have been shown eleven tribes. Where is the twelfth? It may occur to us that Dan seems to be missing. Some commentators do suggest that in 7:12, another unintelligible verse (Shuppim and Huppim again bringing confusion, as in 7:15!), there was a mention of him which at some stage dropped out: 'Son of Dan: Hushim, a single son'.[17] That would make up twelve tribes – and then leave us with yet one more complication: we have still had no mention of Zebulun! What are we to make of this?

The fact of the matter is that the Bible, which often lists the sons,

---

[15] The problems concern (1) the Ephraims of 7:20 and 7:21b–24 – are they the same person, or not? (2) the raid of 7:21 – who killed whom, and where? (3) the line from Rephah to Joshua, in 7:25–27 – whose son was Rephah? For attempts at the answers (which presumably the Chronicler and his readers knew), see Williamson, pp. 80f.

[16] Nu. 27:1–11; 36:1–12.

[17] Ackroyd, p. 41; and so most commentators; and see Gn. 46:23. But see also Williamson, p. 78.

or tribes, of Israel, does so in a number of different ways. It has been reckoned that there are no fewer than seventeen variations in the order of the names. Further, there is no uniformity as to which names are put in and which left out. One factor, however, is almost invariable. (1) Israel's sons numbered twelve.[18] (2) His grandsons Manasseh and Ephraim were adopted as full sons of his own, giving rise to two separate tribes in place of the one which would have arisen from their father Joseph,[19] and making a total of thirteen; but Levi's call to a special ministry separated him from the other tribes, compensated for the doubling of Joseph, and left once more a total of twelve.[20] (3) In the settling of the promised land, Simeon had no clear boundaries, and was absorbed in Judah; but Manasseh split in two, with separate lands east and west of Jordan, so the number of territories turned out also to be twelve. (4) The Chronicler's survey is different again. We can only hazard guesses as to the purpose of his choice of tribes. But we do notice that if, as well as *both* Levi *and* the two sons of Joseph, he has included Dan at 7:12, by omitting Zebulun he keeps the tally to twelve. If on the other hand he has omitted Dan as well as Zebulun, twelve is still the total, if we now count the number of *settlements* referred to (with two for Manasseh).[21]

There is, at all events, no doubt that such a twelve-fold structure, however it may be arrived at, is seen as proper to the true Israel. That outline, together with the broad palette of colours which the Chronicler will be using to fill it in as he goes on with his book, is intended to show us in a variety of ways the people of God as, ideally and in principle, they ought to be.

[18] Gn. 35:22b–26; 1 Ch. 2:1–2.
[19] Gn. 48:5–6.
[20] Nu. 1.
[21] The latest of these lists, the one in Rev. 7:5–8, includes Joseph as well as both his sons, but keeps the total at twelve by (curiously enough) omitting Dan.

# 1 Chronicles 8 – 9

## 3. Fruit

We have been following, as if it were the growth of a tree, the story of the people of God in Old Testament times. Its roots are thrust down deep into the past. Its branches spread wide, to embrace an immense variety of all sorts and conditions of men. And its fruit?

In the groves of the remote Bermoothes', the Creator (says Andrew Marvell)

> hangs in shades the orange bright
> Like golden lamps in a green night.

So shines the fruit of the Tree of Israel: that which declares its nature and shows that it truly is the people of *God*, having with him a real and living relationship. It is a double fruit. God is represented to his people by the king, who is his viceroy, governing them with divine authority. They are represented to God by the priest, who is their mediator, approaching God on their behalf, in all his humanity, which is theirs also. Kings and priests are, of course, to be found among all the nations. But because God himself has so appointed them, Israelite kingship and priesthood together express the two-way relationship with an adequacy which their Gentile counterparts lack. By its fruit the Tree is known.[1]

In the genealogies of the tribes, three stand out because of the amount of space devoted to them: Levi, Judah, and Benjamin. Geographically they will later form the southern kingdom, Judah, on which the Chronicler's attention will focus. But these emphases also correspond to the fruit of the Tree. Levi is the priestly tribe; from Judah and Benjamin arise the kings.

### 1. Kingship

Chapter 8 concerns the tribe of Benjamin. A paragraph about this tribe has already appeared in chapter 7, and the Chronicler might be thought to be a rather untidy writer, who, had he been more

[1] Mt. 7:20.

methodical, would have streamlined his book by cutting out such 'repetitions'. But interestingly, the extra Benjamin material at this end of the survey is balanced, as we have seen, by extra Judah material at the other end. As the former is given not only 7:6–12, but also 8:1–40,[2] so the latter was given not only 4:1–23, but also 2:3 – 3:24. We therefore return for the moment to those earlier chapters.

### a. The finest fruit of kingship

Judah's tribe occupied practically the whole of chapter 2, with its most significant division in the days of his great-grandsons Jerahmeel, Ram, and Chelubai, or Caleb (2:9). The line through Ram, which led to David (2:15), was given pride of place. Then, after the other branches had been dealt with, the Chronicler returned to David, and the whole of chapter 3 was about him.

Now, therefore, it is appropriate to consider in more detail what was only touched on before. Here in chapter 3 is Judah's greatest descendant. How is he pictured? In these early chapters the Chronicler's medium is names. So in 3:1–9 we have a procession of queens and princes, the wives married to David and the sons born to him while 'he reigned' first 'in Hebron' and then 'in Jerusalem' (3:4). In this unusual but simple way is shown the *greatness* of David's kingdom. We can visualize around this extensive royal family the whole life of an oriental court, with its indispensable 'supporting cast' of slaves, soldiers, politicians, and administrators, and with power and glory to match. All this will be developed at great length in the second half of 1 Chronicles. The reign of David is for the Chronicler the golden age. It is seldom far from his thoughts, and is a standing reminder of what Israel can be when she loves godly government.

In keeping with this thought he continues in 3:10–16 with a list of David's descendants, the kings who reigned in Jerusalem through the four centuries from Solomon to 'Jeconiah the captive'. Thus he shows the *vitality* of David's kingdom. The king dies, but the kingdom does not die with him. There are ups and downs in its fortunes, naturally, but 'for better, for worse, for richer, for poorer, in sickness and in health', this union, between an earthly government and the divine power which maintains it, persists. Not until God himself, in the sixth century BC, changes the rules of the

---

[2] And 9:35–44 too, for that matter; but to this we shall come later.

game will the Davidic throne, in that original manifestation, disappear. Indeed in the truest sense it does not disappear even then, but stands unshaken, and will so stand through all time and into eternity. The vitality of that throne which 'shall never, Like earth's proud empires, pass away', that kingdom which 'stands, and grows for ever',[3] will be another of the Chronicler's chief themes in subsequent chapters of his book.

Nevertheless the rules *were* changed.[4] The time came when the kingdom as a political institution was allowed by God to fall to an invader, with a ruin so complete that never again did it take quite the shape it had had originally. The trappings of royalty vanished. And yet the line continued. Jeconiah, captive though he became, was not the end of it, and in 3:17–24 his descendants are listed through the period of the exile and on into the Chronicler's own time. In each generation there was a pretender to the throne, which of course did not exist, since the Hebrew colony round Jerusalem was there only by courtesy of the Persian kings, as one of their many subject peoples. What we have here is, in fact, the *mystery* of the kingdom. That New Testament phrase is altogether apt to describe this, the profoundest of all the Chronicler's themes. Circumstances change almost out of recognition; yet there is continuity. The days when kings of the house of David ruled in Judah belong to another age; yet the sons of Elioenai are here with us in Jerusalem. Royalty does not exist, and yet royalty does exist.

At any rate, the kingly line of David, with all its mysterious and exciting implications, is the finest fruit of the Tree, the greatest of the 'golden lamps' by which it is shown to be a tree of the Lord's planting. To it the Chronicler will be giving many chapters as his work progresses.

### b. The earliest fruit of kingship

We have already seen that outside the general survey of the tribes in chapters 4 to 7 the Chronicler records extra material about a few of them. Just as a separate section about Judah preceded that survey, occupying chapters 2 and 3, so a separate section about Benjamin now follows it, occupying chapter 8.

An emphasis on Judah is understandable, since the royal house of

[3] John Ellerton, *The day thou gavest, Lord, is ended.*

[4] That is, the rules according to which, for a limited period, divine providence makes 'the people of God … a political entity' (McConville, pp. 64f., in a very important passage which relates in the first instance to David's wars but also to much else in Chronicles).

David belonged to that tribe. But why should there be an emphasis on Benjamin? The fact of the matter is that although David and his kingdom are from one point of view the Chronicler's ideal, he regards as even more important the idea of the kingdom *per se*, whether or not its kings belong to the house of David and the tribe of Judah. It is with this in view that the Chronicler embarks on a chapter which from first word to last concerns the Benjaminites (8:1–40), even though in the general survey of the tribes a Benjamin paragraph has already been included (7:6–12).

The first part of chapter 8 presents problems. Because of the obvious differences between the information given in 7:6–12 and that given in 8:1–28, it is on the one hand difficult to see how the two passages can be reconciled, yet on the other hand necessary to assume that both the Chronicler and his readers took such differences in their stride. (Alert and intelligent people who were prepared to let such 'contradictions' stand as part of a historical record[5] presumably had sound reasons for doing so.)

As soon as we move on into the second half of chapter 8, however, our attention is caught in a new way. There are familiar names here. The place called Gibeon (8:29) we may recall from other mentions in the Old Testament story,[6] and the man called Kish (8:30) is remembered as the father of a famous son, who duly appears in this passage – Saul, with *his* son Jonathan and grandson Merib-baal, or Mephibosheth (8:33–34; 2 Sa. 4:4). We know very little about his other descendants beyond what we are told here; but we may note that the dozen generations from Saul which are listed in the rest of the chapter would bring us down roughly to the time of the end of the monarchy, in 587 BC. Perhaps it was in that catastrophe that this Benjaminite family disappeared from the records, 'mighty warriors' though its last representatives may have been (8:40).

Long before that, however, Benjamin had disappeared from a different kind of record. For though it figured throughout Israelite history as one of the twelve tribes, there had once been a brief period when it figured as the *royal* tribe. And this surely is the chief reason why the Chronicler is here giving to Benjamin, as he had already given to Judah, considerable extra space in his book. He uses the words 'king' and 'kingdom', with reference to Saul, only after Saul's

---

[5] On the reasons why factual historical material is necessary for the Chronicler's purpose, see above, pp. 26, 29–30.

[6] Jos. 9; 2 Sa. 21:1–14; 1 Ki. 3:3–15.

death (10:14; 11:2), and reckons it nothing to his purpose to tell again the story of how Israel actually became a monarchy. Like the crucial events of the days of Noah and Abraham and Moses, the crisis by which the rule of the judges gave way to that of the kings is already sufficiently known (1 Sa. 8 – 10), and like those earlier times of crisis, it appears in Bible history as a major turning-point. The Chronicler omits all these things; for, as we have noted, it is the other side of the coin that he wishes us to look at – not the great changes, but the great continuities. So without fuss or fanfare there comes into view, almost unnoticed in the course of a complicated genealogy, the man who first of all the sons of Israel was to embody the idea of the kingdom:[7] 'Ner was the father of Kish, Kish of Saul' (8:33). This man is the first of these 'golden lamps in a green night', the earliest fruit of kingship among the people of God.

## 2. Priesthood

The opening verse of chapter 9 might be taken as a conclusion and summary of the whole first section of the book: 'So all Israel was enrolled by genealogies; and these are written in the Book of the Kings of Israel. And Judah was taken into exile in Babylon because of their unfaithfulness.' But the Chronicler has a few remaining lists to record before he embarks on the narratives which start with chapter 10. And in fact 9:1 brings us not to his own times, but only as far as the deportations to Babylon at the beginning of the sixth century BC. The return of the exiles something over half a century later provides the lead into his last major name-list, since 'the first to dwell again in their possessions ... were ... the Levites' (9:2). Members of other tribes who returned are also listed briefly (9:3–9), and a repeat of the Benjaminite section from the end of chapter 8 rounds off this chapter too, to provide an introduction to the account of the death of Saul in chapter 10. But most of chapter 9 concerns the priestly tribe of Levi. As was the case with Judah and Benjamin, the special importance of this tribe is indicated by the extra space given to it.

The reason is not far to seek. As one of the Chronicler's chief preoccupations is Israel's monarchy, so another is its temple

---

[7] We do not of course take account of the pretensions of Abimelech son of Gideon, in the days of the judges (Jdg. 9:6).

worship; and temple worship, translated into the genealogical language of 1 Chronicles 1 to 9, means Levi. So the Chronicler now adds yet more Levi material (9:10–34) to what may already have seemed, in the survey of chapters 4 to 7, a disproportionately large Levi section (6:1–81).

### a. The historic fruit of priesthood

We recall the contents of that earlier chapter.[8] The branching of the tribe of Levi is there traced through several generations of the descendants of each of Levi's three sons, Gershom, Kohath, and Merari. Kohath's line begins of course with his father, taking us back well before the time of the exodus, to the much earlier time when Levi, along with the rest of Israel's immediate family, first went down into Egypt. But it is with Aaron[9] that the priesthood is first established. The Tree of Israel first bears this fruit when he is consecrated as high priest, and that appointment is a part of the instruction given to Moses at Sinai regarding the whole system of worship there laid down by God for his people. The line of high priests is then depicted as a continuous one through the periods of both judges and kings, right up to the end of the monarchy.

Following this historical outline of the priestly tribe (6:1–30) we noted its function (6:31–53). The levitical priesthood offers praise, service, and sacrifice on behalf of the rest of Israel. Such offerings are acceptable to God, since the system operates in obedience to him – 'in due order' (6:32), 'according to all that Moses the servant of God had commanded' (6:49). By this fruit also, the representation before God of a people rightly related to him, as well as by the fruit which is his viceroys' rule of that people, the nature of the Tree is known.

Thirdly, we saw the extent of Levi's settlement in the promised land (6:54–81). His descendants are scattered throughout the territories of the other tribes, so that the total picture is of this priestly tribe standing for the whole nation 'in things pertaining to God',[10] in every period of its history and every part of its territory.

### b. The continuing fruit of priesthood

Now we turn back from chapter 6 to chapter 9, and in the second

---

[8] See above pp. 37–38.

[9] Apparently Levi's great-grandson (6:1–3); though if Levi and his brothers settled with their father Jacob in Egypt in the 18th century BC, then whether the date of the exodus (and therefore of Aaron) is the 15th century or the 13th – at present a debated question – there must be generations missing in these verses, and 'sons' must mean remoter descendants. Cf. p. 178 n. 6

[10] Heb. 2:17 AV.

major section devoted to Levi we note again the Chronicler's stress on continuity. Even in the first verse of the chapter it can be perceived. He does not quite ignore the exile, as he ignores some great events of Israelite history (Noah is mentioned – just – but not the flood (1:4); Moses, but not the exodus (6:3)). But he gives it the most cursory of glances, and by verse 2 it is over and Israel is back home again, the unbroken thread of its life continuing almost as if nothing had happened.

The curious phrase at the end of 9:2, 'Israel, the priests, the Levites, and the temple servants', is perhaps intended as a summary of what follows. 9:3–9 tell us something of the 'Israel' which the levitical priesthood now represents. It comprises various families and groups, but we observe, and store the observation for future reference, that it includes people not only of Judah and Benjamin, but also of Ephraim and Manasseh. For his remaining fifty-six chapters the Chronicler will be concentrating almost exclusively on Judah and Benjamin, not so much because they are both, as we have seen, royal tribes, as because they formed the southern kingdom which held to the generally godly line of David when the other tribes, notably Ephraim and Manasseh, broke away to form the northern one. But now after the exile the Chronicler sees emerging once more, however diminished, his cherished ideal of the true Israel, which is drawn from north as well as south.

9:10–13 list those of the returning exiles who serve Israel as priests, and 9:17–34 those who serve as gatekeepers, singers, and other 'temple servants', while between these two sections, in 9:14–16, is a list of those who (although all three groups were of the tribe of Levi) carried the name 'Levite' as a special designation. All of this tribe who return to live in Jerusalem are involved in one way or another with the centralized worship of Israel. Their 'second temple', built on the ruins of Solomon's grand original, is also a somewhat second-rate temple when compared with its predecessor. But in it the sacrifices and services take place as of old, with its priesthood providing continuity with the past even though there has been a break in its worship.

## 3. A fruitful Tree to the end of time

'You will know them by their fruits.'[11] A tree demonstrates that it is an apple tree by bearing apples, an orange tree by bearing oranges;

[11] Mt. 7:16.

the nature of this Tree, the people of God, is demonstrated likewise by the fruit it bears, the double fruit of kingship and priesthood. If these really are the people of God, then by definition there will be a true relationship between them and him, and that in both directions: they related to him in proper worship, which necessitates the priesthood, and he related to them in proper government, which implies the kingship.

And this is an unchanging truth. Wherever and whenever God's people really are God's people, the double fruit must be there to prove it. So these early chapters not only foreshadow two of the Chronicler's chief themes, kingship and priesthood, but also show one of his main characteristics. He constantly challenges his readers with the paradox of what is, and is not. That is to say, he tells them that where the real Israel is, there the kingly and priestly tribes will be flourishing; or, in terms of his later chapters, that where the real Israel is, there will be the power of David's throne and the glory of Solomon's temple. 'But', his readers protest, 'they are not! The glory has gone, and the power is non-existent! What is the point of setting before us this model, this ideal, when for us it is so remote and meaningless? Or are you telling us that for lack of it our standing as God's people is in doubt?'

In order to understand this paradox, let us imagine an Old Testament Israelite living in the days of his nation's greatness, the period which is at the centre of the Chronicler's story. We must see him as a real flesh-and-blood person, with body, mind, and spirit — in particular, spirit, so that although his culture and ours are very different, at the deepest level his needs and ours are the same. Let us see him, indeed, as a man of spiritual insight. Where will he find that those deep needs are met? He looks to Jerusalem. There in God's temple the high priest stands, offering sacrifices on behalf of the people; there on God's throne the king sits, dispensing justice for the wise government of the people. Our spiritually-minded Israelite is aware that the blood of bulls and of goats cannot in itself take away sin,[12] but he is also aware that the God who appointed such sacrifices is a God who hates sin, and who presumably intends that one day it will actually be done away; the priestly sacrifices

---

[12] Heb. 10:4. The whole context in Hebrews (7:11–25; 8:7–13; 9:6–10; 10:1–18) indicates for us how such a worshipper could, and should, have understood the meaning of the Old Testament sacrifices, and how he might have known himself to be justified by faith, as we are.

must therefore, he believes, be a kind of God-ordained picture of that, and so he has faith, not in the animal sacrifices as such, but in whatever ultimate Fact it may be for which they stand. He believes that what these sacrifices point to is the removal of his sins, so that he may become acceptable to God. It is then clear to him that as he in this way comes to God, so God's government comes into his life in the form of the righteous, benevolent, and powerful rule of the kings of Israel, who sit on the throne as God's viceroys or representatives to his people, just as the priests stand at the altar as the people's representatives to God.

This is all very well for, say, the tenth century BC. But let us now imagine another man, this time living in the Chronicler's own period, several centuries later. He too believes himself to be a member of the people of God, and is aware of his own need for a right relationship, in both directions, between himself and God. How can that exist, though, when circumstances have changed so much? Priests are offering sacrifices in Jerusalem, it is true, but Solomon's temple has gone, and with it much that would once have been thought essential for the proper worship of God; while the rule of the kings has ceased altogether. Yet man's need, first to be made right with God and then to live rightly under him, is still the same. To that need the Chronicler addresses this sermon of his, based on Israelite history. At the centre of the life of the people of God there *must* be the priest and the king: only round these two figures will the rest of the picture fit into place. And even if there is no one actually playing either or both of these parts, yet still it is only round an empty space of the priest-and-king shape, as it were, that the picture of God's true people can be built up. Whether or not David reigns enthroned and Abiathar presides at the altar, there must be the acceptance before God, and the rule of God, which these stand for.

If, lastly, we picture a man of our own day, with the same basic human needs, the Chronicler preaches to him the same answers. His Chronicles are an old story from a bygone age, but their message is unchanging. The message is, indeed, what he is preaching to us ourselves, and to all men in every age everywhere. Let us hear what, through him, 'the Spirit is saying to the churches'.[13] The great need is that man should be first brought into, and then kept in, a right relationship with God. To this end, God has fostered the growth of

[13] Rev. 2:7, 11, *etc.*, JB.

the Tree which is his people; and among them, by the vital sap of these spiritual principles, by the great continuities, he has caused its precious fruit to appear 'like golden lamps in a green night'. The pattern was first established in the days of David, when the double line of Israelite priests and kings began. There would one day come forth the last and greatest fulfilment of the pattern, in a way the Chronicler could never have imagined. Or could he? Did he perhaps understand that neither the priest-and-king-shaped gap, nor the succession of men of Israel who filled it, could ever in the end achieve the real union of God with his people, unless the truth which they signified were one day to become incarnate Fact? Did he, like Abraham, look 'into the future, far as human eye could see',[14] and there see the day of Christ, and rejoice?[15] For king and priest were, of course, to merge in the single figure of our Lord Jesus Christ, whose eternal priesthood and kingship would 'bring in everlasting righteousness'.[16] Realized or unrealized before the time, he is in fact the one who actually makes all his people, whether 'BC' or 'AD', truly the people of God. It is he who fulfils the Chronicler's great vision: 'One church, one faith, one Lord'.

[14] Tennyson, *Locksley Hall*.
[15] Jn. 8:56.
[16] Dn. 9:24.

# Part Two
# DAVID, THE MAN OF WAR
# (1 Chronicles 10 – 29)

## 1 Chronicles 10 – 12

## 4.  The unity and individuality of the people of God

With his first nine chapters the Chronicler has introduced his ambitious re-presentation of Israel's history as a sermon. Drawing on ancient material, much of which is familiar to us from the earlier books of the Bible, he has already indicated his major concerns. He will be focusing on the kingship and the priesthood – that is, as it will turn out, on the throne of David and the temple of Solomon – and he will be selecting and simplifying, as he preaches on the story of these things, so as to bring out unchanging principles and ultimate truths.

David is the subject of the next twenty chapters, through to the end of 1 Chronicles. They do not however provide a biography of him, still less a character study. To find David depicted with 'warts, and everything',[1] we must go to the books of Samuel and Kings. This is not to say that the Chronicler intends to flatter David. Both writer and readers know those older books, and to attempt in this new account a whitewashing job on a character with many blemishes (which is what some would say we have here) would be singularly pointless. Everyone knows from Samuel/Kings what David was 'really' like – on occasions impulsive, lustful, heartless, indulgent. But he was also, just as 'really', the greatest of all the kings of Israel, and the new portrait is the official one of David as he embodies the kingship. To this end the Chronicler, though nowhere departing from the truth, is unashamedly selective in what he writes.

The first point in this sermon on David concerns the relationship between the man and the nation. We are asked to consider him, as the people's king, and afterwards his subjects, as the king's people.

## 1.   The people's king (10:1–14; 11:1–9)

Let us again put ourselves in the position of the first readers of this book, and think what David would have meant to them. By their time, that is in the fourth century BC, most of the world the Chronicler was describing was dead and gone. None of it was more decidedly dead than the glorious reign of David. Yet though the glory had departed (cf. 1 Sa. 4:21–22), neither his nation nor his ideals were actually extinct. And the Chronicler's message was that the principles laid down in David's reign were still the only ones around which the life of the people of God could be organized if it was to have any value and meaning. David was no more, yet the place he once occupied – the David-shaped blank – still had to be recognized as the necessary core of that life.

So 'he being dead yet speaketh',[2] and events of the distant past affect people living long afterwards, as starlight shines tonight which left distant galaxies thousands of years ago. In fact, if we go on to ask what all this has to do with us, so many centuries later still, the answer is that for us David 'means' not only as much as he meant for them, but far more. In the intervening years the David-shaped blank has again been filled, this time by one who

---

[1] 'I desire you would use all your skill to paint my picture truly like me, and not flatter me at all ... roughnesses, pimples, warts, and everything': Oliver Cromwell to the court painter Peter Lely.

[2] Heb. 11:4 AV.

outshines even David in the glory of his kingship, and who (as we have seen)[3] fulfils the other half of the pattern too by being priest as well as king.

To 'great David's greater Son'[4] we shall return. In the meantime it is clear that the people's king provides the focus of their unity. In the tenth century BC the life of Israel centres on David himself. In the fourth century the person is long gone, but the principles he embodied are still valid. In the first century AD those principles will be once again embodied, this time perfectly and permanently. Around this core the people of God crystallize.

### a. His character highlighted (10:1–14)

But where is he? Not mentioned till the very last verse of this chapter – 'the LORD ... turned the kingdom over to David the son of Jesse' (10:14). The whole chapter seems to be not about David at all, but about his predecessor Saul. Why start with *him* – especially when, as we shall see, the Chronicler is so good at editing out of his narrative the incidents which do not suit his purpose? This surely, one would think, might have been omitted, not only because the Chronicler wants to focus on David and this is merely Saul, but because he also wants to focus on glory, and Saul is a disaster.

But notice just how he does edit his material. 2 Samuel 3:1 tells us that 'there was a long war between the house of Saul and the house of David; and David grew stronger and stronger, while the house of Saul became weaker and weaker.' Our writer includes in his account neither this verse itself, nor any hint of the slow decline of the house of Saul both before and after his death. He concentrates on the single calamitous event, and adds a moral: the reason for Saul's downfall was that 'he was unfaithful to the LORD ... did not keep the command of the LORD ... did not seek guidance from the LORD' (10:13–14). It was because of this, we are told, that God replaced Saul by David. What are the implications?

One is that such disloyalty to God will always result in catastrophe,[5] and can only be remedied by devotion like David's. Again and again the Chronicler will illustrate this in his narrative, and surely sees the same principle at work in the exile and the

---

[3] See above, p. 50.

[4] James Montgomery, *Hail to the Lord's Anointed*.

[5] Comparison with 1 Sa. 31:6–10 shows how the Chronicler heightens the disaster in subtle ways; see Williamson, p. 93f., and McConville's perceptive comments on Saul, pp. 15–18.

restoration which belong to his own times.

But we must also see in this picture of Saul a foil to set off the character of his successor. Saul has been unfaithful and disobedient, and has not sought the Lord; David, by contrast, will be faithful and obedient, and will seek the Lord. This character fits him to be a true ruler over the people of Israel. Where God and his viceroy are of one mind, the people will prosper. The older history had made this point about the character of David, and it is taken up in the New Testament, in a passage which like Chronicles is 'preached history': 'I have found in David the son of Jesse a man after my heart, who will do all my will.'[6]

The account of the death of Saul having highlighted, by contrast, the character of the one who succeeded him, we are next shown the effect of this character.

### b.   His people gathered (11:1–3)

Both Samuel/Kings and Chronicles speak of a steady growth in David's power once he had been recognized as king: 'David became greater and greater' (11:9; 2 Sa. 5:10). But as we have seen, the earlier rise in David's fortunes and the decline in those of Saul and his family (2 Sa. 3:1)[7] are omitted by the Chronicler (except for the hint at the beginning of 11:2), and so far as the former is concerned he fastens instead on the particular occasion when 'all Israel gathered together to David' to anoint him king at Hebron.

We may note four things in this gathering of the people. First, they recognize David's oneness with them: 'We are your bone and flesh'. Though he is as it were sent from God to rule his people, nevertheless from the human point of view his origins are among them. Secondly, they honour his achievements: 'It was you that led out and brought in Israel'. They 'remember ... all the hardships he endured'[8] and the solid results that came from those exertions and sufferings. Thirdly, they accept his covenant: 'David made a covenant with them ... they anointed David'. He proposes the terms, they indicate their acceptance by the anointing with oil which is the equivalent of a coronation. Fourthly, they acknowledge his commission: all this has been 'according to the word of the Lord by Samuel'. The Chronicler and his readers know well the story of Samuel's visit to Bethlehem (1 Sa. 16), where at God's direction he

---

[6] Acts 13:22; cf. 1 Sa 13:14.     [7] See above, p. 53.
[8] Ps. 132:1.

chooses of all the sons of Jesse the youngest, David, to be the eventual successor to Saul. That story does not need to be repeated here; the Chronicler needs only to remind us that all this happened as God had said it should, and the people acknowledged it as his plan.

Psalm 89 turns the whole event into poetry, and makes all four points. *'Thou didst speak ...* and say: "I have set the crown upon *one who is mighty*, I have exalted one *chosen from the people*. I have found David, my servant; with my holy oil *I have anointed him ... my covenant* will stand firm for him." '[9]

Having been thus enshrined in the Psalter, the great king-making is lifted to a higher plane by being fulfilled in the New Testament. The pattern foreshadowed in David is clearly seen in David's greater son. Jesus too is one with his people: he and they 'have all one origin ... He is not ashamed to call them brethren ... He himself likewise partook of the same nature ... He had to be made like his brethren in every respect'.[10] His achievements too are to be honoured: he is the pioneer of our salvation and of our faith,[11] and we praise him for all that he has done and endured on his people's behalf. His covenant is to be accepted: we 'hail the power of Jesus' name ... and crown Him Lord of all',[12] fully aware that the initiative has been his, and that we are simply responding to the terms of grace. And his commission too is to be acknowledged: at conception, birth, baptism, transfiguration, and resurrection his authority, like David's, has been sealed by a word from God.[13]

'Unto him', then, the prince of the house of Judah, 'shall the gathering of the people be.'[14] 'All Israel' – we note a favourite phrase of the Chronicler's – is 'gathered together to David at Hebron' (11:1), and it is 'all Israel' (11:4; the Chronicler re-words his source, 2 Samuel 5:6) which then goes with him to the conquest of the city which is to be his capital.

*c.   His city established (11:4–9)*

This place is given four different names in the space of only two

---

[9] Ps. 89:19, 20, 28.

[10] Heb. 2:11, 14, 17. The passage is explaining how Christ had to become man in order to be a 'faithful *high priest*'; but he is still the God-Man, and with the same object, now that he is reigning as *king*.

[11] Heb. 2:10; 12:2.      [12] Edward Perronet, *All hail the power of Jesus' name.*

[13] Lk. 1:32; 2:11; 3:22; 9:35; Rom. 1:4.

[14] Gn. 49:10 AV.

verses. It is tempting to think in terms of source-criticism, and to visualize the Chronicler cobbling together a phrase from each of four original writers, J (who always called the place Jebus), S (who called it Jeru-Salem), Z (who thought of it as Zion), and D (who preferred City of David)! In fact the Chronicler would have been familiar with all the names, and the varied usage might well indicate here – as, no doubt, in other passages where such theories are applied more seriously – not different authors, but different overtones.

The name 'Jerusalem', for example, seems increasingly, as the Bible story progresses, to stand for the eternal city – eternal in a way that Rome, pretending to that title, could never be. This is the home of God and his people in the world to come,[15] and at the other end of Scripture its predecessor Salem was the home of the mysterious priest-king Melchizedek, 'a priest for ever', having 'neither beginning of days nor end of life'.[16]

'Jebus', on the other hand, is the historical city, the home of an old Canaanite tribe called the Jebusites. Jebus is the past; but to say it was 'dead and gone' would be incorrect: it is dead, but by no means gone, and somewhere deep beneath the streets of modern Jerusalem is a layer of Jebusite rubble, representing the hard facts that underlie all biblical theology.

'Zion' is the name used again and again in Scripture when the city's spiritual meaning is in view. In particular, a score of references in the Psalms speak of it thus. On Zion's hill God enthrones his king;[17] his greatness, love, and praise are made known there;[18] with gospel grace he adopts Gentiles and pagans as 'natives' of Zion;[19] the strength of its situation pictures the security of his people.[20]

The strong city of Psalm 125 leads to the last of the four names: 'David dwelt in the stronghold; therefore it was called the city of David.' He had been strong enough to capture it (11:4–6), and he was strong enough to keep it (11:7–9). The king, the throne, the stronghold: the power which holds the people together as a unity, bound in one, as it were, within the 'complete circuit', the 'surrounding wall' (11:8 NIV)[21] of the city of David. Thus at the

---

[15] Rev. 21:2ff.
[16] Gn. 14:18; Heb. 7:3.
[17] Ps. 2, used often of Christ in the New Testament.
[18] Ps. 48.    [19] Ps. 87.    [20] Ps. 125.
[21] If this is what the phrase *ūˊad–hassābîb* means; commentators agree only on the obscurity of the verse.

heart of the new kingdom is a city both eternal and historical, the repository of spiritual truth and the seat of strong government.

For the first readers of Chronicles all this must have been a difficult truth to grasp. It was all very well to say that around a king of that sort, reigning over such a city, God's people would find their true unity; but no such king existed in their day, and they had to work out the application of the sermon to such principles as did govern their lives. But for New Testament believers the picture has come back into focus. We do have a king enthroned among his subjects, and can see something of the inner meaning of these chapters. The implication of 10:1–14, that David's character is the opposite of Saul's, highlights also the character of Christ. *He* is the man after God's heart, who fulfils all his will. Where God's people are what they ought to be, it is only because this Man, in whose words and works alone the heart and will of God can truly be known, is at the centre. Where he is not proclaimed and obeyed, the church will disintegrate. But where he *is* acknowledged, there, as in the events of 11:1–3, his people will be gathered to him. Like Israel of old, men and women will recognize how he is one with them, understanding human nature from the inside; what he has done for them, in the victory which has delivered them from their enemies; the covenant he offers to them, asking only that they should accept his rule; and the divine word which has sent him among them, as the climax of all that God has been saying down the years. They will recognize these things, and as they do so they will be drawn to him. That is, the preaching of the great doctrines of incarnation, redemption, grace, and revelation have a magnetic power which attracts and unites. Thus, as in 11:4–9, the city of the great king is established. We have come to the heavenly Jerusalem, whose walls are salvation and whose gates are praise.[22]

> I rejoiced with those who said to me,
>     'Let us go to the house of the LORD.'
> Our feet are standing
>     in your gates, O Jerusalem!
> Jerusalem is built like a city
>     that is closely compacted together.
> That is where the tribes go up,

[22] Heb. 12:22; Is. 60:18.

> the tribes of the LORD,
> To praise the name of the LORD
>   according to the statute given to Israel.
> There the thrones for judgment stand,
>   the thrones of the house of David. [23]

## 2. The king's people (11:10–47; 12:1–40)

The king, then, is the centre around which the people are bound into a unity: 'one church, one faith, one Lord'. This common identity does not mean, however, that they lose their individuality. They have the same loyalty, but they do not all think alike. They speak the same language, but do not all sound alike. They are one, yet they are immensely varied. There lies ready to hand in Samuel/Kings a passage which well conveys the variety of character to be found among the king's people. There, it comes much later in the story of David (2 Sa. 23:8–39). But if it is right to see the theme of these chapters as 'the unity and individuality of the people of God', then it is appropriate that the Chronicler should bring forward this passage, the list of David's mighty men, and include it here.

We have seen 'all Israel' come to make David king; in the same way, the thing that unites the mighty men is their loyalty to him. But what a diversity of loyal individuals! And in the king's service, and therefore (to illustrate the point) in the Chronicler's record, there is room for each and every one. To bring some order out of what may seem merely a miscellany of names, we might distinguish eight groups.

### a. *The outstanding (11:11–14)*

'Jashobeam ... was chief of the three' (11:11), says the RSV, preferring this description of Jashobeam's group to the MSS which read 'the thirty' or 'the captains'. The Chronicler does speak of 'the three mighty men' (11:12), even though he seems to mention only Jashobeam and Eleazar by name; but Samuel/Kings has the full story, and it looks as though at some stage in the transcribing of the book a copyist's eye slid from one Philistine gathering (2 Sa. 23:9) to the next (2 Sa. 23:11) and in the process missed Shammah. An unfortunate slip, in the circumstances: the very reason for recording

[23] Ps. 122:1–5 NIV.

these names was that they were the most notable of all David's warriors – leaders of the calibre always needed by God's people, and unfailingly provided for them by God. Such people are to be recognized and honoured (and *not* overlooked).[24]

### b. The adventurous (11:15–19)

The names of this trio have been forgotten, but what they did was unforgettable. It took place when David was no longer a shepherd boy in Bethlehem, but before he had become king in Hebron or Jerusalem. He had made the cave of Adullam his headquarters at the time when every man's hand was against him, and he was in danger both from the Philistines and from Saul's Israelite army. Even in those early days, at least seven years before he established himself in Jerusalem (see 1 Ch. 29:27), these three unnamed heroes had proved their valour, and their devotion to David, as they conceived the ridiculous and splendid notion of fighting their way through the enemy lines, and back, simply to gratify his whim for a drink from the well he had known in childhood. They stand as examples of all those in the history of God's people whose service for the king, though sometimes foolhardy, has nevertheless been imaginative, valiant, and daring.

### c. The overshadowed (11:20–25)

Here, as in 11:11, it is hard to know what exactly the figures were. Perhaps the NIV rendering of 11:21 best represents the original: Abishai 'was doubly honoured above the Three and became their commander, even though he was not included among them'.[25] On the other hand, the RSV translation says that both Abishai and Benaiah 'did not attain to the three'. What is hard then, if this is what the Chronicler means, is to find the right word to describe them. 'Second-class' is quite misleading, and 'second-rate' even worse; they were second to none except the three supreme heroes. Benaiah was renowned for a number of great deeds; the meaning of 'ariels' is not certain (11:22 RSV; 'champions' is NEB's guess), but who having once read it could fail to remember the incident of 'a lion in a pit in a snowy day'?[26] Abishai's fame rested upon one

---

[24] See Eph. 4:11; Heb. 13:7; and note the ironic Hebrew meaning of the name: Shammah is 'There'!

[25] This would accord with what is said elsewhere about Abishai (2 Sa. 2:17–24).

[26] 11:22 AV; another of the graphic references, so frequent in these chapters and similar to those with which the genealogies are studded (*e.g.* Nimrod, Jabez; see pp. 30, 33), which anchor the Chronicler's narrative in the popular memory of his readers.

particular exploit, greater than any of Benaiah's. Perhaps the word is not 'second' anything, but 'overshadowed' – 'made apparently less important by others' brilliance'.[27] 'It takes more grace than I can tell To play the second fiddle well'; but where would the orchestra be without the second fiddles?

### d. The unremembered (11:26–47)

It is not clear how this list relates to the 'Thirty' mentioned earlier (11:15, 25),[28] or to the parallel list in Samuel/Kings, which ends with Uriah the Hittite (11:41; 2 Sa. 23:24–39). One might call this group 'the anonymous', except that 'unnamed' is precisely the wrong way to describe them – the names are practically the only thing we *do* know about them! So thousands in the king's service are known to their fellow-warriors in other times and other places by their names alone; millions more, indeed, lack even that niche in the wall of fame. Nonetheless God had set his seal on them: 'The Lord knows those who are his'.[29] It is a sobering thought that we ourselves, around whom (we tend to assume) the world revolves, are not even names to far the greater part of the church militant. With the church triumphant it is, no doubt, a different matter. But, in the famous words from the Apocrypha, in this world 'some there be, which have no memorial; who are perished, as though they had never been ... Their bodies are buried in peace; but', valued by and intimately known to God, in his heavenly record 'their name liveth for evermore'.[30]

### e. The discerning (12:1–7)

This passage, like the one about the three adventurous warriors who fetched the water from Bethlehem, refers to the time when Saul was still on the throne. The background events are described in 1 Samuel 27. The discerning eye that made them accurate marksmen with both bow and sling is evidenced in another sense by the fact that they were 'Benjaminites, Saul's kinsmen', and yet came to the aid of the fugitive David. In those days of enmity between the two men, blind tribal loyalty would have ranged these warriors behind the reigning king, with whom they had ties of blood-relationship. But something – a sharp eye, politically and spiritually? – indicated to

---

[27] See *overshadowed* in Concise Oxford Dictionary.
[28] And possibly in other verses; *cf.* the versions of 11:20–21.
[29] 2 Tim. 2:19.　　　[30] Ecclus. 44:9, 14 AV.

them that the future lay not with him but with David. The leaders of this band actually came from Saul's own town, Gibeah. We may picture them observing their kinsman and neighbour, asking questions, weighing the alternatives: 'Which way is right? The party line, or is God call us to one which is likely to be misunderstood, unpopular, and dangerous?' They made the choice, and 'came to David at Ziklag'.

### f.  The valiant (12:8–15)

Even earlier than the Benjaminites' coming to Ziklag was the arrival of these Gadite troops in the days when David was camping in strongholds in the wilderness (1 Sa. 23 – 26). Fierce as lions and 'swift as gazelles', they were reckoned to be 'mighty and experienced warriors' (12:8), and 12:14 is probably not about their rank ('the lesser [were each] over a hundred and the greater over a thousand', RSV) but about their reputation ('the least was a match for a hundred, and the greatest for a thousand', NIV). 12:15, though also a debated verse, illustrates their valour, whether it refers simply to the crossing of a river so flooded that it was making even the tributary valleys on both sides impassable (so most commentaries), or whether the Gadites in the course of their march put to flight the inhabitants of all those valleys (so most versions).

### g.  The inspired (12:16–18)

This band of soldiers from Benjamin and Judah has something special about it. Not at first sight, however, since David's initial reaction to its coming is one of suspicion: for some reason he fears possible treachery. Perhaps this is the Chronicler's way of recalling to his readers' minds a grisly incident, even further back in the history of Samuel/Kings than the circumstances of the last two paragraphs: the betrayal to Saul, by Doeg the Edomite, of an entire priestly community, and its subsequent slaughter (1 Sa. 21 – 22). In fact David has nothing to fear from this 'Thirty'. Their support for him is unfeigned, and is demonstrated in a particularly memorable way. A phrase is used in this passage which occurs only three times in the whole Old Testament: concerning Gideon the judge,[31] Zechariah the prophet,[32] and, here, Amasai the warrior (12:18). According to most of the translations, 'the Spirit came

[31] Jdg. 6:34.
[32] Not of course the author of the book of Zechariah, who lived much later; see below, p. 113. This prophet we shall meet in 2 Ch. 24:20.

upon Amasai'. But the verb which the Chronicler uses actually means that the Spirit of God *clothed himself with* Amasai. Through this man, in no other way distinguished by the Chronicler among David's warriors,[33] God speaks to David a prophetic message of encouragement.[34] In one way unexpected, in another it is a kind of insight which should not surprise God's people, as his still-speaking Spirit reminds them through unlikely mouthpieces of what his Word has already told them: where God's favour rests, and what the consequence of that is (12:18).

*b. The cautious (12:19–22)*

We might even call them 'the tardy'. From an incident which reminds us of the earliest days of David's conflict with Saul, the Chronicler now moves to one at the very end of Saul's reign. The background to the fighting between Israel and the Philistines, in which David almost found himself in action on the side of the latter, and in which Saul was soon to die, is described in 1 Samuel 29. Not until the eve of the battle of Mount Gilboa (1 Sa. 31) – until, in other words, it was obvious which way the wind was blowing – did this band of Manassites throw in their lot with David. He was by that time clearly the man of the future, and Saul was equally clearly doomed. Only then did they make a decision made much earlier by brave men of other tribes. One is reminded of Jesus' parable of the labourers in the vineyard. Why should those who join in at the eleventh hour be put on an equal footing with those who, like Amasai's troop in the last paragraph, 'have borne the burden of the day and the scorching heat'?[35] There is an apparent unfairness, which in the gospel story is intended to teach a lesson about the sovereign grace of God. The workings of divine grace will be a major theme in a later chapter of this book. But there is also a shrewdness about the cautious men of Manasseh which is a gift not to be despised. We may be sure that the king values it and uses it for his own purposes.

The roll-call of the troops 'who came to David in Hebron, to turn the kingdom of Saul over to him' (12:23), sums up the whole of this

---

[33] Except that he was, or was to become, 'chief of the thirty'; and if he is identical with the Amasa of 2 Sa. 17:25; 19:13, he was in those histories a noted military commander.

[34] Williamson (p. 108) brings out the possible importance of the time and place of this assurance of divine favour.

[35] Mt. 20:9–12.

section concerning the unity and individuality of the people of God. Even the summary list of 12:23–37 does not consist merely of names and numbers: *individuals* (Jehoiada, Zadok) are specially noted, as are distinguishing points about the background and character of each tribe's contingent. Yet at the same time the Chronicler is at pains to tell us that representatives of every tribe *united* in David's support. Our three chapters conclude (12:38–40) with an impressive picture of 'all these, men of war' together with 'all the rest of Israel' coming to enthrone the king, with 'full intent' and 'a single mind'.[36]

This picture of the beginning of the Davidic monarchy stands in contrast to what has gone before. In the time of the judges, the people of God formed politically a kind of loose federation of tribes, an 'amphictyony'. To call it the 'United States of Israel' would not be altogether inaccurate, but any notion of a strong central federal government would be wide of the mark. The tribes went their independent ways, with mutual suspicions and recriminations, quarrelling among themselves and unable to pull together. The very individuality which should have been an ornament of a united nation was tending to make that nation fly apart: 'every man did what was right in his own eyes'.[37] This was as improper a model for the life of the people of God as, at the other extreme, a regimented dictatorship would be. The ideal to strive for is that expressed in New Testament terms by Paul's three great chapters in 1 Corinthians on the 'varieties of gifts' which Christians are expected to use 'for the common good' and in loyalty to 'the same Lord'.[38] For us, as for ancient Israel, the enormous diversity to be found among the king's people is integrated, drawn together into a unity, around the people's king.

[36] 'The Chronicler relates that the trickle of men who joined David at Adullam became a flood before Saul's reign was over' (Payne, p. 32). In the preceding pages Payne has listed the reasons why the description in 12:1–22 of David's ever-increasing support is 'more plausible than many biblical scholars will allow'.

[37] Jdg. 17:6; 21:25.

[38] 1 Cor. 12 – 14; 12:4, 7,5.

# 1 Chronicles 13, 15 – 16

## 5. Changeless grace in changing circumstances

It is not possible at one and the same time to consider the Chronicler's themes successively and to follow his narrative in order. He likes to intertwine his chief themes, with the result that either we work steadily through the books and find ourselves shifting from one subject to another and back again, or we pursue one particular subject at a time and find that we have to skip chapters to do so.[1] Although our study of the first main section of the two books (1 Ch. 1 – 9) has taken the chapters in order, we have seen already how the topic of priesthood (the tribe of Levi) moves from chapter 6 to chapter 9, while that of kingship (the tribes of Benjamin and Judah) links chapters 2, 3, 4, and 8. Again in the latter part of 1 Chronicles, the story of David, the themes intertwine, and here a thematic approach seems important enough to suggest that we should for once sit loosely to the chapter order. The ark, the symbol of God's changeless grace in changing circumstances, is the subject of chapters 13, 15, and 16; chapter 14 gives advance notice of a different subject, David's foreign policy and international relations, which is to reappear later on. We shall first consider the three 'ark' chapters, therefore, and afterwards link chapter 14 with chapters 18 to 20.

Moses had been instructed long before[2] about the making of the gold-plated box which was known as the ark of the covenant, and which from his time onwards was the heart of Israelite religion and worship. It contained a number of articles dating back to those great days when God met his people in the desert of Sinai. The New Testament mentions this[3] and indicates that the ark, like the rest of the tent and its furniture, contained also much spiritual meaning. That meaning is brought out by the Chronicler as part of his story of David.

[1] See the diagram on p. 87.
[2] Ex. 25; 37.
[3] Heb. 9:1–5.

As the priests of Israel, according to the ritual of their worship, proceeded stage by stage through courtyard, outer curtain, holy place, and inner curtain, into the holy of holies where the ark rested, so we in four exploratory steps may see its meaning progressively revealed.

## 1. The characteristics which the ark possesses (13:1–14)

Certain things which the Chronicler wants to stress concerning the ark are brought out in the narrative of this chapter. He does not need to describe its physical appearance; although none of his readers will ever have seen it,[4] they will know the descriptions of it in Exodus 25 and 37. Nor does he need to explain why it is, at the beginning of David's reign, in the town of Kiriath-jearim, for they will know from Samuel/Kings the story of how it was taken into battle as a talisman by the Israelites, captured by the Philistines, passed from one Philistine city to another like a hot potato leaving burnt fingers wherever it went, and at last returned to its homeland, coming to rest eventually in that southern Israelite town (1 Sa. 4:1 – 7:2). The Chronicler's concern is to show how it is brought out from the obscurity of those twenty years at Kiriath-jearim to a place of honour in Jerusalem. So for us the characteristics of this ancient relic are brought out of the shadows and set plainly before us in the events here described.

### a. Its importance (13:1–4)

It is David who convenes a mass meeting, and David who there proposes the bringing of the ark to Jerusalem. He as king is at the centre of his nation's life. As the king is the magnet holding a people who would otherwise scatter, so he is the motor driving them if they will not move when they should. The kingship has both functions, 'to hasten or control'.[5] In chapters 10 to 12 David is bringing Israel under his control; in this chapter he is hastening his people into action.

The gathering is large, but also (more importantly) comprehensive. 'Every leader ... all the assembly ... all the people' come together. The older history simply describes David setting forth

---

[4] Not even the high priest of the day, who alone had the right to enter the holy of holies (Heb. 9:7); for the ark had been lost when the first temple was destroyed, and its place in the second temple was empty.

[5] J. E. Bode, *O Jesus, I have promised.*

with 'all the people who were with him' (2 Sa. 6:2), but the Chronicler wants to make a particular point, and a slightly different one. Not simply all those who happened to be with David, but representatives of the whole nation, set out for Kiriath-jearim, because they had all *agreed to do so.'* So this Old Testament story embodies the New Testament principle of the 'two or three' (Mt. 18:15–20): a thought in the mind of one individual is found to be the common thought of several, and thus those who are asking 'if it is the will of the LORD our God' conclude that it is, and 'the thing [is] right in the eyes of all' (13:2, 4).

David proposes, then; the people agree; and God ratifies. In this way the excursion to Kiriath-jearim is mounted. But the object of it is more to the point than the method. All is planned with a view to the reinstatement of the ark. The intentions of the king, people, and God converge on the ark. So important is this gilded box considered to be.

### b. Its charisma (13:5–8)

It does more than engage the attention of David and his people. It fires them with enthusiasm. This quality of 'excitingness', the 'charisma' of the ark, is seen in the description of the second great gathering, not now to deliberate over what to do, but actually to do it. What is in mind is nothing more than a march from Jerusalem to Kiriath-jearim and back, a round trip of seventeen miles or so. Yet from one end of the country to the other, from the Shihor in the south to the 'entrance of Hamath' in the north,[6] the imagination of 'all Israel' is caught by the idea. Planned as a procession, in the event it becomes a positive carnival. To this celebration the people come flocking, in even greater numbers than for the consultation of 13:1–4. There is something about the ark, or what the ark stands for, that makes God's people want to dance and sing. It is not only important; it is exciting.

### c. Its holiness (13:9–13)

The third characteristic of the ark is made plain by a strange incident which introduces a jarring note into this story of joy. The great company arrives at the home of Abinadab in Kiriath-jearim

---

[6] The Shihor was the river reckoned as the boundary between Canaan and Egypt. The 'entrance' to the state of Hamath, Israel's northern neighbour, lay between the mountain ranges of Lebanon and Hermon. See Jos. 13:3–5.

(13:7), where for twenty years past the ark has been kept. From the 'house on the hill' (as the old story twice calls it) the precious golden box is brought forth, to be set on a new cart hauled by oxen and driven by Abinadab's sons.[7] Then, as the returning procession draws level with Chidon's threshing-floor, the oxen stumble, the cart jolts, the ark seems about to slide off, Uzzah reaches out a hand to steady it – and the Lord strikes him dead.

David's anger seems entirely understandable! There could scarcely be a more effective way of quenching the joy of the occasion. But he is not unversed in the ways of God. God's action may make David angry, but Uzzah's action must have made God angry in the first place. So David's anger gives way to fear. However important and exciting the ark may be, it is clear that there is also something perilous about it. The fate of Uzzah is a fearful warning against over-familiarity with God. His attitude to the thing should have been as reverent as his attitude to the Person. That, indeed, is the meaning of holiness. The ark belongs to God. It is specially his, consecrated to him. Therefore it is to be regarded with appropriate awe, and treated with appropriate respect. It is holy.

### d. Its goodness (13:14)

So 'the ark of God remained with the household of Obed-edom'. That memorable day did not reach its intended climax; there was no triumphal arrival in Jerusalem. Alarmed at the ark's lethal holiness, David (reflecting no doubt the general dismay at Uzzah's untimely death) put it down there and then, at the house of Obed-edom the Gittite, who became its custodian for the next three months.

In that time one more characteristic of the ark was demonstrated. Everyone who had taken part in the unfinished festival had seen how dangerous the things of God can be when the careless mishandle them. Yet the coming of the ark to Obed-edom's home brought three months of unstinted blessing.[8] Surprisingly, perhaps, its devastating holiness is found to go hand in hand with a positive and enriching goodness. We may be sure that it was set down with the utmost reverence in the house of this man from Gath, whose pagan Philistine relations had already learned by experience a greater

---

[7] A number of the details are omitted by the Chronicler, but would be known to his readers from the parallel passages in 1 Sa. 7:1–2 and 2 Sa. 6:3–5.

[8] 'See the *completeness* of God's work when things are as they should be,' says the Chronicler's sermon, as it adds a phrase to Samuel/Kings: 'the Lord blessed not only Obed-edom and his household but *all that he had* (2 Sa. 6:11)'. See above, p. 55.

respect for the ark than the Israelites themselves had (see 1 Sa. 5:8ff.).

Is there a capricious magic about this biblical picture of the ark, which makes us view it with some scepticism? No more than there is in our own prosaic experience of a natural power such as electricity, highly beneficial or highly dangerous depending on whether or not it is approached with an understanding of its nature. In the case of the ark, the dealing out of destruction on the one hand and blessings on the other is similarly related to an understanding of what it is, and not to the use or non-use of correct magical formulae.

At this point the reader may be impatient about one obvious question which is increasingly demanding an answer! But before the Chronicler deals with this, he intends to develop a theme arising from chapter 13 – the holiness of the ark, which caused the death of Uzzah – as he expounds the events which took place three months later, when the ark finally did reach Jerusalem. A different subject, David's relationship with the surrounding nations, begins in chapter 14 to be interwoven with the Chronicler's other threads. To that we shall return in due course. For the present we move on to chapter 15, and take up again the story of the ark there.

## 2. The attention which the ark deserves (15:1 – 16:3)

A general attitude of respect for the ark is not in itself sufficient. On its own, it is analogous to the approach to Christ which calls him 'Lord, Lord' but does not do what he says.[9] A notion of what we think reverence might involve has to become a conviction, in both heart and mind, of what God says it actually does involve.

### a. Ancient ceremony (15:1–15)

The 'outbreak against Uzzah'[10] causes David to reflect on how *ancient* the ark is. 'It was because you, the Levites, did not bring it up the first time', he says (15:13 NIV), 'that the LORD our God broke out in anger against us. We did not enquire of him about how to do it in the prescribed way.' There are ancient rules which govern the handling of the ark. A proper respect for it means obeying those rules. This is why David has re-enacted the particular principle in 15:2: 'No one but the Levites may carry the ark.' And, though there may have been ignorance about what the rules were, there was no

[9] See Lk. 6:46.
[10] The meaning of the place-name Perez-uzza (13:11 NIV, mg).

doubt as to where they were to be found: when eventually it was brought to Jerusalem, 'the Levites carried the ark of God upon their shoulders with the poles, *as Moses had commanded according to the word of the LORD*' (15:15).[11] As the ark dates back to Moses' time, so do the regulations about it; and to implement them David calls on the Levites, who trace their family lines back to that same period and beyond.

Even in these days of built-in obsolescence, most of us have household appliances which we hope will last for some years, and not need to be discarded at the first sign of trouble. With that in mind, we are glad to keep for reference when necessary the original instructions from the maker. It would be foolish, finding such a booklet which had been mislaid or forgotten, to throw it away as if its age made it useless. To David, the ark for all its antiquity is a central feature of his people's religion, and so he goes back to the maker's instructions to find out about its proper handling.

Then with pomp and ceremony he assembles representatives of 'all Israel' once again, contingents from the three great Levite families, and the chief priests and 'heads of the fathers' houses of the Levites', and requires the proper ritual for their personal preparation and for the carrying of the ark (15:3, 4ff., 11–12, 14–15). In this way he sees to it that all is as the ancient law decrees.

### b. *Modern worship (15:16 – 16:3)*

Yet, like the famous Anglican hymn book, the worship that surrounds the ark is to be both 'ancient and modern'. The principles underlying it are rooted in the past, but the expression of them is very much of the present. The difference between the orchestra of 15:19–22 and that of 13:8 is not in its composition, but (naturally, in the circumstances) in its more detailed and careful ordering. For all that, the vigour of its music-making was thoroughly uninhibited, as the narrative goes on to show (15:25–29). We do not know whether the music was new in the sense of being composed for the occasion, any more than we know the meaning of the terms Alamoth and Sheminith (15:20, 21).[12] But we may be sure that in every sense that mattered Israel was singing 'to the LORD a new song'.[13]

---

[11] *Cf.* Nu. 3:5–10, 27–31; 4:1–15.

[12] 'Alamoth (*'alāmôṯ*) means "girls"; Sheminith (*š*ᵉ*mīnîṯ*) means "eighth" ... the majority opinion is that Alamoth means the treble range, and Sheminith therefore the tenor or bass' (Derek Kidner, *Psalms 1 – 72* (Inter-Varsity Press, 1973), pp. 40–41).

[13] Pss. 96:1; 98:1.

So David sees to it that the ark is given the best in contemporary worship, as well as the closest attention to its historical background.

15:1–24 is a revealing example of one kind of material that specially interests the Chronicler: what will in due course become the temple worship, lovingly and painstakingly detailed (see 1 Ch. 23 – 28; 2 Ch. 3 – 7, 29 – 31, 35). He has inserted this passage into the older history, between the note that the LORD has blessed Obed-edom's house (2 Sa. 6:11) and the record of David's going to fetch the ark (2 Sa. 6:12b). Picking up the Samuel/Kings narrative at that point; he rewrites the following verse. The earlier account said that 'when those who bore the ark of the LORD had gone six paces, he sacrificed an ox and a fatling' (2 Sa. 6:13), implying perhaps that as soon as the ark had been picked up and its progress had resumed without anyone being struck down as Uzzah had been, a thankoffering was in order. The Chronicler spells out the implication. This time 'God helped the Levites' (15:26); the careful attention given both to the principles and to the practice of the ritual relating to the ark meant that now his favour was assured.

After dilating so much on the procession arrangements, the Chronicler goes to the other extreme: he mentions very briefly the scorn of David's wife Michal at the sight of 'David dancing and making merry' (15:29), and omits the altercation between the two which followed (2 Sa. 6:20–23). In the incident as Samuel/Kings recounts it our sympathies may well be with Michal. Perhaps for our author she is simply a representative of the house of Saul, showing that it is still not in tune with the mind of God; whereas in giving the ark the attention it deserves, David is.

### 3. The truth which the ark enshrines (16:4–36)

The question which was outstanding after we had considered the characteristics of the ark[14] should wait no longer for an answer. It concerns, of course, the relevance of all this to the Chronicler's readers. It is all very well for him to write so enthusiastically about Israelite worship in the days of David; but he is centring it on the very thing which, with all their attempts to revive true worship after the exile, they do not actually possess! The temple rebuilt, the priesthood restored, sacrifice recommenced – but the ark has disappeared, and even if they wanted to give it the honours which

[14] See above, p. 68.

the Chronicler seems to be commending, they could not; it is not there to be honoured.

He would surely say that the very absence of the ark makes in these chapters the kind of point which he wants to make throughout his great sermon. What matters is not so much the thing itself (in this case, indeed, it cannot be) as the truth which the thing enshrines. This ark, which in the days of David was so important, so exciting, so electric with holiness, so rich with blessing; this ark, which deserved the best worship of David's own day because it was still venerable with the aura of a bygone day – what does it actually stand for? What does it mean?

This will be the subject of the greater part of chapter 16. But a clue has already been planted in the closing verses of chapter 15. No less than four times over it is there called 'the ark of the covenant' (15:25, 26, 28, 29).

### a. The ark of God means the covenant of God (16:4–6)

Once the ark has arrived in Jerusalem and been installed in the tent prepared for it, some of the Levites previously involved in the procession are appointed to continue the worship in music. It goes without saying that it is not the ark itself which is being worshipped. The ministry of Asaph and his fellow-musicians is 'to invoke, to thank, and to praise *the LORD, the God of Israel*'. This God is unique among the gods of the nations. He is Yahweh, the one who came to rescue his people from slavery in Egypt and to make them his own through the great encounter at Sinai. There he decreed that he would be their God, and they his people, for ever. That was his covenant, and 'the LORD' – Yahweh – is his covenant name. 'The LORD', therefore, is the object of the continual praise of Israel, and once more, as if to clinch the point, the ark which is the focus of this praise is called 'the ark of the covenant of God' (16:6).

It is no coincidence that the many-sided genius of the king includes musicianship and poetry. He knows what he is about as he sets the tone for worship in God's holy place through all the years to come (16:7). In a text to be found also in the book of Psalms, as we shall see, the covenant is mentioned three times (16:15–17), while the meaning of the covenant is the theme of the entire song.

### b. The covenant of God means the grace of God (16:7–36)

The musicians have been appointed 'to invoke, to thank, and to praise the LORD', and their psalm does exactly that. It is a composite poem, bracketing the whole of Psalm 96 between parts of Psalms 105 and 106, and its grand subject throughout is the God of the covenant.

In 16:8–22 (Psalm 105:1–15) we celebrate first the deeds of Yahweh and his wonderful works (16:8–13), then his words, his judgments and covenant and promise (16:14–18), and then both together – what he did and said on his people's behalf in the time of their weakness (16:19–22). In 16:23–33 (Psalm 96) our praise is directed to his greatness (16:23–27) and his worth (16:28–33). The song ends (16:34–36) with the opening and closing words of Psalm 106 (verses 1, 47–48), as a personal cry in which the singers take hold of the covenant relationship for themselves: 'Yahweh, you are "the God of our salvation": we have praised you for all that you have done and said in the past; now we ask you to act and speak on our behalf also.'

But notice throughout the psalm where the emphasis lies. It is *his* deeds, *his* words, *his* greatness and worth. The covenant is a great scheme of blessing set up entirely for his people's benefit, but entirely on his own initiative. In a word, it is a covenant of *grace*. The corollary of their being 'few in number, and of little account' (16:19) is that the grounds of his covenant are to be found not in them at all but in him alone: in terms of the memorable definition of grace in Deuteronomy 7:7–8, he loves them simply because he loves them.

That is the truth which the ark enshrines. Yet even now we have not penetrated to the very heart of this holy place. The final verses of chapter 16 lift the veil and give a glimpse into the holy of holies, and we see as it were the real ark, that truth concerning it which most deeply affects those who would be God's people.


## 4. The promise which the ark conceals (16:37–43)

We may grant that the important thing about the ark is not the object itself but the truth it stands for, and yet we may still feel there is something slightly odd about the Chronicler's preoccupation with it. His fourth-century readers might well have sensed this oddity. There was more to it than the fact that this article, which he apparently regarded so highly, was not there in their temple. There was also the fact that even when it had been there, it had been far from being the most obvious feature in the practice of their religion. No one but the high priest ever even saw it, and he only once a year. Much more obviously central, indeed constantly and obtrusively so, was the whole system of altar and sacrifice. But the Chronicler is subtly changing this emphasis. His David is much involved with the offering of sacrifices (15:26; 16:1–2, 39–40), but the altars are set up because the ark is there, and not vice versa. He is showing us that the ark takes precedence over the altar: that is, that in the nature of things the gift of grace must precede the response of faith; and the promise contained in that truth – a New Testament promise, a gospel promise, if ever there was one – he reveals as the final secret of the ark by means of the short paragraph which rounds off these chapters.

### a. Grace distinct from faith

The events described almost make his point for him. 'David left Asaph ... before the ark of the covenant of the LORD', now installed in Jerusalem (15:1–3), and 'left Zadok ... before the tabernacle of the LORD *in the high place that was at Gibeon*, to offer burnt offerings to the LORD upon the altar' (16:37, 39–40).

If the ark is a symbol of God's grace, and the altar a symbol of man's response, the relation between the two is instructive. They are normally inseparable, for man cannot respond until God has given him something to respond to, and conversely to God's action in grace one expects there to be a human reaction. As if to illustrate this, through all the centuries that elapse between the making of the tabernacle in Moses' time and the destruction of the temple in Zedekiah's, the ark and the altar are practically always found together. But not *quite* always. And it so happens that the formative period of the early monarchy, from which the Chronicler is preaching spiritual fundamentals, is precisely the period when the two were separated. The divine grace represented by the ark of the covenant and the human response pictured by the offerings at the altar are two distinct things. If they are invariably linked, we are in danger of misunderstanding the relationship between them. So people readily assume that where there is much religious observance, or much Christian activity, or even much 'faith', there God's grace is bound to wait upon it. Where the altar is, there the ark is bound to be. But grace is not in fact bound: not to religion, not to good works, not even to the work of 'faith'. It is perfectly possible for the altar to be at Gibeon while the ark is in Jerusalem.

## b. Grace independent of circumstances

Indeed, even as the ark of the covenant will not necessarily be found where the sacrifices are being offered, so it does not have to be in *any* particular location. In this respect also the Chronicler is stripping away misunderstandings which seem to conceal the truth about God's grace. Once the ark had been firmly ensconced, not just in the tent provided by David but in the temple built by Solomon, it gave rise to a belief which, though in one sense true, could easily lead to false conclusions. This is the thought expressed in so many psalms: 'The LORD has chosen Zion ... : "This is my resting place for ever"';[15] 'The LORD loves the gates of Zion more than all the dwelling places of Jacob'.[16] So deeply rooted did this notion become in the minds not only of Israelites but also of neighbouring peoples, that a thousand years later a Samaritan woman would tell Jesus – *O sancta simplicitas*! – that the very distinction between Hebrew religion and others was a matter of what we might call geographical grace: he as a Jew, she said, would naturally hold that 'in Jerusalem is the place where men ought to worship', while '*our* fathers worshipped on this mountain', Gerizim.[17]

But history told how the ark had in fact travelled to all sorts of places. Indeed it had been specifically designed to be portable,[18] and had spent the first forty years of its existence accompanying the Israelites on their constant journeyings in the wilderness of Sinai. Even after the people were settled in the promised land, it seems to have continued its travels: it turns up now at Gilgal,[19] now at Bethel,[20] now at Shiloh.[21] Captured by the Philistines, it makes the round of their five cities, as potent a sign of God's presence among unbelievers as among believers. Returning to Israelite territory, it finds another temporary home at Bethshemesh, and then moves to Kiriath-jearim. There the Chronicler takes up its story. The last two stages before it reaches Jerusalem are enough to provide him with evidence that God's grace operates, whether for bane or blessing, regardless of where it may be. It is 'a fragrance from death to death' at Perez-uzza, 'a fragrance from life to life' at the house of Obed-edom.[22] It does not have to be in Jerusalem before it can be effective.

---

[15] Ps. 132:13–14.  [16] Ps. 87:2.
[17] Jn. 4:20; and see below, p. 129.  [18] Ex. 25:14.
[19] Jos. 4:19.  [20] Jdg. 20:26–27.
[21] Jos. 18:1; 1 Sa. 4:3–4.  [22] 2 Cor. 2:16.

This aspect of grace has always scandalized those who like to have God's workings contained within the familiar and the comprehensible. In New Testament times, a more deadly misunderstanding than that of the Samaritan woman is evinced when Stephen, like his Master before him, is accused by Jews in Jerusalem of wanting to 'destroy this place'.[23] His answer, recounted at length in Acts 7, is, in a nutshell, that when man dictates to God the circumstances in which grace is to work and in which he is prepared to respond to it, he is at best a fool and at worst a rebel. The building of Solomon's temple was, as we shall see, a project dear to the Chronicler's heart. But he indicates here that he would have endorsed fully the thought that seems to lie behind Stephen's words in Acts 7:47: 'Solomon ... built a house for [God]' – and one could have wished, from this point of view, that he had not: such dangers are there in believing that God's grace is tied to particular places or circumstances.

### c. Grace greater than its symbols

So we come to the last enigma. For the Chronicler has been preaching the glories of the ark of the covenant *to people who no longer possess it*. For years the tangible reminders of the great period of Israel's kingship and priesthood have been slipping, one by one, from their grasp. They build another temple, and later try to set up another royal house, but the fact of the matter is that practically the whole structure of Davidic Israel has evaporated around them. 'The cloud-capp'd towers, the gorgeous palaces' have dissolved, 'and, like this insubstantial pageant faded, leave not a rack behind.'[24] The readers of this book ask therefore the most obvious of all the questions, and receive the profoundest of all the answers. 'Why preach to us about the ark?' they say; 'we have no ark.' And the Chronicler replies: '*You do not need an ark.* Grace is not bound to your religion or your faith: it precedes them, and they are simply a response to it. Grace is not bound to particular places or circumstances: man must be prepared for God to come down to him anywhere. And grace is not bound to its symbol, the ark, either. Grace is *free*. God is pouring out his grace upon you here and now, ark or no ark, and will be doing so when the entire system of Old Testament Israel, priests, kings, and all, is ancient history. Never say, therefore, that if you go here or there, if you do this or that,

---

[23] Acts 6:14; *cf.* Mk. 14:57-58.
[24] Shakespeare, *The Tempest*, IV.i.152ff.

God will be bound to bless you. His grace is bound to nothing at all except his own love and goodness. Fortunately so; because while everything else is changing and unreliable, that is constant.'

# 1 Chronicles 14, 18 – 20

# 6. The fame and fear of the king

Again, for the moment, following a particular thread rather than the whole fabric of the Chronicler's narrative, we return now to chapter 14, and shall then move forward to chapters 18 to 20.[1] The keynote of these four chapters is struck in 14:17: 'The fame of David went out into all lands, and the LORD brought the fear of him upon all nations.' They deal, in other words, with foreign affairs – with his international relations and influence. In the nature of the case, they mention a number of military campaigns, and David's 'great wars' (22:8) are to have far-reaching and unexpected effects on the later history of Israel.[2] But their immediate result is to add a necessary colour to the Chronicler's picture of David's own time. After considering the way he sets forth this aspect of David's reign, we shall try to see how his sermon applies lessons from it to his own contemporaries, and then to discover its underlying truths and its relevance for every age.

## 1. The Chronicler depicting past time

It is always worth noting how he treats his source materials. In this brief survey we shall see something of the structure of these central chapters of 1 Chronicles, and what he puts into them.

### a. The structure of the section
Chapters 10 to 12 showed us the king with his people gathered round him, their unity and their individuality. That section was

[1] See below, pp. 86–87.    [2] See below, pp. 93–94, 99–100.

followed by the beginning of the 'ark' narrative, in chapter 13. But by the time the Chronicler gets to 13:14 (the ark's stay of three months with Obed-edom), he is well on through his main source book, Samuel/Kings, and has reached 2 Samuel 6:11. So before continuing with the story of the ark, he uses the three-month gap, as it were, as an appropriate place to insert a passage from earlier in that book: 2 Samuel 5:11–25, which now forms the greater part of 1 Chronicles 14.

It may be that the statements in 14:2 about the establishing of David and the exalting of his kingdom are meant as headlines, to be amplified in the rest of the chapter. At home, he is established as his family, and therefore his household, grow. Abroad, his kingdom is exalted as friend and foe alike (Tyre, 14:1; Philistia, 14:8ff.) come to recognize his stature.

To the transcription from Samuel/Kings is added a sentence presumably from the Chronicler's own pen. He had rounded off the story of Saul's last fight against the Philistines (1 Sa.31:1–13 = 1 Ch. 10:1–12) with a personal verdict: 'For his unfaithfulness … the LORD slew him' (1 Ch. 10:13–14). So now he rounds off the story of David's early fighting, as king, against the same enemies (2 Sa. 5:11–25 = 1 Ch. 14:1–16) with the analogous, but contrasting, comment that 'the fame of David went out into all lands, and the LORD brought the fear of him upon all nations' (14:17).

These paragraphs about David's international relations, drawn from further back in the older history, are used to introduce the subject. The Chronicler will return to it further on. For the moment, however, having planted the theme here in chapter 14, he concludes in chapters 15 and 16 his narrative about the ark. Next, in chapter 17 he introduces yet another theme, the temple. That in its turn is then held over for the more detailed treatment later, while chapters 18 to 20 take up our present subject again.

Chapter 14 is based, as we have seen, upon 2 Samuel 5. These other three 'foreign affairs' chapters (18–20) are a compilation of the relevant parts of the rest of 2 Samuel. Chapters 8 and 10 of that book are reproduced here;[3] most of chapters 11 and 12 is excised, and the cut ends (11:1 and 12:26) are stitched together; then nearly nine chapters are skipped, until the Chronicler alights on 21:18–22,

---

[3] Among the various small changes, the addition of 1 Ch. 18:8 (how Solomon later used in the temple bronze captured by David in one of his campaigns) indicates one of the Chronicler's special interests.

which will form the close of his own chapter 20.

The passages he leaves out concern David's personal relationships, some creditable, others less so. The strife, immorality, and murder which marred David's reign are all omitted. A superficial judgment might be that the Chronicler is attempting to whitewash his character. This cannot however be his purpose, since his readers will know David's faults as well as he does. But these personal matters are not his concern. Rather, he is deliberately portraying David the king, not David the man. It is the king's reputation and influence which form the content of the four chapters we are considering.

## b. *The content of the section*

'So David reigned over all Israel; and he administered justice and equity to all his people.' 18:14 stands at the centre of this section, as David sits enthroned at the centre of his kingdom. The nation thus organized around its ruler was the first great image of David's reign to be set before us, in chapters 10 to 12. What now are we to visualize as its effect on the surrounding nations? How do they react?

The great Phoenician seaport of Tyre, to the north of Israel, is friendly. 14:1 indicates the personal contacts between its king, Hiram, and David, which were to develop considerably in the reign of Solomon (2 Ch. 2). On the other hand, the coastal settlements of the south, the 'Pentapolis' or Five Cities of the Philistines, continued to be hostile, as they had been when Saul was king (1 Ch. 10) and before that when Samson was judge.[4] More space (14:8–16) is given to the example of hostility than to the example of friendship, although both contribute to 'the fame' and 'the fear' of the king (14:17).

This is to be the basic pattern also for chapters 18 to 20. The more detailed information in those chapters concerns half-a-dozen of the surrounding nations. The events described begin and end with a series of campaigns against the Philistines, include one against Ammon, described at length, and concern also Moab, Edom, Amalek, and the Aramaean peoples of Zobah, Damascus, Maacah, and Mesopotamia (all 'Syrians' in the RSV). In this long catalogue a single paragraph, corresponding to a single verse in chapter 14, suffices to note those who side with David (there Tyre, here Hamath).

[4] Jdg. 13 – 16.

In other words, most of David's neighbours are opposed to him, though some ally themselves with him. Even his enemies, however, are forced to recognize his power ('The LORD brought the fear of him upon all nations'). All of them, in varying degrees, are subjected to him. The defeat of the Ammonites is particularly thorough and humiliating,[5] and may be described in such detail because of the perfidy of their king Hanun; we have no other record of the previous alliance between David and Hanun's father Nahash (19:2), but such a thing would be in keeping with the fact that the latter was certainly an enemy of Saul's (1 Sa. 11). In the same way, earlier conflicts and alliances are recalled in the final paragraph of this passage, where the Philistine 'giants' are finally overcome 'by the hand of David and by the hand of his servants' (20:8). Thus the accounts of his military achievements come full circle, and we are reminded of the most famous of all of them; for though the Chronicler has chosen not to include it, neither he nor his readers will be unfamiliar with the story of David's encounter, years before, 'with Goliath the Gittite' (20:5; cf. 1 Sa. 17).

Yet not every nation is drawn by 'the fear of him' into conflict with him. For Hiram of Tyre, as we have seen, 'the fame of David' leads to political and maybe personal friendship ('Hiram always loved David', said the older history (1 Ki. 5:1)). There will even be a recognition – how clear, we have no way of knowing – not only of Israel's king but of Israel's God: 'the king of Tyre answered in a letter which he sent to Solomon, "Because the LORD loves his people he has made you king over them ... Blessed be the LORD God of Israel, who made heaven and earth"' (2 Ch. 2:11–12). Tou of Hamath is likewise on excellent terms with David, and sends his son Hadoram with greetings and gifts (18:9–11). With such matters in mind, we may recall an earlier passage which is normally, perhaps, given no more than a cursory glance, and notice that the list of David's mighty men includes Zelek the Ammonite, Uriah the Hittite, and Ithmah the Moabite (11:39, 41, 46); while here in 18:17 appear Cherethites and Pelethites, with whom Samuel/Kings associates also a band of six hundred Gittites (2 Sa. 15:18). What are we to make of all these Hittites and Gittites? Simply this – that they have come into the service of the king of Israel from foreign, generally hostile, nations; and the last group, which seems actually

[5] Though probably not as cruel as in the un-amended text, 'He sawed them with saws' (and also 'made them pass through the brick-kiln', 2 Sa. 12:31 AV, RV).

to be David's personal bodyguard, originates (when re-translated) from Crete, Philistia, and even specifically the Philistine city of Gath, home of his first great adversary Goliath.

Thus in an antagonistic world there are some nations, and in enemy nations there are some individuals, drawn to the side of God's king. But all alike, friend or enemy, acknowledge the fame and fear of David.

### c. A psalm for David's time

Psalm 60 was traditionally held to belong to the period we are considering. It is not easy to fit together the accounts in the three books,[6] but according to its heading the psalm was thought to relate to a war between Israel and Aram,[7] when David was king and Joab his commander-in-chief, and to a slaughter which followed in the Valley of Salt. The heading may not be part of the original work, and many believe its setting is quite different. But the heart of it is surely the truth which the Chronicler wants to demonstrate from that period of history. The cry of verses 1 to 5 fits the context of a dismaying (though in the event temporary) setback: the kind of thing which he, intent on the ultimate victory, would in any case omit from his summary of the wars. But in the turmoil of panic and doubt, God's answer is clear (verses 6–8), and this the Chronicler would vigorously endorse. The word of God has gone forth from his sanctuary, from the city of David: just as every part of Israel belongs to him, so every surrounding nation is in his power. Some accept God's king, many reject him, but all ultimately must acknowledge his fame and fear, for the Lord is with him.

## 2. The Chronicler preaching to his own time

In turning history into a sermon, the Chronicler edits his material considerably, as we have seen. In this section, he has edited out the long, disgraceful tale of David's family troubles.[8] There would be no point in his trying to make David look faultless; his readers are quite well aware of the king's failings. He might more justifiably be accused of making David seem rather inhuman – little more than a

---

[6] Ps. 60; 2 Sa. 8:3–14; 10:6–19; 1 Ch. 18:3–13; 19:6–19.

[7] *I.e.* the 'Syrians' of Mesopotamia (Naharaim, the 'Two Rivers') and of Zobah.

[8] Between 20:1a and 20:1b he has omitted the greater part of the two chapters on David's adultery (2 Sa. 11:2 – 12:25), and between 20:3 and 20:4 nearly nine chapters about the crimes of David's sons and the ensuing civil war (2 Sa. 13:1 – 21:17).

relentless winner of wars. But the real problem about this as a sermon is not that the king is perfect, nor that he is unreal, but that he is cruelly irrelevant.

### a. Royal power as it seems to be

'David ... established ... over Israel', and 'his kingdom ... highly exalted' (14:2), may have been historical facts in the tenth century BC, but by the fourth century BC nothing remotely like them exists any longer. In David's time, Israelite territory stretched 300 miles 'from the Shihor of Egypt to the entrance of Hamath' (13:5); by the Chronicler's time it has been drastically curtailed, and is a tiny fraction of what it once was. In the old days it was ruled by a great king-emperor; now instead of a monarch of its own, it has a mere governor responsible to the distant Persian capital. Then, it had the finest armies in the Near East; now it has none at all. Then, its reputation – 'the fame and fear of the king' – was immense; now it does not even have an independent existence.

In other words, the time *of* which the Chronicler writes is a day of great things, but the time *in* which he writes is a 'day of small things'.[9] What then is the point of his harping on the great days of old? Is it simply nostalgia, a vain hankering after past splendours? Or does he have in mind some sort of restoration of the old 'land of hope and glory' – 'Wider still and wider Shall her bounds be set; God who made thee mighty Make thee mightier yet'?[10] In his time the royal power of David seems not to exist. Yet if his depiction of it is intended as sermon material, a yearning for it as it once was can hardly be serious, and an urging that it might again be striven for can hardly be realistic. What then *does* it have to do with us to whom, here in the Chronicler's time, the sermon is being preached?

### b. Royal power as it really is

Apparently, the royal 'fame and fear' is a cruel mockery. But really, it is a glorious fact. It is in these days, the days of Israel's eclipse, that Scripture sets the stories of Daniel, Nehemiah, and Esther. When Israel is nothing and Babylon is all, Daniel stands up fearlessly in the Babylonian court and declares that 'the Most High rules the kingdom of men, and gives it to whom he will'.[11] When Israel is nothing and Persia is all, Nehemiah demonstrates before his

[9] Zc. 4:10.
[10] A. C. Benson, text for Edward Elgar's *Coronation Ode* (1902).
[11] Dn. 4:17, 25, 32.

opponents that it is God who governs the politics of the Persian empire: 'The king granted me what I asked, for the good hand of my God was upon me'.[12] And in a book, and a world, where God's name is not even mentioned, Esther's story shows his hand unmistakably at work behind the scenes, controlling every twist and turn of the plot. The dates and historicity of all three books have of course been disputed. But that fact should not be allowed to obscure this consideration – that the sovereign power of God, which is made plain in one way when it is embodied in the Davidic monarchy, is in another way made even plainer when it is stripped of its earthly trappings. Daniel, Esther, and Nehemiah are examples of those who 'won strength out of weakness'[13] – who found, indeed, that God's 'power is made perfect *in* weakness'.[14] And the Chronicler and his readers have in their own experience seen the implementing of the astonishing statement of Cyrus of Persia: 'The LORD, the God of heaven, has given me all the kingdoms of the earth, and he has charged me to build him a house at Jerusalem' (2 Ch. 36:23). Whether Cyrus understood or believed his own words is beside the point. They expressed a vital truth: that is, that David's power did not belong only to David's own lifetime, or even to the 400-year period during which he and his descendants ruled a political kingdom. What those centuries saw was but one representation of the rule of *God*, exercised *through* David and his successors. 'On the throne of *the LORD*' sat each king in turn (29:23), and it did not perish even with the last of them; while the greatest of them, David and Solomon, are depicted by the Chronicler as ideal rulers, their glories magnified and their many sins simply omitted, in order to illustrate the greatness of the heavenly King whom they represent. 'God governed the events of history', says McConville, 'to impart to the kingdom of Israel, at least once, a splendour which was fit to symbolize his own.'[15]

### c. A psalm for the Chronicler's time

If Psalm 60 may be related to the past time which the Chronicler is depicting, his preaching to his own time might well recall Psalm 72. As with the earlier psalm, the heading of this one is a subject of debate. But the sense in which it is 'of ' Solomon – by him, or about

---

[12] Ne. 2:8.  [13] Heb. 11:34.
[14] 2 Cor. 12:9.  [15] McConville, p. 110.

him, or neither – is not our present concern. It is a prayer for the reigning king, and one which is not a hesitant requesting of the unlikely, but a confident claiming of the impossible. 'May he live while the sun endures, and as long as the moon, throughout all generations! ... May he have dominion from sea to sea, and from the River to the ends of the earth!'[16] Such conviction do the words carry that we are not disposed to regard their language as mere extravagance. But what is the serious meaning of such a prayer?

Although the psalm is usually dated after Solomon, certainly after David, there could have been good hope even in their day of a literal fulfilment of these desires, in the sense that, even as the generations passed away, the Davidic rule continued and the Davidic realm expanded. But paradoxically, it was when the line of kings came to an end and their realm was wiped off the map, that the extravagances of the psalm became realities. For then it became clear in a new way that the sovereign power of God continued and expanded still. 'Those vessels soon fail, though full of thy light, And at thy decree are broken and gone; Thence brightly appeareth thy truth in its might, As through the clouds riven the lightnings have shone.'[17]

As the Psalmist pictured 'the kings of Tarshish and of the isles ... the kings of Sheba and Seba' bowing before the Lord's throne,[18] so David had already seen the kings of Zobah and Ammon acknowledging its authority, and so now, astonishingly, the Chronicler's generation realizes that the kings of Babylon and Persia have yielded to the same power. The only difference is that in his time it is not embodied in an actual 'royal son'.[19] Whether it will ever be so again is not known to the men of the fourth century; although they hope it will, and presume that the psalm will be ultimately fulfilled in the coming Messiah.

## 3.  The Chronicler foreshadowing our time

The centuries pass by, and we, 2,300 years later, find ourselves in a situation like yet unlike. The Messianic hope has come true, and in a sense history repeats itself. The throne has again been set up in the person of a flesh-and-blood king, a 'son of David'. But he, though

[16] Ps. 72:5, 8.
[17] J. B. de Santeuil (translated by Isaac Williams), *Disposer supreme, and Judge of the earth.*
[18] Ps. 72:10.    [19] Ps. 72:1.

83

alive with an endless life, is like his fourth-century ancestors no longer visibly enthroned in Jerusalem. This is why the Chronicler's situation so plainly foreshadows our own.

### a.  Our time in secular terms

For us, as for him, the people of God no longer count for anything in terms of secular influence among the kingdoms of this world. That is not to say that they have never tried to do so. As a political power, the Christian Church made a determined effort over more than a thousand years to be as famed and as feared as the Davidic monarchy had previously been. From the days of Constantine its progress in this respect is one of the most obvious facts of history, through the empires of Christianized Rome and Byzantium to the notion of 'Christendom' which continued to unite even the fragmented map of mediaeval Europe. But by the territorial decline of the Papacy into the Papal States of Italy, and then into the tiny area of the Vatican City, we may measure the general decline of the political pretensions of God's New Testament people. Where the name 'Christian' is now used in this way, for a faction in a Lebanese civil war or a party in a West European election, it has practically nothing to do with the true people of God.

Similarly, the Church is no longer the cultural force it has been in the past. If it is the Catholic Church which on the whole has been active in politics, culture has perhaps been the preserve of the Protestant churches. But here too the influence has waned dramatically. The old 'Christian' virtues of thrift and hard work, of philanthropy and public morality, once permeated much of our society, as a genuine effect of the influence of God's people. Now they are widely regarded either as hypocrisy, to be dismissed, or as truth which has sadly been lost.

In secular terms, the fame and fear of the king – of King Jesus, that is – are a caricature. We have to look elsewhere to see whether there is in our age any analogy to the reverence which was felt for David throughout the world of his day.

### b.  Our time in spiritual terms

By the time the Chronicler wrote, the secular glories of the kingdom had disappeared, and another age had come into being. In that new age, although God's people still existed they had been deprived of the power they once wielded over the rest of their world. Yet in a world now politically and culturally dominated by pagan empires, the fame and fear of the true king shone with a lustre all the more remarkable.

And so it is in our time. In secular terms, the kingship of Christ no longer means anything to this modern age. Measured by such a yardstick, the kingdom of the world has replaced the kingdom of our Lord and of his Christ, instead of the other way round.[20] Yet in another sense the fame and fear of the king still spread, with wider influence and deeper effect than ever. In spiritual terms his name is made known to the hearts and minds of men everywhere, as the gospel is preached all over the globe. As before, most oppose him, but many accept him. The circumstances seem less promising than in David's day, but then we have a greater king. Ammon and Moab, Edom and Syria, prove to be his enemies, but Tyre and Hamath become his friends. The Philistines as a nation reject him, yet there are some 'Pelishtim' – Pelethites – who accept him, even a band of Gittites from Goliath's home town. The important thing is that his fame is going out into all lands, and the fear of him is brought upon all nations. The day is drawing nearer when at the name of Jesus every knee shall bow, and every tongue confess that Jesus Christ is Lord.[21]

### c. A psalm for our time

In whatever sense Psalm 60 may be 'of David', and Psalm 72 'of Solomon', both would be very much to the Chronicler's purpose at this stage of his sermon. The circumstances in which Psalm 87, 'of the sons of Korah', was written are a matter of debate. But it uses an extraordinarily prophetic picture to make the same lesson live for our own time.

These lines concern the register of the people of Zion, David's royal city. Those entered in it include nations notorious amongst Zion's enemies; for 'Rahab' means Egypt, and we realize with hindsight that the Psalmist has named the first and the last great oppressors of Israel in Old Testament history (Egypt and Babylon), together with representative opponents, as well as friends, of the Davidic monarchy itself. The astonishing thing foreseen in this psalm is that men from all nations come to 'know' the Lord; that is, they recognize or acknowledge him, with the whole new rela-

[20] Rev. 11:15.
[21] Cf. Phil. 2:10-11.

85

tionship which that implies; and they are then registered not simply as allies, nor even as friends, but explicitly as *natives* of Zion.

We have no means of knowing exactly what the Psalmist understood by either the people or the concepts that appear in Psalm 87. But it cannot escape our notice that to know God, to acquire a second, spiritual, citizenship, and to be born again, are all New Testament descriptions[22] of a profound change in the human heart: that which follows the willing response to the fame and fear of the king.

# 1 Chronicles 17, 21 – 22

# 7.   Gifts for the house of God

With chapter 17 the fourth great theme of the Davidic section of Chronicles emerges. The first was that of the Nation, the people and their king, dealt with in three successive chapters (10–12). The second theme, the Ark, appeared in chapter 13, but its introduction was immediately followed by the appearance of a third, the 'fame and fear of the king' – what we might in one word call the theme of Testimony: how the Nation is seen by its neighbours. That began in chapter 14. Chapters 15 to 16 revert to the Ark narrative and complete it, and then, before the Testimony thread is taken up again, this fourth theme, the Temple, is introduced here in chapter 17. (Notice that as the Testimony chapters develop the Nation theme, setting it against a new and wider background, so the Temple narrative takes up the Ark theme, setting that too in a new and more elaborate context.) Then, after our introduction to the Temple, we have three more chapters dealing with the Testimony (18–20), before the two final chapters on the Temple (21–22).

---

[22] Jn. 17:3; Phil. 3:20; Jn. 3:3, 7

The interweaving of these themes may be set out thus:

| Nation | 10–12 | | | | |
|---|---|---|---|---|---|
| Ark | | 13 | 15–16 | | |
| Testimony | | 14 | | 18–20 | |
| Temple | | | 17 | | 21–22 |

Again, it seems simpler for our purposes to unravel the threads which the Chronicler has woven together, in order to consider his themes one by one.

We may note four significant verses here which will help us to follow the 'Temple' thread.

'Now when David dwelt in his house, David said to Nathan the prophet, "Behold, I dwell in a house of cedar, but the ark of the covenant of the LORD is under a tent"' (17:1). In David's heart is the desire to build a house for the ark too, and Nathan encourages him in the project. That at least is Nathan's immediate human reaction. But it has to be revised in the light of a divine message to him the same night. It is to be not David, but his son Solomon, who will build the temple for God's ark. What God will do for David, however, is infinitely grander, and brings forth from David a response which is one of the great prayers of the Bible (17:16–27).

After chapters 18 to 20 have fully developed the Testimony theme, the return to the Temple theme introduces another prophet, Gad. 'The angel of the LORD commanded Gad to say to David that David should go up and rear an altar to the LORD on the threshing floor of Ornan the Jebusite' (21:18). What lies behind this command is the national census which David ordered, and which (for reasons we shall consider later) provoked God to punish him. A plague swept through Israel, stopping just short of Jerusalem. The terrifying vision of the 'destroying angel' standing between heaven and earth, his drawn sword stretched out over the city, indicated the place where the plague had halted. David and his 'elders' saw it as they were perhaps on their way to Gibeon, to beg God's mercy with the offering of sacrifices at the altar of the 'high place' there. It was seen also by Ornan and his sons as they were threshing wheat, for it was at the threshing-floor that the angel seemed actually to be standing.

At that point the desire of 17:1 and the command of 21:18 converged; and 'David said, "Here shall be the *house* of the LORD God and here the *altar* of burnt offering for Israel"' (22:1). So he set about the initial plans and preparations for the building of the temple. From the start he associated Solomon with the project, knowing that he himself would never see it completed, but envisaging the finished house as 'the sanctuary of the LORD God', where 'the ark of the covenant of the LORD and the holy vessels of God' would be 'brought into a house built for the name of the LORD' (22:19).

We have already seen that the ark represents covenant grace, God making the first loving move towards man before there can be any answering move from man to God. Although in practice this outgoing love never fails to evoke a response, in principle it needs no such response in order to exist. In other words, the ark does not actually need a temple to house it. 'Did I speak a word with any of the judges of Israel, ... saying, "Why have you not built me a house of cedar?"' (17:6). Yet it is right that man should respond to God's grace; and the temple, though in a sense superfluous, will nevertheless be the corporate expression of Israel's response.

What will contribute to the building of this house? The people of God will bring to it many gifts in the normal sense of money and talents. But we shall find that besides these a variety of unexpected contributions figure in the chapters we are considering. The first of them does not require wealth or skill, but is something with which anyone can respond to the grace of God.

## 1. Devotion (17:1–27)

Although David's desire is not actually expressed in 17:1–2 – 'I dwell in a house of cedar, but the ark ... is under a tent' – it is as easy for us as it is for his prophet Nathan to see what is in his heart. His intentions and his sincerity are plain.

But the reply given through Nathan shows that God's intentions are somewhat different from David's, and in doing so it gives David a clearer view of the truth, the grace, and the plan of God. The *truth* (17:4–6) is that, as I have said, a temple to house the ark, the symbol of God's gracious presence, is strictly unnecessary. Had God wanted such a thing, he would have asked for it; but, in point of fact, at no time between the exodus and the monarchy had he done so. Indeed, he had specified that the shelter for the ark should be not a permanent house, but a movable tent. As later times would see, there were positive dangers in the former idea.[1] God is too great for

---

[1] *Cf.* Je. 7:4; Acts 7:44–50; and see above, p. 73–75.

there to be particular places where he can be pinned down as more really 'present' than elsewhere. Whatever else it may be, the temple is not that.

Secondly, the *grace* of God is made clearer to David (17:7–10). Notice how often the pronoun 'I' occurs in this passage, which reaches its climax in the declaration that 'the LORD will build you a house'. David wants to do something for the Lord, and we may be sure that that desire is appreciated. But the fact is, says the Lord, that what I do for you is infinitely more important than anything that you can do for me; our whole relationship from start to finish is based upon my grace; I have done this, and this, and this for you, and if there is to be any house-building at all, it will be first and foremost that *I* will build *you* a house.

So thirdly, the *plan* of God is made clearer (17:11–14). The house is to be built, but it will be Solomon's work, not David's, and moreover it will be as nothing compared with the kingdom, the throne, the adoption, and the mercy which will be God's gifts to Solomon: 'I will confirm him in my house ... for ever.' 'My thoughts are not your thoughts, neither are your ways my ways, says the LORD. For as the heavens are higher than the earth, so are my ways higher than your ways and my thoughts than your thoughts.'[2]

In the message of 17:4–14 God is responding to the emotional side of David's personality. David's impulse to build a temple was a matter of the emotion – which, be it understood, is to be seen as a virtue, not a weakness. But God, while appreciating the sincerity of such desires of the heart (as we should call them), responds to them by stretching the mind. His object is 'To teach our faint desires to rise' – our greatest enthusiasm is a faint thing, on the divine scale – 'And bring all heaven before our eyes.'[3] Although it is not only the 'broken and contrite heart', but any movement of the heart towards himself, that he will not despise,[4] yet to enlarged desires he seeks to add enlarged understanding.

To his great credit David, so far from being vexed, is delighted with this response from God. The memorable prayer of 17:16–27 is in effect a repeating back to God of what God has said to him, and the core of it is 17:23b: 'Do as thou hast spoken.' In that brief phrase lies a profound truth about the believer's practical devotional life. Prayer is never more effective than when it claims from God what he

[2] Is. 55:8–9.  [3] William Cowper, *Jesus, where'er thy people meet.*
[4] Ps. 51:17.

89

has said he will do in any case. The winds of emotion can easily drive the ship off course, but provided the rudder and sails are properly set it is those very winds which will drive it in the right direction. So God's revealed words correct and actually harness the impulses of the heart, and the wise believer will bring emotion and revelation together as he comes before God: 'Thou, my God, hast revealed to thy servant that thou wilt build a house for him; therefore thy servant has found courage to pray before thee' (17:25).

That kind of contribution to the building of God's house, the devotion of the heart, is not hard to understand. But as we move on from chapter 17 to chapter 21, we find a contribution of a very different kind.

## 2. Evil (21:1–18)

There are dark mysteries here. Without warning or preamble, Satan comes on the scene. Only at the end of the New Testament is he fully identified as the dragon, the serpent, the devil, and the deceiver.[5] In the Old Testament he appears three times, and the appearance here is like that in the Book of Job.[6] In each case he incites to evil,[7] but the evil that he brings about is both permitted and limited by God. Indeed the account in Samuel/Kings says that it was actually the Lord who in anger prompted David to the disastrous course of action which followed (2 Sa. 24:1).[8]

There is something mysterious too about this sin of David's. Certainly 'to number Israel' (21:1) could be a dangerous thing. The law of Moses threatened punishment if a census were taken without each person numbered paying a 'ransom' for himself to the Lord.[9] Perhaps the sin would lie in imagining that it was the numbers of able-bodied men of military age (21:5) which constituted the strength of the state, whereas in fact each individual, the nation itself, its wars, and its very destiny are all in the hands of God. The older history had made this clear – 'the LORD saves not with sword

---

[5] Rev. 12:9; 20:2.

[6] Jb. 1:6ff. The other reference is Zc. 3:1–2, to which the picture 'Satan stood up' relates.

[7] With 21:1; cf. Jb. 2:3 NIV.

[8] The census was going to anger the Lord; but something else had angered him already. Both accounts say that the punishment was directed 'against Israel', not in the first instance against David. Keil and Delitzsch (*The Books of Samuel*, p. 503, on 2 Sa. 24:1) see 'guilt on the part of the nation ... in the rebellions of Absalom and Sheba against the divinely established government of David', known to the Chronicler and his readers from 2 Sa. 15 – 20.

[9] Ex. 30:11–16.

and spear; for the battle is the LORD's' (1 Sa. 17:47) – and the Chronicler will underline it repeatedly (2 Ch. 13:18; 14:11; 16:8; 20:15). At all events either the census itself or the spirit in which it was conducted was a grave sin, which not only displeased God (21:7) but even scandalized Joab, who is not noted in these histories for a particularly scrupulous conscience (21:3, 6).

But the God whose anger had given rise to the temptation, and whose displeasure was renewed when David so deliberately yielded to it (21:4a), was to turn all these things to good. Three times David expresses his distress and deep contrition (21:8, 13, 17), God halts the plague with which he has been punishing Israel, and it is out of this whole harrowing process of sin, punishment, and repentance that there emerges the command to 'rear an altar to the LORD' (21:18). As on those other occasions when the Old Testament reveals to us the doings of Satan, in the poetry of Job and the prophecy of Zechariah, we are taken behind the scenes, to be shown something of the workings of evil and of the way in which God overrules it for good. For the building of the altar will become an integral part of the great temple project. This is not of course an excuse, still less a justification, for sinning. To say that we may 'do evil that good may come', and 'continue in sin that grace may abound',[10] is no part of a biblical faith. But when we do sin, God can take that sin and its evil effects and transmute them into something which will contribute to his glory.

So the two contributions come together, each according to the word of the Lord. The devotion of David's heart leads to the promise through Nathan of the eventual building of a house for the ark (17:12), and the evil resulting from David's sin leads to the command through Gad to set up the altar (21:18). The two converge in David's own words in 22:1: 'Here shall be the house ... and here the altar'.

This declaration is followed at once by a passage describing the third kind of contribution.

## 3. Materials (22:2–5)

The actual word – 'David provided *materials* in great quantity' (22:5) – is not in the original,[11] but it does sum up the paragraph. Here are

[10] Rom. 3:8; 6:1.
[11] 'David made extensive preparations' (NIV).

gifts for the house of God in a quite concrete sense, a practical and comprehensive list, stone, metal, and wood.

We notice first the sheer amount of material gathered. This is pointed out in a variety of phrases: 'great stores of iron ... quantities beyond weighing ... without number ... great quantities'. With regard to such gifts, David is determined that so far as he is concerned there shall be no shortage in work done for the glory of God.

Secondly, the source of it is noteworthy. From one point of view, of course, it was David who 'provided' it all. But he used immigrant labour in the preparation of it, and he had no qualms about accepting much of it from his heathen neighbours. It is true that the story of Abraham, which illustrates so many principles of the life of faith, shows the church saying to the world, 'I would not take a thread or a sandal-thong or anything that is yours, lest you should say, "I have made Abram rich"'.[12] David however is in the position, not of Abraham refusing to be beholden to the king of Sodom, but of Moses or Nehemiah, more than willing to accept the riches of Egypt and Persia,[13] as we realize when we note a third feature of this paragraph.

That is the object of the amassing of all this material. 'The house ... is to be built for the LORD', and its 'fame and glory' – and therefore his – is to be known 'throughout all lands.' Here we glimpse, intertwining with the Temple theme of these chapters, the Testimony theme of chapters 14 and 18 to 20. This is why David need not share Abraham's scruples. Once the city of God is established there need be no hesitation about bringing into it 'the glory and the honour of the nations'.[14] They cannot infect it; rather, it will disinfect them. There is nothing that cannot be laid under contribution for the building of God's house, once the gift can be recognized as belonging to God before it belonged to Sidon and Tyre. 'Everything created by God is good, and nothing is to be rejected if it is received with thanksgiving; for then it is consecrated by the word of God and prayer.'[15]

Finally we observe that these verses illustrate a principle which holds good in all ages. David's material gifts of bronze and timber do not need to be spiritualized in order to make a point for us. Our equivalent of the Jerusalem temple – something constructive done

[12] Gn. 14:23.   [13] Ex. 12:35–36; Ne. 2:7–8.
[14] Rev. 21:26.   [15] 1 Tim. 4:4–5.

for the glory of the Lord, embodying faith's response to grace – may not be a building at all. But we are told here that whatever it may be, thoroughly practical donations in cash and in kind will be expected from us. The New Testament churches are taught this in 2 Corinthians 8 and 9, where Paul devotes two whole chapters to the matter of giving. It is seen put into practice in Acts 11:27–30, where Luke recounts how the new and probably suspect church in Antioch (the first congregation ever which was not mainly composed of real Hebrew Christians!) gave as prime proof of its genuineness the alacrity with which it dipped into its pocket when need arose.[16]

## 4. Talents (22:6–16)

Here we have gifts according to the other common meaning of the word. At the end of the paragraph we are told that just as there is an abundance of materials, gifts of that kind 'without number' (22:4), so there is 'an abundance of workmen: stonecutters, masons, carpenters, and all kinds of craftsmen without number' (22:15). But in fact the whole passage has to do with abilities. It is not only the workmen who are 'skilled' in their various crafts. David's son Solomon is himself a greatly gifted man.

Mentioned a few times in earlier chapters, he is here brought into the mainstream of the narrative at a point where the chief subject is the building of the temple, for that is to be his supreme memorial. The gifts of his personality are chiefly to be devoted, according to the Chronicler's reading of history, to that great aim. His largeness of mind, his knowledge of the natural world, and his fame as a writer of songs and proverbs, are celebrated in a passage in Samuel/Kings (1 Ki. 4:29–34). The Chronicler omits this, and goes behind such expressions of Solomon's brilliance to describe him simply as 'a man of peace', endowed by God with 'discretion and understanding' (22:9, 12).

The 'man of peace' here stands in contrast to his father David, who is described as a man of war (22:8). As a matter of historical fact, that was how the circumstances of the two reigns worked out. The first had been a time of warfare, in the second the Lord gave 'peace and quiet to Israel' (22:9). But the phrases 'man of peace' and 'man of war' mean more than that. Each man has a character well suited to the period in which he lives. David cannot honestly say

[16] See below, pp. 113–114.

concerning his own disjointed time, 'O cursed spite, That ever I was born to set it right!'[17] The fact is that he is a born fighter, a general, a charismatic leader of men, a destroyer of enemies and a winner of victories. These are his gifts.[18] Solomon on the other hand not only lives in a time of peace, but is gifted with the arts of peace. He is the diplomat, the statesman, the ruler and judge. To him may be applied Isaiah's prophecy of a much later 'branch' of the roots of Jesse: 'the Spirit of the LORD shall rest upon him, the spirit of wisdom and understanding, the spirit of counsel and might, the spirit of knowledge and the fear of the LORD.'[19] These are *his* gifts.

They are gifts in the sense that Solomon will give them, devote them, to the building of the temple. But they are also gifts given *to* him in the first place. It is the Lord who will declare him to be a man of peace and will grant him discretion and understanding. For there is no contribution that we can make to the temple which was not in the first place given to us. In the famous words of David to which we shall shortly come, 'all things come from thee, and of thy own have we given thee' (29:14).

There remains one other contribution to the house of God. For it we turn back to a passage which just now was left to one side. David had sinned in ordering a census, God had sent a plague as punishment, the destroying angel had swept over Israel as far as a point just north of Jerusalem; and 21:19 – 22:1 describes what happened next, and the remaining gift to be contributed to the building of the temple.

## 5.  The site (21:19 – 22:1)

It might well seem at first glance that this of all things cannot be called a gift for the house of God. Ornan the Jebusite, owner of the

---

[17] Shakespeare, *Hamlet*, I.v. 188.

[18] He is also, as we have noted already (p. 52) and as Samuel/Kings makes clear, a man of passion and cruelty – 'a man of blood' (2 Sa. 16:8). In that passage, Shimei is wrong to accuse him of 'the blood of the house of Saul', but there is guilt in abundance on David's head quite apart from that. As so often, the Chronicler does not deny such things, but sidesteps them, and links David's bloodshedding specifically with the wars he has fought (22:8) – wars which the Lord himself has been fighting, through his viceroy, to free the temple-building age of Solomon from the fear of enemies (17:8; 22:9–10). 'That David is not blamed for being a man of war is clear from the comment that appears twice in chapter 18: "And the Lord gave victory to David wherever he went" (vv. 6, 13)' (McConville, p. 63). 'The designation of David as a "man of wars" ... does not imply culpability. Similarly the description of Solomon as a "man of rest" ... is not meant to congratulate him upon a moral quality' (McConville, pp. 77f.).

[19] Is. 11:2. The whole chapter will repay reading in this connection.

threshing-floor which was to become the site of the temple, had indeed wanted to give it, and everything that went with it – 'I give it all' – but David had insisted on paying for it (21:23–24). Nevertheless it *was* a gift, and the greatest gift of all, as the narrative will make clear.

God's halting of the plague provides one of the most dramatic scenes in the Old Testament. The 'sword of the LORD' in the hand of his angel (21:12) has been cutting down the people of Israel in their tens of thousands, as the plague marches southwards through the land. Then, as it reaches the old Jebusite threshing-floor, the Lord says 'Enough'; and simultaneously, it seems, the angel becomes visible to human eyes, 'standing between earth and heaven, and in his hand a drawn sword stretched out over Jerusalem' (21:16). He is seen by David and the Israelite elders, who have (if we may judge by 21:29–30) just set out from the city to go to Gibeon. He is seen by Ornan and his sons at the threshing-floor itself (21:20). At the command of the prophet Gad, David and Ornan meet where the angel has halted, and David says, 'Here shall be the house of the LORD God and here the altar of burnt offering for Israel' (22:1).

Here, by divine command, is to be the site of the temple. It is a gift not from Ornan but from God. The grace of God, in giving this to his people as the place where ark and altar are to be brought together, is a thing to be wondered at. 'Here shall be the house': where? On a hill top on which, eight hundred years before, another sacrifice had been offered, and another disaster averted, and God had shown himself the giver of life from the dead. For when the Chronicler comes to record the start of Solomon's work on the temple, he will tell us that the building is 'on Mount Moriah' (2 Ch. 3:1), surely intending that his readers shall make the connection between that and the only other occurrence of this name in Scripture. It is the place where once Isaac lay bound on an altar, as good as dead beneath the knife poised in his father's hand, and where in the nick of time God prevented the sacrifice and gave Abraham his son back from death.[20]

A still more remarkable connection, of which the Chronicler was not aware unless he had prophetic foresight, should be plain to us who have hindsight. 'Here shall be the house': where? On a hill above the city of David, at the northern end of which, a thousand years after, the ultimate sacrifice was offered and the plague was

[20] Gn. 22:1ff.

finally halted. The mound called Calvary lay beyond the city wall, outside the temple site, but the area was all Moriah.

The place, and the events which happened there, twice as foreshadowings and the third time as fulfilment, were God's gift to his people. All other contributions pale into insignificance beside this one.

> 'Were the whole realm of nature mine,
> That were an offering far too small;
> Love so amazing, so divine,
> Demands my soul, my life, my all'[21]

– yet even that offering is nothing compared to the prior offering of God's own Son, the greatest of the sacrifices of Mount Moriah – the 'wondrous cross On which the Prince of glory died', to which the last verse of Isaac Watts' hymn is simply a response. Paul, as we have noted, writes two whole chapters about the grace of Christian giving. But he ends them, rightly, with the words 'Thanks be to God for *his* inexpressible gift!'[22]

# 1 Chronicles 23 – 27

## 8.  A people prepared

Dismaying lists of names are once again the order of the day. The kind of material which made up the first nine chapters of the book seems also to dominate the five which follow David's preparations for the temple (1 Ch. 23 – 27). But we have already seen how important such lists are in the Chronicler's overall scheme, and shall see it again here.

In considering this section we shall work our way through the

---

[21] Isaac Watts, *When I survey the wondrous cross.*
[22] 2 Cor. 9:15.

Chronicler's content and method to his purpose. That is, we shall ask ourselves in turn the three questions what, how, and why. We shall then be in a position to work back from the writer's purpose, which is in fact the chief question, to look again at his method, and finally to review in greater detail the section's content.[1]

## 1. Content: what is presented

The introductory verses 23:1–6a[2] lead into what is basically a long account of David's organization of the tribe of Levi for its special functions in the life of Israel as a whole. Four categories are to be described: the staff of the sanctuary (that is, before Solomon's time the tabernacle, and then the temple) from 23:6b onwards; the musicians from 25:1; the gatekeepers from 26:1; and the 'officers and judges' from 26:20.

The five chapters actually range more widely than this. With the basic material, mostly 'genealogies' in the sense of family connections within the tribe of Levi, several extra paragraphs of a different type are combined. In the list of sanctuary staff we find also an account of their work, and in addition a good deal about the particular clan within the tribe of Levi which, being descended from Aaron, became the priestly line.[3] In the list of musicians there is as well as the division according to families a different division of the same people, according to the order in which the lots for their duties fell. In the list of gatekeepers is included a note about the intriguing character Obed-edom,[4] and a paragraph about the allocation of duties at the gates. To the list of Levite 'officers and judges' are added further lists of national and regional officials of various kinds, ranging far and wide across practically all the tribes of Israel.

Such in brief is the content of our present passage. We shall return in due course to consider it at greater length. To do so with understanding, we need next to ask how the Chronicler puts together this material and integrates it with his work as a whole.

---

[1] This chiastic ('cross-over') scheme is common in the arrangement of Old Testament writings. See above, p. 27 n. 8.

[2] Williamson indicates that a new sentence, indeed a new paragraph, should start halfway through 23:6: '... in divisions. Concerning the sons of Levi, Gershom, Kohath, and Merari: ...' (Williamson, pp. 160f.).

[3] 'Priests and Levites' became the usual distinction (e.g. 23:2), but meant in fact 'priestly (=Aaronic) Levites and non-priestly Levites'.

[4] See below, p. 106.

## 2. Method: how it is presented

Standing back to view the total architecture of Chronicles, we see the reigns of David and Solomon at the centre, flanked by a long introduction and a longer sequel, which span all sacred history from Adam to the Chronicler himself. It is less easy to see at a glance where the pivot of the story is. Solomon's reign begins in one sense in the first chapter of 2 Chronicles, following the death of David in the last chapter of 1 Chronicles, so that the midpoint of the Chronicler's work falls neatly just where it divides into its traditional halves. But already in the first book, in 28:1, David has called a national assembly for the handing over to Solomon not only of the temple project, but also, it would seem, of the royal power (29:22ff.). Already, indeed, even here in 23:1, Solomon has been officially associated with his father on the throne, in what some believe to be the earlier 'king-making' implied by 29:22.[5] And even before that Solomon and the glorious prospects of his reign have come on the scene in 22:6ff.

In other words, the two reigns seem to blend and overlap, with Solomon coming gradually to the fore. In chapter 22 the turmoils of David's reign, and his own preparations for the temple, are finished (22:14, 18), and Solomon enters the main story;[6] then he is presented as king from 23:1, though David does not cease to be king till 29:28; and Solomon's sole reign begins there, at the end of the first book.

In the seven chapters of the overlap, 23 to 29, David summons two assemblies, the second (28:1) perhaps more formal than the first (23:2).[7] It is with the earlier of the two that our five chapters are concerned. As the kingdom begins to be transferred from David to Solomon, it is first necessary for the nation to be organized, so that the new king finds 'a people prepared' (Lk. 1:17).

The basic account of David's organization of the Levites into the four categories of 23:4–5 provides the framework for the Chronicler's extended treatment. He will, however, as we have seen, go far beyond that simple Levitical outline, because of the purpose he has in view. To this we now turn.

---

[5] *E.g.* Curtis & Madsen *in loc.* But see below, p. 117.

[6] His name has appeared several times already, for other reasons.

[7] The wording differs: 'gathered together' (23:2 RV), 'assembled' (28:1 RV).

### 3. Purpose: why it is presented

One thought governs the Chronicler's presentation of Israelite history at this point: the handing over of the kingdom from David to Solomon. The transfer is very much more than a mere bequest from father to son. The two men, their reigns, their policies, are described in such a way as to bring out certain types of likeness and certain types of contrast. No doubt each will have resembled the other physically as father and son, and culturally as men born in the same age and country. The likenesses that interest the Chronicler are not these, however, but rather the fact that each man in turn takes on the role of the chosen ruler of God's people. On the other hand, they also no doubt differed from each other in a thousand ways, as distinct individuals of two different generations. But the significant contrast between them, to the Chronicler's mind, is the one we have already remarked on – that David is 'a man of war' (28:3 RV) while Solomon is 'a man of peace' (22:9).[8]

The transition period from David's reign to Solomon's is, in other words, the passing of a nation from war to peace. More correctly and fully, it is a movement away from the circumstances and necessities of the one and towards the circumstances and possibilities of the other. It has been David's function to win the wars: it will be Solomon's task to establish the peace. The first reign sees the clearing of the ground, the second sees the work of construction. One king quells opposition, the other gains admiration.

We need to remind ourselves that it is not a case of David's doing wrong and Solomon's doing right. When the Chronicler quotes the word of the Lord to David, 'you shall not build a house to my name, because you have shed so much blood' (22:8), while the earlier history quotes Solomon: 'David my father could not build a house for the name of the LORD his God because of the warfare with which his enemies surrounded him' (1 Ki. 5:3), the first is not a reproof, and the second is not an excuse; both are statements of fact. Nor do they contradict each other. They are saying that the building of the temple is a project which belongs not to a period of turmoil but to one of tranquillity. Solomon will be primarily a man of *rest*; the Lord will give him *rest*, the undisturbed conditions for temple-building, before he gives him the richer gift of *peace* (as well as quiet!).[9] For

---

[8] See above, pp. 93–94.
[9] 22:9 RV. 'Rest', notice, not 'peace'; the RSV is misleading.

David the project is inappropriate. But what he *can* do is to make preparations for it.

This he does in three ways. We should understand that his wars, the very things which disqualify him from the project himself, are themselves a preparation. His is the responsibility of disarming the enemies of Israel precisely in order that there shall be a period of rest in which his successor can 'build a peace'. Secondly, Solomon will be building the literal temple, and David makes quite concrete preparations for that, as we have seen (22:2–5). But there is a third kind of building. The people of God itself will be built up under Solomon's wise government; and for that too David prepares, by the organizing of the community of the Israel described here in chapters 23 to 27.

The temple of stone is a model of the living temple of God's people. The two were set side by side in the message God gave to David through Nathan: 'You shall not build me a house ... [but I] will build you a house' (17:4, 10). The kind of house which David wanted to build, and which Solomon did build, was planned to its last detail, had wealth and care lavished upon its making, and fitted together in all its parts to become a magnificent expression of praise to God. And so it was to be with the house which God duly built for David, the living house of Israel. To entitle this section the 'organization of the Levites' is to make it sound like bureaucratic regimentation. It is rather to be seen as a scaffolding for that house, a structure to enable God's people to function as they ought. Not for nothing is the metaphor taken up in the New Testament, where the Christian Church is 'God's temple',[10] 'a holy temple in the Lord',[11] 'living stones ... built into a spiritual house'.[12]

Needless to say, the Chronicler's readers could have raised the same question about this picture (the community of Israel as David had organized it) as about the rest of his sermon: 'What relevance has this for us? Some parts of it, for example the twenty-four divisions of the priesthood, do accord with what we have now; but for the rest...! The complexity of it, the extent, the numbers, the wealth it all implies!'

'True,' rejoins the Chronicler: 'in many ways that ancient world is nothing like ours. But that (I say it again) is to make you look for the *principles*. This is how the people of God ought to be. Whenever

[10] 1 Cor. 3:16.    [11] Eph. 2:21.    [12] 1 Pet. 2:5.

they are emerging from turmoil and being built anew, there must be this kind of care, this kind of thoroughness, this kind of devotion to duty and sense of community.'

So remembering now his purpose in writing, we consider his method once more.

## 4. Method: the 'how' again

Looking previously at his method, we saw how he orders his story, working in the account of the organization of the Levites at the point where the David period begins to overlap the Solomon one. This time we shall see, to change the metaphor, how he paints his picture.

He is concerned with three things which can be confused, but which though closely related are really distinct: fact, truth, and right. First, the basic composition of the picture is *fact*. He is not interested in fabrication, or even in the making of plausible 'faction'. It is nothing to his purpose to invent a fiction which illustrates a principle, if he cannot find an example of the principle's actually being embodied in a fact somewhere in Israelite history.

It is not surprising, therefore, to find scattered through these chapters touches of realism of the kinds that we have noticed before. We are told for instance that Zechariah, one of the chief *gatekeepers*, was also incidentally 'a *shrewd counsellor*' (26:14) – the kind of bizarre sidelight which is surely fact because no-one would think of inventing it. Another tell-tale mark of actuality is the kind of passing reference which cheerfully leaves the reader with an unanswered question, unless he happens to know the historical answer provided elsewhere in Scripture. Why, for instance, alone among the forty-odd people listed in chapter 27, do we find successors named for Asahel (27:7) and Ahithophel (27:33–34)? In fiction one would scarcely find such an oddity; in fact, one knows from Samuel/Kings the reason for it, namely that both men died in the course of David's reign (2 Sa. 2:18–23; 2 Sa. 17:23). Such pointers as these indicate how the Chronicler bases his 'historical preaching' on history as it was, rather than on history as he would have liked it to be.

Is that really correct, though? Is it not undeniable that an element of fantasy enters into the way he recounts history, even if he does incorporate into it all sorts of individual facts? There are ways and means of glamorizing a collection of facts so that the impression it makes is far from the truth. Quotations from hostile theatre critics can easily be reproduced out of context to extol the very play they were vilifying!

But the Chronicler is as much concerned with *truth* as he is with fact. When he selects his material, putting this in and leaving that out, it is not in order to distort the truth, but to expose it. As we have remarked before, he may omit facts; but when he does so, it is not in order to suppress them, for the simple reason that everybody knows them anyway. He is in effect saying: 'I shall not put on to my canvas the ugly building which we all know is there, spoiling the view. The landscape I am painting existed before the building appeared, and will still exist after it has vanished; and I intend to depict the lasting truth of this scene.'

Then again, he makes no bones about putting together historical material drawn from several different periods – 'new things and old co-twisted, as if Time were nothing'.[13] If we ask whether the various lists of Levites and other officials relate to the situation in David's time, or to that before his time, or to that after his time, the answer is probably 'Yes'! We are asking the wrong kind of question. As Williamson says, 'The allusions of the differing verses' (and he is speaking only of the passage 26:20–32) 'seem to stretch throughout the period of the monarchy and into the post-exilic period.'[14] The many-layered result has a depth of truth which would have been lacking in a description of things as they were at one given time. Carved in marble round London's Albert Memorial are famous artists, writers, and musicians from many lands and eras. Each figure represents as accurately as possible an actual person – that is, a fact. The complete frieze does not represent an actual meeting of all these people; that is not, nor ever could have been, fact. But it does represent genius, in the persons of 169 of the world's great men, and that is truth.

Thirdly, the Chronicler is concerned with *right*. He wants to show the preparation of Israel for Solomon's reign not only as a matter of historical fact and as a matter of spiritual truth, but also as a correct and legitimate process. All must be seen to belong. So his framework consists of a genealogical register, the four-fold list of Levites who with their various tasks are yet bound together by

[13] See above, p. 35 n. 7.
[14] Williamson, p. 172.

family ties. He is of course interested in showing that the organization of the Israel of his own time is as it should be. He is perhaps more deeply concerned that God's people of every age should be the right kind of people, should be undertaking the right kind of service, and should have the right kind of relationships; and all this under royal direction, since it is to be in David that the proper authority is to be recognized for the rest of Israel's history.

## 5. Content: the 'what' again

So we return finally to the content of chapters 23 to 27. Bearing in mind the Chronicler's purpose and method, we are now in a position to review the whole passage.

He makes three introductory points. First, David reaches an honourable old age (23:1).[15] This is the caption for the next seven chapters, which will take us to the end of 1 Chronicles. We know that many intrigues and follies spoilt David's last days (see 1 Ki. 1); but the Chronicler omits them, because in the perspective of history the chief characteristics of David's and Solomon's reigns will be seen to be respectively conflict and rest; and once the theme becomes 'preparations for the peaceful reign of Solomon', notes of further turmoils, though historically true, would obscure the spiritual truth of the sermon.

Secondly, an assembly is called, and this caption (23:2) introduces the five chapters we are studying, 23 to 27. The Chronicler's basic outline deals with Levites, that is members of all families of the tribe of Levi except that of Aaron. But Aaron and his descendants were of course the priests of Israel, and the Chronicler wishes to include them also in his survey of David's organization of the people. In fact, his view ranges far beyond Levi. He wants to show that the whole people is to be prepared, and prepared in both the religious and the secular spheres, for the reign of David's successor, and so tells us that David 'gathered together all the leaders of Israel, as well as the priests and Levites' (23:2 NIV).

Thirdly, the Levitical register is introduced. Its four categories are listed in order of size: 24,000 sanctuary staff, 6,000 'officers and judges', 4,000 gatekeepers, and 4,000 musicians (23:3–5). The paragraph should end 'David organized them in divisions' (23:6a).[16]

[15] This is the meaning of the phrase 'old and full of days'; cf. Gn. 25:8; Jb. 42:17.
[16] See p. 97, n. 2.

The Chronicler will afterwards rearrange the order of the four lists to demonstrate what the priorities should always be in the life of God's people: first the sanctuary staff, then the musicians, then the gatekeepers, then the 'officers and judges' – *i.e.* starting at the centre with God, and working gradually outwards into secular life.

The triple introduction thus leads to the first of the lists (23:6b–24:31). 'The sons of Levi ... who were to do the work for the service of the house of the LORD' (23:6b, 24): that is its subject. Into the basic family records of Gershom, Kohath, and Merari, bound together by the genealogical father-son connections, the Chronicler makes two pairs of insertions. A brief note reminds us that Moses' line was counted with the rest of the (non-priestly) Levites, while Aaron's was set apart for the priesthood (23:13b, 14); then later a long account is included (24:1–19) of how the twenty-four divisions of the priests were shared out between the family of Ithamar and the more numerous sons of Eleazar, in a 1:2 ratio. The circumstances surrounding the death of Aaron's two elder sons, Nadab and Abihu (24:2), are not mentioned. We need not imagine that 'the embarrassing reason' for it 'is suppressed',[17] since readers would be expected to know the story of Leviticus 10:1–2. Rather we may see here again the omitting of facts which would hinder a presentation of the main truth, as we noted in 23:1.

The Chronicler's many-layered technique, presenting a picture of Israel which has a peculiar and almost three-dimensional depth, may be the most remarkable feature of the section concerning sanctuary staff. We cannot help noticing it in the other pair of additions to this first list. So far we have noted two insertions to do with the priests; now we have two extra passages about the non-priestly Levites. They comprise a statement by David about their duties in the house of the Lord (23:25–32), and a list of the 'heads of fathers' houses' (24:20–31). The former seems to combine two kinds of duty which the introductory note kept separate, namely sanctuary assistance and music.[18] Such an interpretation could point towards different dates for the two passages. That might also explain why the minimum age for Levite service is thirty in the introduction (23:3) and twenty elsewhere (23:24, 27). And something like it is clearly behind the differences between the original list of heads of fathers' houses in 23:15–24, recording the headships of Shebuel, Rehabiah,

---

[17] *Pace* Williamson, p. 163.
[18] David's statement could of course be referring to both groups at once.

and their contemporaries, and the additional one in 24:20–31, recording those of their sons.

We move on from the list of sanctuary staff to the list of musicians (25:1–31). Here again the basic material is bound together genealogically (25:1–6). The twenty-four music-leaders are grouped by family, as sons either of Asaph or of Heman or of Jeduthun. The additional passage (25:7–31) sets out the rearrangement which followed the casting of lots, so that for the most part the three families took turns.

Perhaps the chief point to note in this chapter is the orderly thoroughness which is commended when God's people prepare to sing his praises. Is there no place here then for spontaneous worship? Of course there is; three times in 25:1–3 the function of the musicians is said to be 'prophesying', meaning that they are open to whatever unexpected ministry the Spirit of God may put into their mouths. But in the same verses they are also said, three times, to be 'under ... direction'. The freedom is within a framework.

The question again arises as to whether the Chronicler has to resort to invention to make his point, or whether history makes it for him. The last nine of Heman's fourteen sons (25:4) provide a good opportunity for considering the matter in this context. The most uninstructed Bible reader would probably have the feeling, if he had worked painstakingly through the whole of 1 Chronicles up to this point, that even the hundreds of Hebrew names he had grappled with already did not include any quite like these. There is an oddity about the list that catches the attention. Who that has once rolled his tongue round the syllables 'Romamti-ezer' would ever forget them? Like most Bible names, these have meanings, and the meanings can actually be strung together to make sentences that look rather like a verse or two of a psalm: 'Be gracious to me, Yahweh' (Hananiah), 'Be gracious to me' (Hanani), 'You are my God' (Eliathah), and so on.[19] To many commentators the greater part of the list seems frankly artificial; and it could be held, on this view, that the writer has invented nine extra Levites to back up his contention that there must be a twenty-four-man leadership of the temple music. He does however seem to have historical backing for the large number of Heman's sons, a divine promise which he assumes his readers know about (25:5). In addition, if he were inventing names he would surely have aimed at greater verisimili-

[19] *Cf.* Myers, *1 Chronicles*, pp. 172f.

tude; these are so unlikely that they must be real! Finally, such naming is not unknown in other historical contexts. The custom of some parts of English society in the seventeenth century comes to mind, reflected in the characters of Bunyan's *Pilgrim's Progress* (Facing-both-ways, Valiant-for-truth, and so on) and in extreme form in the pretended author of Macaulay's *Battle of Naseby*, Obadiah Bind-their-kings-in-chains-and-their-nobles-with-links-of-iron. It would be of a piece with the whole message of the Chronicler if he were here saying: 'These are the preparations which were once actually made for the praises of God by his people, and from this historical example we should deduce a principle which ought always to obtain in such matters.'

The third list is that of the gatekeepers (26:1–19). The information about Levite families is here interwoven with a paragraph about Obed-edom (26:4–8) and one about the allocation of the gatekeepers to their duties (26:12–18). Obed-edom raises interesting issues. Could there be two men of the same name, the Levite who appears here and is presumably the gatekeeper who was also appointed as a singer for the bringing of the ark to Jerusalem (15:18, 21, 24), and the Gittite in whose house the ark had stayed for the previous three months (13:13–14; 15:25)? It seems unlikely that the Obed-edoms in the two successive verses 15:24 and 15:25 are two different people.[20] Perhaps only one person is in view – '*the* Obed-edom', specially blessed by God[21] – and either he was both a Levite and a Gittite (born of the tribe of Levi but living in the city of Gath), or else he was of a different tribe (maybe even another nation) but became a kind of 'honorary' Levite. If so, the writer stresses that he can be legitimately included among the gatekeepers by giving him, like the rest, family connections, and by referring to God's blessing on him, and to the number and ability of his sons and grandsons. It is important that things are seen to be done properly even (indeed especially) where there may be thought to be irregularities.

The description of how the gatekeepers' duties were allocated (26:12–18) brings again to the fore the Chronicler's use of fact. Strangely enough, it is the very word which no-one now understands which indicates how historically reliable the account is. The 'parbar', whatever it may be, is with other items in this paragraph

---

[20] Although this does seem to be the case with the name Shimei in 23:9–10.
[21] Compare 26:5 and 13:14.

the kind of detail which betrays the exact knowledge which a contemporary would have of the layout of the sanctuary.[22]

Finally we come to the list of 'officers and judges'. Here the Chronicler clearly means us to widen our perspectives. Even in his primary material, the notes of Levite families involved in this work (26:20–32), he goes beyond the expected bounds, not only geographically ('the oversight of Israel westward of the Jordan', 26:30) but also functionally ('for all the work of the LORD *and for the service of the king*', 26:30b – presumably affairs secular as well as religious). The added material (27:1–34) goes further. The twelve commanders, or high officials, who served a month at a time through the year, were appointed from many tribes, not just that of Levi (27:1–15). Over and above these, leaders were appointed specifically for the twelve tribes (27:16–22). Although Gad and Asher are omitted from this register,[23] this is because both Levi and the two Joseph tribes, Ephraim and Manasseh, are included, and so are both halves of Manasseh, as though they were separate tribes. As we have seen before,[24] the twelve-fold structure of the nation is more important than any particular arrangement of the tribes; and twelve tribal leaders are one way of saying that 'all Israel' is the Chronicler's concern. David's stewards (27:25–31) show in yet another way how comprehensive is his organization of his country. We notice incidentally that they are twelve in number. Lastly his own closest associates, his inner cabinet, are named (27:32–34).

So ends this long section, five chapters which at the outset may have looked as unfruitful as any in the book so far. Indeed, something we came across in the previous section may have made us wonder whether such lists were not only barren but actually poisonous: remember the damage caused by David's census in chapter 21! But the difference between that numbering and this one must surely lie in the motives behind them. So far as we can tell, the earlier one was to boost the confidence and pride of man; this has an eye to the glory of God. Such an object requires a people in every respect prepared for his service.

[22] In my youth, as an exercise in the memorizing of Scripture my Bible class leader would often propose this as the most unforgettable (and obscure) of verses: 'At Parbar westward, four at the causeway and two at Parbar' (26:18 AV)! It may be pointed out that even if 'parbar' is a word of Persian origin, it could still be an updating for the Chronicler's readers of something which did exist in David's time; *cf.* p. 16, n. 10.

[23] And Aaron inexplicably included, 27:17.

[24] See above, pp. 39–40.

# 1 Chronicles 28 – 29

# 9. The great continuities

With what might be called 'the Second Assembly of Jerusalem' the Chronicler completes his story of David, we reach the halfway mark in his book, and in a real sense the heart of his message is laid bare. The reason is this. David's reign has been the age of great achievements, whereas the Chronicler's time is 'the day of small things', as certain also of his own prophets have said.[1] When two periods of history are so very different from each other, what can the later possibly learn from the earlier? It is the Chronicler's conviction that there *are* lessons to be learnt, and it is his task to interpret David to an age when there is no more David. His readers are still David's people, and his object is to fill out for them the rich meaning of what may seem to be now no more than a tenuous connection. Therefore this point in the story is of special interest. David is about to leave the stage. Every reader knows that the reign of Solomon is to follow, and that the glories of war will be succeeded by the greater splendours of peace. But the fact remains that it will be a world without David. And in that crucial respect it will have lessons of prime importance for these people of a later age, whose cry is precisely that the Davidic stories have no relevance for them because they too live in a world without David.

What then does David bequeath to the Israel whose existence will continue after his death? Solomon's accession is no doubt the subject of these chapters (29:22b), but it is David who has stage-managed the ceremony (28:1ff.), and David's words which provide the Chronicler with the basis for his sermon at this central point. What is his message to those who will survive and follow him? The fabulous reign comes to an end: what continues? 'Only connect,' says the Chronicler; '– never imagine that our age is unrelated to the one that preceded it'; and from David's farewell to his kingdom our preacher expounds a series of great continuities. When David is gone, what will still be here?

---

[1] Zc. 4:10.

## 1. Still the Lord is here to be acknowledged (28:2–8)

The temple is a central theme in Chronicles, as we know, and the handing over of the temple-building project by David to Solomon is clearly central to these chapters. Some therefore would say that this is the chief tie-rod that joins David's reign with the centuries that follow. But David's tent, or tabernacle, was there before Solomon's temple, and was itself only erected as a dwelling-place for something which existed long before it, namely the ark of the covenant. This, as we have seen, stands for God's gracious providence, and in its very history illustrates a prime spiritual truth. *The ark was there first.* Yahweh, the covenant Lord, has taken the initiative; and the corollary of that is the same in the Old Testament as it is in the New – that since he, the Salvation of God, 'is before all things', then 'in him all things hold together'.[2] What David had already said to Solomon (22:7–13) he now says to Israel as a whole: that though times change, the God of Israel is still the Lord, the One who is behind and before and over all.

This is the burden of his opening speech. 'I had it in my heart to build a house of rest for the ark ... But God said ...' (28:2–3): David proposes, but God disposes. He looks back over his own ancestry and recognizes that it was the Lord who chose Judah out of Israel, and Jesse out of Judah, and him, David, out of the sons of Jesse (28:4). David's own sons have been given him by the Lord (28:5a). David's kingdom, and Solomon's after him, are actually the kingdom of the Lord (28:5b). Solomon's great work in building the temple has been decreed by the Lord (28:6a). Solomon himself is the Lord's adopted son, and his future is guaranteed by the Lord (28:6b–7).

For all the greatness of David, here is a God who is greater still. 'Thou dost beset me behind and before, and layest thy hand upon me. Such knowledge is too wonderful for me; it is high, I cannot attain it.'[3] This is the God whom David 'bequeaths' to Solomon, and to Israel. It is inconceivable that a God so great should ever fail his people. When David is dust, and even when twenty kings in succession after him have come and gone and the day of the kingdom itself has given way to the 'day of small things', still the Lord is here to be acknowledged.

---

[2] Col, 1:17.    [3] Ps. 139:5–6.

## 2. Still the plan is here to be followed (28:9–21)

An omnipotent God who thus oversees all things might seem to leave little room for human endeavour. In fact, however, the story envisages the genuine action of man's will. There are plans and thoughts in the human heart which the Lord searches out and understands, and man's whole-hearted, willing service is a thing both possible and desirable (28:9).

But the important thing is that the plans of men should be aligned with the plan of God (28:11).[4] Here, of course, the divine plan referred to is that of the temple; but the Chronicler's readers will recognize that it is meant to illustrate a general principle. The point, the Chronicler tells them, is that you should know what it is that 'the Lord has chosen *you* to build', that as the Lord surveys your plans they should be found in line with his plan, and that you should then 'be strong' and go ahead 'and do it' (28:10).

God's plan for his people's service is remarkably detailed. This characteristic brings with it two lessons which may seem to conflict, but which in fact complement each other. The plan details the structure of the temple building itself (28:11) and of its surrounding courtyards and adjacent buildings (28:12), the duties of its staff (28:13a), the making of its furniture and utensils (28:13b–18a), and in particular the construction of the 'golden chariot of the cherubim' for the Most Holy Place where the ark is to rest (28:18b).

As we shall see in due course (2 Ch. 3 – 4), Solomon followed his instructions in every respect. But before we jump to conclusions as to the spiritual lesson of the detailed nature of God's plan, it is worth noting two further facts. One is that Solomon, though a man of brilliance and flair, at no point in this narrative seems to find it irksome to fit in with someone else's plan. The building became known as 'Solomon's temple', and he clearly left on it the imprint of his own imagination; so either the plan handed down to him accorded exactly with what he himself wanted to do anyway, or else the details laid down left him sufficient freedom to express the exuberant mind which the older history attributes to him (1 Ki. 4:29–34). The other fact to note is that the later temple, the one built after the exile and known to the Chronicler and his readers, actually differed in many details from Solomon's. Yet the

---

[4] The word for 'plan' in 28:9 (*yēser*) is different from that in 28:11 (*tabnît*). But the RV makes even clearer the point that man's 'imaginations' must be brought into line with God's 'pattern'.

Chronicler, though he dwells at length on the earlier construction, nowhere seems to be hinting that the later one ought to have been built (or ought now to be rebuilt) according to the original specification.

With these things in mind it seems we are to understand this double lesson from the detailed nature of the temple plan: that as we seek to find and follow God's way, in one respect the detail matters, and in another respect it does not. On the one hand, we are sometimes tempted to think that he is not concerned with it. We may be feeling independent, or neglected, or despairing; we may even be drawing false conclusions from the Bible's teachings about his greatness. Any of these states of mind may lead us to discount his interest in 'the forks, the basins, and the cups' (28:17). Then we need the reminder that detail does matter to him; indeed, that in New Testament terms the very hairs of our head are numbered.[5] He who is concerned with the grand overall scheme is concerned equally with all that goes to make it up. On the other hand, it can be spiritually unhealthy to imagine that in every single circumstance of life there is just one choice which is right and all others are wrong. There must be many of God's servants who are haunted by the fear that at some point they may, perhaps unwittingly, have got some crucial detail wrong, and been relegated from then onwards to God's 'second-best' will. A biblical view of the process of Christian maturing would seem on the contrary to allow for areas in which particular choices are genuinely left to the 'temple-builder', who thus (again in New Testament terms) has his 'faculties trained by practice to distinguish good from evil'.[6]

This is not to say, however, that every detailed decision is not allowed for. The plan is real, however much latitude it may allow us at particular points. We are at liberty within it, but we are not at liberty to go outside it. And it is good for us to realize that we need it, and that what we might take into our heads to build for God's glory might be not at all the appropriate thing. David was a man of enormous gifts, yet it was God's plan, not one of his own, that he handed on to his son. Solomon was a man of unexampled wisdom, yet it was God's plan, not one of his own, that he set about implementing. If even they need such guidance, how much more do the men of the second temple, the Chronicler's people, and how much more do we!

[5] Mt. 10:30.      [6] Heb. 5:14.

111

To follow the plan is a liberating thing, not a restricting one, any more than a game's progress is restricted by its rules or a train's by its track. And obedience to the plan makes for confidence. It is here that David quotes a great saying which like so much else in Chronicles reaches out to both past and future, and expresses another of Scripture's unchanging truths. 'Be strong and of good courage ... Fear not, be not dismayed; for the LORD God, even my God, is with you' (28:20a). It was so in the days of Moses and Joshua,[7] and it will be so in the days of the Letter to the Hebrews.[8] And here this four-times-repeated exhortation and promise are uttered in the context of God's plan for his building: 'He will not fail you or forsake you, until all the work for the service of the house of the LORD is finished' (28:20b). The blessing of God's presence is related directly to obedience to the plan.

Solomon's temple rose in glory, adorned its age, and then with the turning of history fell in ruin. Yet still the plan of another temple, the building up of God's people, is here to be followed. The principle holds good. The necessity for obedience to the detailed instructions of God is one of the great continuities.

## 3. Still the challenge is here to be accepted (29:1–9)

Up to now, in the proceedings of the Second Jerusalem Assembly, David has spoken chiefly to Solomon and only incidentally, by way of setting the scene, to the gathered representatives of the nation (28:1). At this point he turns to them with the direct challenge which is implied by what has been said so far, concerning the Lord's presence and plan. It is a great work that has been set before Solomon, who, despite God's choice of him and the majesty and wisdom which will one day be his, is as yet 'young and inexperienced' (29:1). Hence the challenge to commitment which is directed to the rest of them.

It has been accepted by David himself (29:2–5). 'I have provided ... so far as I was able' (29:2 RSV) could sound as though David were apologizing for a rather paltry contribution! When we read of the quantities of material he had already amassed in the official fund, as well as the munificent gift from his own private purse, we may prefer the RV of this verse: 'I have prepared with all my might'. The challenge is thereupon accepted by his people also, through their

[7] *Cf.* Dt. 31:7–8; Jos. 1:6, 9.   [8] *Cf.* Heb. 13:5.

representatives (29:6–9). The leaders' giving is willing, whole-hearted, and free, and that and the general response of joy – one of the passages which give the lie to the notion of the Chronicler as a cold man, interested only in organization and structure – show with what enthusiasm it is taken up.

Among the gifts is mentioned a sum of '10,000 darics of gold' (29:7). This takes us at once across the generations to the Chronicler's own time. The word *daric* is an anachronism so far as the gifts for the first temple are concerned. It is a coin of the Persian Empire, first minted in the reign of Darius I, five centuries after David, and certainly known to the Chronicler's readers. In this way the generosity of their ancestors is brought to life for them, much as it might have been indicated in terms of pounds or dollars in a modern translation. There is every reason why the challenge and the response should be put in this 'up-to-date' way by the Chronicler. His world is that which has seen the building of the second temple. In spite of the lavish financial support with which that project was set in hand,[9] it tended from then on to progress in fits and starts. To the accounts in Ezra and Nehemiah we need to add the straight talking of the last prophetic books of the Old Testament. 'The word of the LORD came by Haggai the prophet, "Is it a time for you yourselves to dwell in your panelled houses, while this house lies in ruins?"' The Lord spoke also through Zechariah: ' Let your hands be strong, you who in these days have been hearing these words from the mouth of the prophets, since the day that the foundation of the house of the LORD of hosts was laid, that the temple might be built.' And he spoke through Malachi: 'Will man rob God? Yet you are robbing me. But you say, "How are we robbing thee?" In your tithes and offerings.'[10] Israel after the exile was faced with the same sort of challenge to commitment as the Israel of the early monarchy had been. And it was still to be met in the same practical way: the giving of oneself, expressed by the giving of one's wealth.

A crude way of expressing spiritual devotion? Well, God seems to set a good deal of store by it. It reappears brazenly in the world of the New Testament, in a passage I have already referred to briefly.[11] Acts 11:27–30 is a deceptively simple account of a prophecy of impending famine, which encourages the Christians to whom it is addressed to send financial help to one of the areas of need. But there

---

[9] Ezr. 1:2–6; 2:68–69.    [10] Hg. 1:3–4; Zc. 8:9; Mal. 3:8.
[11] See above, p. 93.

is more to this than meets the eye. For these Christians were the church of Antioch, and the congregation which had come into being at Antioch was the first church in the world which was not primarily Jewish. The mother church in Jerusalem had literally never seen anything like it, and there must have been Hebrew Christians who doubted whether such a phenomenon could be a true church at all. No wonder a deputation was sent to see what was going on.[12] Barnabas was sufficiently convinced when he 'saw the grace of God' at work in Antioch. But how is this new congregation to vindicate itself publicly as a true gathering of God's people? The answer of the New Testament is, *by rising to the challenge of the temple.* 'Who then will offer willingly?' cried David in the days of the first temple, and the Chronicler in the days of the second. The third temple, the New Testament one, is no longer a building but a people; yet in its thoroughly practical need to be supported by gifts in cash and in kind, it provides the same down-to-earth test of a true devotion to the Lord. 'The disciples' at Antioch 'determined, every one according to his ability, to send relief to the brethren who lived in Judaea; and they did so'.[13]

The Chronicler is once more driving home the perennial lesson. 'Who then will offer willingly?' (29:5). There is no generation of God's people, least of all our own, which can afford to sidestep the issue. Although so much has changed in the world, still the challenge is here to be accepted: for the work of God, for the benefit of the 'temple' which is his people, are we prepared to give – to give the gold and silver and precious stones (29:7–8), and to give the whole heart (29:9)? In the words of 29:5, which brackets the two givings, the outward sign together with the thing signified, 'Who then will *offer willingly*, consecrating *himself* today to the LORD?'

## 4. Still the joy is here to be expressed (29:10–22a)

Blessing and worship, an abundance of offerings for sacrifice, total involvement, and a celebration with 'great gladness': again the supposedly austere Chronicler relishes the delight of the occasion (29:20–22a). Again, too, we remember that he is writing for an age which is perforce far less lavish in its festivities, an age which in response to this narrative, as to so many others, might grumble 'It was all very well for them!' So it is necessary that here also, for the

[12] Acts 11:19–24.    [13] Acts 11:29–30.

benefit of the 'day of small things', the Chronicler should bring out the inner principle which holds good even in changed circumstances. In a passage more memorable than the mere description of the festival, he gives us David's prayer at the climax of its opening ceremony (29:10–19). It is David's words here which pinpoint the cause of this next 'great continuity', the perennial joy that God's people should know.

What words they are! As so often seems to happen, verses whose whereabouts in Scripture we cannot quite recall, but whose content is quite unforgettable, turn out to be the work of the Chronicler. A dull writer, they say, yet how many gems wait to be unearthed from his unfamiliar pages! 29:11 and 14 are a case in point. A conflation of parts of the two verses is used in worship all over the Christian world, among thousands who have no idea where the words come from. Instead of the RSV, I quote a version which for this reason is perhaps better known: 'Yours, Lord, is the greatness, the power, the glory, the splendour, and the majesty; for everything in heaven and on earth is yours. All things come from you, and of your own do we give you.'[14] It is a precious thing of undimmed lustre and undiminished value.

And it is, we must not fail to notice, an expression not only of constant joy, but of the constant source of joy. We live in a time in the church's history which tends to value Christian experience more than the cause of that experience. So it is important to grasp that the believer's joy, which is a responsive emotion, can be an abiding thing only because God's bounty, which gives rise to it, is itself an abiding thing. Only when we can pray, with understanding and assurance,

> O may *this bounteous God*
> Through all our life be near us,

can we go on to praise him for the consequence:

> With *ever joyful hearts*
> And blessed peace to cheer us.[15]

This is what David celebrates. The immediate reason is Israel's gifts for Solomon's temple: 'All *this* abundance that we have

---

[14] The Holy Communion Service, the *Alternative Service Book 1980* of the Church of England.

[15] Martin Rinkart (tr. Catherine Winkworth), *Now than we all our God.*

provided for building thee a house for thy holy name comes from thy hand and is all thy own' (29:16). But he does not fail to draw the wider lesson: '*All* things come from thee, and of thy own have we given thee' (29:14). Recognizing God's prior gifts to him, David must give himself back to God in true, sincere, consecration: 'In the uprightness of my heart I have freely offered all these things' (29:17b). So must Israel: 'Now I have seen thy people, who are present here, offering freely and joyously to thee' (29:17c). So must Solomon: 'Grant ... that with a whole heart he may keep thy commandments, thy testimonies, and thy statutes' (29:19). So must all God's people, in all ages before and since. 29:18 brings together past, present, and future, with a vision which is central to the Chronicler's message: David speaks to the Lord as his own real and present covenant God, addresses him as the God of his fathers, Abraham, Isaac, and Israel, and prays that his people may be kept in the same spirit of devotion for ever.

All this lies behind the 'great gladness' of that assembly (29:22). It is plain that however circumstances may alter, the Chronicler sees no need for such joy ever to become a thing of the past, if only God's people will learn to count their blessings, to learn in whatever state they are, to be content,[16] and to recognize in every day's events the bountiful goodness of the covenant-keeping God of their fathers. He underlines the point by reminding us how transient were even the glorious days of the early monarchy: 'We are strangers before thee,' says David, 'and sojourners, as all our fathers were; our days on the earth are like a shadow, and there is no abiding' (29:15). Indeed so far as human life is concerned there is not.

> Yet, God the same abiding,
> His praise shall tune my voice;
> For, while in him confiding,
> I cannot but rejoice.[17]

## 5.  Still the king is here to be enthroned (29:22b–30)

How different these chapters are from the Samuel/Kings account of David's last days! 1 Kings 1 and 2 are a sad end to a proud story. They portray an old man in failing health. He has to be nursed; he can be deceived; were it not for a little group of faithful friends his

[16] Phil. 4:11.    [17] William Cowper, *Sometimes a light surprises*.

authority would be ignored. Without the vigilance of his wife Bathsheba and his counsellor Nathan the prophet, his eldest surviving son Adonijah would have taken the kingdom against David's wishes, and Solomon, the designated heir, and his faction, would have suffered; as it was, the tables were turned and the plot overthrown, and it was Adonijah's party which suffered. Either way, it was a situation of intrigue which reflects badly on the closing years of what had been a glorious reign.

There is no indication here in Chronicles of such a sorry decline. Some time certainly elapsed between the Second Jerusalem Assembly and David's death, but whatever follies and miseries came into the story in that interval, the Chronicler does not record them. We are to remember David as he was at the time of the Assembly, with (as was said of Moses) 'his eye ... not dim, nor his natural force abated'.[18] As it were in the same breath, and at any rate with no note of an intervening decline, the Chronicler tells us that 'King David rose to his feet' to address his ringing words to his people (28:2), and that 'he died in a good old age, full of days, riches, and honour' (29:28).

He is not falsifying the tale. As we have frequently noted, it would scarcely be possible for him to do so, since the facts are so well known. What he is doing is making a radical selection from those facts. We may see one pointer to his deliberate policy of omitting whatever might confuse the main issue, in his reference to Solomon's being made king 'the second time' (29:22b). 23:1 ('When David was old and full of days, he made Solomon his son king over Israel') should be taken as a general heading to the whole long section of seven chapters (23 – 29); as an account of a particular ceremony, it is quite unsatisfactory. The first 'coronation', which is implied by the mention here of a second one, is surely the affair spoken of not in 23:1, but in 1 Kings 1, an emergency measure hastily contrived to forestall Adonijah's usurpation of the kingdom. We know this anyway from Samuel/Kings, and it would not suit the Chronicler's purpose to repeat it. Instead he points us to the public, official, and universally acknowledged 'second time' as being the occasion which carries his message. It is the kingship which is important, the 'royal majesty' which though Solomon's in an unprecedented way (29:25), belongs to the throne regardless of the person who may occupy it at any given time.

[18] Dt. 34:7.

In this way the continuity is stressed yet again. 'Thus David the son of Jesse reigned over all Israel ... Then he died in a good old age, full of days, riches, and honour; and Solomon his son reigned in his stead' (29:26–28). The king is dead, long live the king. The cross-currents are ignored as the great tide of God's purpose is being described. For it is 'the throne of the kingdom of the LORD over Israel' (28:5) which each king occupies in turn. '*Thine* is the kingdom, O LORD' (29:11). The Chronicler was writing in an age when for Israel not only the power of David and Solomon, but the political kingdom itself, was a thing of the past. He wrote of the majesty of kings when there were no kings, and cried up their glories all the more for that. And as this paradox of what is, and what is not, is forced upon our attention, it becomes clear what he is driving at. The confident prayers of Psalm 72 (we have noted them already)[19] are something more than pious exaggeration, when we ask who it is that really, behind all the appearances, sits on the throne – especially when we ask the question with New Testament hindsight:

> Give the king thy justice, O God,
> and thy righteousness to the royal son!
> ... May he live while the sun endures,
> and as long as the moon, throughout all generations!
> ... May he have dominion from sea to sea,
> and from the River to the ends of the earth!
> ... May his name endure for ever,
> his fame continue as long as the sun!
> May men bless themselves by him,
> all nations call him blessed![20]

Through all the discouraging days for which our book is written, even when God's people seem of small account, their God reigns. Even when there is no throne in Jerusalem, there is a throne, and it is the Lord's. Even when the kingdom of David and Solomon is no more than a tale in a book of old chronicles, still the King will be here to be enthroned among his people. He is the greatest of all the continuities. He will always be here; for the Chronicler, if it is not David's son, then it will be David's Lord who reigns; for a later, more blessed generation, it will be seen that the two figures merge, and that the true King will be miraculously both David's Son and David's Lord.[21]

[19] See above, p. 82–83.     [20] Ps. 72:1, 5, 8, 17.
[21] Mt. 22:41–46.

# Part Three
# SOLOMON, THE MAN OF PEACE
# (2 Chronicles 1 – 9)

## 2 Chronicles 1 – 2

## 10. Solomon establishes himself

Twice 'made king' already in his father's lifetime,[1] Solomon takes royal power fully and finally after David's death. Those who divided into two what was originally the single book of Chronicles were no doubt right in seeing this as the most appropriate place at which to do it. It is a point of the most acute interest. David is the central figure of the book, the man after God's own heart (as Samuel/Kings had called him),[2] and in many respects the ideal by which all later ages are to be measured. But he is the central figure, not the final one. The book does not end with him; indeed we are not even halfway through. The Chronicler is very interested in what is to

[1] See above, p. 117.
[2] See 1 Sa. 13:14; Acts 13:22.

follow the reign of David, for, as we have seen, a world with no more David in it is precisely the kind of world for which he is writing.

Scripture casts Solomon in more roles than one. It is the older history which depicts him largely as David's son, a man with human weaknesses not unlike his father's. Of course the Chronicler knows about these, but in his picture of Solomon's reign he has other concerns. For him the new king will be from one point of view David's complement, the other half of a double kingship, filling up what was lacking in the previous regime and doing things that his father could not have done. From another, Solomon is David's successor, in the sense that the reign of David laid down certain principles as to the proper government of God's people, and to Solomon falls the task of trying to implement those principles in new circumstances.

The question is, therefore, what will Solomon *do*? Granted that the Lord is the real King, and that his rule is one of the great continuities which survive all the changes of human life, it seems he still intends to operate at one remove, and to delegate responsibility to his servants. How will Solomon rise to this?

With vigour, says the Chronicler. Having been present with a mere walk-on part, so to speak, in the last two chapters of 1 Chronicles, now after the death of his father the new king springs into action. The conviction that the Lord reigns should lead not to an inactivity which masquerades as trust, but to an active response which first asks what, under God, our own responsibilities are in his kingdom, and which then sets about fulfilling them.

So Solomon acted. He 'established himself in his kingdom' – 1:1 is a kind of headline to what follows (2:1–2 is another) – and the greater part of these two chapters describes what in practical terms the response of faith made him actually *do*. They provide in this way a blueprint for all who find themselves expected to undertake responsibility among the people of God.

## 1. Solomon seeks the Lord (1:2–6)

The Chronicler records as the very first event of the new reign that Solomon and the assembly sought 'it', or 'him' – the pronoun at the end of 1:5 could refer either to the Lord, as the RSV (following the Greek and Latin versions) assumes, or to the altar, the subject of the previous sentence.[3] If the altar is the object of Solomon's 'search', it is only because there he wants to meet the Lord, so the sense is the same in either case.

The plain statement of this half-verse is filled out by the writer's geographical note in 1:3–5. The point was made at the beginning of David's reign, and we noticed it at the time;[4] now it is the subject of a brief but explicit contrast. The events of 1:2–13 had already been recorded in Samuel/Kings: 'The king went to Gibeon to sacrifice there, for that was the great high place ... At Gibeon the LORD appeared to Solomon in a dream by night; and God said, "Ask what I shall give you"' (1 Ki. 3:4–5). The wisdom Solomon then requested was promised to him, and much more besides; and after the incident 'he came to Jerusalem, and stood before the ark of the covenant of the LORD' (1 Ki. 3:15). The Chronicler rewrites this, setting the place-names side by side to bring out their significance. Solomon went to Gibeon, 'for the tent of meeting of God ... was there', and 'the bronze altar ... was there'; but as to the ark of God, David 'had pitched a tent for it in Jerusalem' (1:3–5).

The ark represents God's covenant with his people, and is thus the symbol of his initiative of grace; at the altar man responds in faith. The earlier history tells us that Solomon 'offered up burnt offerings and peace offerings' before the ark also (1 Ki. 3:15), but the Chronicler omits this, stressing the theological point that according to its inner meaning the altar rather than the ark is where such offerings are most appropriately made. Both are meeting-places for God and man, and as we have seen they are normally to be found together; so they were for centuries before the time of David and after the time of Solomon, reminding us that *in practice* grace and faith are inseparable. But for that short period one was at Jerusalem and the other at Gibeon, and being separated they illustrate the necessary truth that, *in thought*, grace and faith are to be distinguished.

In the Chronicler's narrative, the assembly of 1 Chronicles 28 – 29 precedes the action of 2 Chronicles 1 – 2. David's reign closes with an affirmation of the great continuities – what God is and will always be, what he does and will always do. On the prior facts of the nature and character of God the promises of the covenant are based.

---

[3] The same verb, *dāraš*, is used of the ark in 1 Ch. 13:3; 15:13 (to neglect = not to seek, not to concern oneself with), and of God in 1 Ch. 21:30. See below, pp. 215–216.

[4] See above, p. 73.

Here is, as it were, the ark. So Solomon's reign opens with the response of the believing heart. The second book begins, theologically and not just geographically, at Gibeon, for 'the bronze altar that Bezalel the son of Uri, son of Hur, had made, was there' (1:5a). The previous two chapters focus on what God does; these two turn our attention to what man will do in response. And Solomon rises to the occasion.

His seeking of God, pinpointed in the words of 1:5b and illustrated by the Gibeon-Jerusalem note of 1:3–5a, is described in a series of deft touches in the course of the paragraph. First, it is not what we might call an agnostic seeking. Perhaps the word 'seek' is misleading; apart from its slightly old-fashioned flavour, it can be taken to imply that one does not know exactly where to look for the thing one seeks. But there is no doubt in Solomon's mind. He is not embarking on a treasure-hunt; the altar is in no sense lost or hidden; he goes to seek not what he hopes he may find, but what he knows he will find. The point is stressed. Gibeon is the place, and Solomon knows it: the tent of meeting is *there*, the bronze altar is *there*, so Solomon goes *there* (1:3, 5–6). In many things, perhaps, in the experience of the seeker after God it is right for him to confess ignorance or doubt. But when God has told us clearly where we may find what we seek, then to ignore his map in the name of a 'reverent agnosticism' is not only folly but rebellion. If we are truly seeking the Lord, then more often than not we shall have to acknowledge that we do know the way to Gibeon, and we do know what we shall find there.

And that brings us to the second characteristic of Solomon's action. It is not an empty-handed seeking. His destination is an altar, and an altar exists for offerings and sacrifices. At Gibeon Solomon intends to present to God a thousand burnt offerings (1:6). The sacrifices are in themselves costly. In the tradition of the Israelite faith they signify something yet more costly, namely the entire consecration to God of the offerer's own heart, and we may take it that in the event that is what they do represent for Solomon himself. It is easy to be cynical about Solomon. If one is not in sympathy with the Chronicler's purposes, one might say that he is going to gloss over the most notorious fact in the great king's story, which was precisely that his heart was *not* wholly devoted to the Lord, but shared with his pagan wives, and then with the gods which those wives worshipped and with the ways of the world over which those gods presided (1 Ki. 11). But at the beginning it was not so. The Chronicler is not intending to suppress facts. What he does say is that there was a genuine whole-hearted devotion to God in the young Solomon; and if it was tarnished in later years, as the Chronicler and everyone else know it was, then the older Solomon was to that extent untrue to his calling, and the narration of such facts would not help to make plain the great principles which the Chronicler wishes so tirelessly to teach. At Gibeon there can be no doubt that the new king embodies one of those principles. The true seeking of God can never be empty-handed, least of all if the seeker is one upon whom great responsibilities are laid. Burnt offerings, a thousand burnt offerings, are called for.

Finally, this is not a solitary seeking. Solomon, like David before him, has called together representatives of 'all Israel' (that favourite phrase of the Chronicler's), and he 'and all the assembly with him' set out for Gibeon (1:2–3). He is here not an individual person, but a responsible leader. This is the public Solomon rather than the private one. And recognizing his responsibility, he shares it with his people. He sees the necessity of involving them in the lessons to be learnt, the principles to be enacted. How much the leader's temper is forged in solitude, in his private dealings with his God, is something which in the nature of the case his people may never know. But he has a duty also to take them with him in the explicit 'search' for God which is their common duty, and which is in fact not so much a seeking, as a grasping of promises and a responding in obedience.

Solomon comes then to the altar before the tent of meeting at Gibeon. He comes with his assurance that, according to promise, God will meet him there. He comes with his offering, which expresses the sincerity of his purpose. He comes with his fellow-Israelites, with whom his calling as ruler is inescapably bound up. But he is as yet, so to say, 'seeking'. We pass on to what follows the memorable day at Gibeon.

## 2. Solomon asks the blessing (1:7–13)

'In that night God appeared to Solomon, and said to him, "Ask what I shall give you"' (1:7). How, we might ask, is Solomon's asking meant to be a model for *action* on the part of those in equivalent situations, when it is so plainly a *re*action to God's initiative? Solomon presumably had no idea that God was going to make him such an offer; is the principle then that we do nothing about asking for God's blessing until he 'appears to us', as it were, and tells us to do so?

Well, he has done just that. Not as a dream-figure, but as the Word made flesh, he has commanded 'Ask, and it will be given you'.[5] He has promised that the answer will be 'good things'.[6] He has spelt out the message through the words of his apostle: 'In everything by prayer and supplication with thanksgiving let your requests be made known to God.'[7] It is by no means out of place for God's servants today to take it that his words to Solomon are equally his words to them. Samuel/Kings stresses at the beginning and at the end of the incident (1 Ki. 3:5, 15) that 'it was a dream'; the Chronicler omits this – we must not imagine that God was making Solomon a private and unrepeatable offer.

Let us see then how the blessing is asked.

We note first that the very terms of the offer expect Solomon to put his request into words. It may seem to be a humble and spiritual attitude which prays only for the vaguest generalities, or even hands the matter back to God as though 'Your will be done' is the only fitting prayer for the pious man. But the mind of God and the mind of man ought both to be involved in such praying. The more we know of the mind of God, the more specific our requests will be, while yet staying within the bounds of his expressed will. The very thing Solomon asks for here, for instance, is the subject of an unequivocal New Testament promise: 'If any of you lacks wisdom, let him ask God, who gives to all men generously and without reproaching, and it will be given him'.[8] And with regard to the mind of man, we are not so unfamiliar with the workings of it that we cannot see the value of being made to think through the question of what we should like God to give us. Although it was perfectly obvious what blind Bartimaeus desired of him, Jesus still asked 'What do you want me to do for you?',[9] and the possible reasons are worth pondering.

Perhaps the little prayer of Jabez was planted way back among the genealogies (1 Ch. 4:10) as the seed which, having grown through the centuries, was here to burst into bloom, at a crucial point in Israel's history, with its fruit ripening eleven years later (*cf.*

[5] Mt. 7:7.   [6] Mt. 7:11.   [7] Phil. 4:6.
[8] Jas. 1:5.   [9] Mk. 10:51.

1 Ki. 6:37–38 with 2 Ch. 3:2) in Solomon's magnificent and highly specific prayer in the dedication of the temple in chapter 6.

First, then, his asking is framed in his own words; and next we note that it is based on God's character (1:8–9). This God is the *sovereign* God, who raised up David and has now raised up David's son in his place. He is very much the God for the days when Jerusalem is no longer the seat of kings – the one called by Daniel, for example, the 'Most High', who 'rules the kingdom of men, and gives it to whom he will'.[10] He is the *constant* God, who has shown 'great *ḥeseḏ*' to David; *ḥeseḏ* is the word which the RSV translates 'steadfast love', and which in itself implies unswerving constancy, made still firmer here by the epithet 'great'. This faithfulness is the quality demonstrated by God when he acts in sovereign power to establish Solomon as David's successor, for that is what he promised he would do (1 Ch. 17:11–14). He is the *all-knowing* God, who may be presumed to understand the size of the task he has given to Solomon, and therefore the wisdom Solomon will need to carry it out! As the request is consciously spelled out, so are the grounds for believing that it will be answered.

Thirdly, it is directed to the heart of the matter (1:10–12). The things which the king might have asked for – riches, honour, long life – are the superficial trappings of kingship. The core of it is a man who is in himself right for the job. And since he is God's king ruling God's people, his request for wisdom and knowledge is a seeking to be the right man, with the right qualities, which comes very close to the seeking for righteousness which Christ likewise teaches to be of first importance. The results will be the same, whether promised on the hillside by Galilee or at the tabernacle at Gibeon: 'Seek first his kingdom and his righteousness, and all these things shall be yours as well'.[11]

Lastly, Solomon's prayer is governed by no selfish motive, but by the needs of the nation for which he is responsible. The sense of his involvement with the rest of Israel over-rides all personal considerations. A people 'as many as the dust of the earth' (1:9), 'so great' (1:10), 'over whom I have made you king' (1:11), Israel is, along with God's greatness and his own inadequacy, Solomon's prime concern. It is small wonder that a prayer framed so thoughtfully, based so solidly, directed so rightly, and motivated with such

[10] Dn. 4:17, 25, 32.
[11] Mt. 6:33.

concern for his fellows, brings Solomon the blessing he asks, and much more besides, from the God who 'is able to do far more abundantly than all that we ask or think'.[12]

### 3. Solomon faces the world (1:14–17)

In the Chronicler's source book this paragraph came at the end of nearly ten chapters describing Solomon's reign, and only just before his moral downfall was recounted (1 Ki. 10:26–29). The Chronicler brings it forward to include it in these foundation chapters, for it indicates another way in which Solomon established himself as king. 1:14–17 is all that is said at this stage concerning the foreign relations of Israel. It is enough to show a marked contrast with such things as they were in David's day. Then it was an almost unrelieved tale of warfare, when even with the few nations that were friendly to David it was a matter of military treaties and alliances, while the rest were enemies to be fought and defeated. All that must have seemed a wilder, cruder world, when viewed from the lush pastures of Solomon's reign; as the Victorian ladies observed after watching Sarah Bernhardt in Shakespeare's *Antony and Cleopatra*, 'How very different from the home life of our own dear Queen' – except that in this case it was not home affairs, so to speak, but foreign affairs. Solomon's were really quite different from David's. Trade, not warfare, was the thread that ran through all *his* international relations.

The mention of the riches that accrued to Solomon through these massive commercial enterprises follows aptly enough on the heels of God's promise in 1:12, and leads equally aptly into the account of the building of the temple (chapters 2 – 4). It may be questioned however whether these are the Chronicler's chief reasons for inserting the paragraph here. 1:15 indicates that the spiralling wealth did not simply enrich the king himself, nor was it all channelled into the temple-building fund. *Jerusalem* was enriched; and a deeper connection with the preceding paragraph may be seen in the fact that as there Solomon's prayer was primarily for the well-being of his people, so here the unasked extra blessing of riches is shared by his people.

Perhaps, indeed, the enrichment of king and nation is something the Chronicler wants us to notice for its own sake. It has echoes in

[12] Eph. 3:20.

the poetry of the Old Testament, and in the eschatology of the New, which we should not ignore. We have turned more than once to Psalm 72, that great celebration of the Davidic kingship, and do so again now to remind ourselves of one salient aspect of the greatness of God's king: that 'the kings of Tarshish and of the isles render him tribute', and 'the kings of Sheba and Seba bring gifts'.[13] Even more splendid is John's vision of the New Jerusalem, and of that too, as of Solomon's Jerusalem, we are told that 'the kings of the earth shall bring their glory into it ... they shall bring into it the glory and honour of the nations'.[14]

All this is of great importance for the Chronicler's generation, compelled as it is to live in a secular world. Solomon's subjects scarcely had to face the question; they were cushioned against it – their king faced it on their behalf. But the Chronicler, and we, have to face it, and we may learn from these histories the ambivalent attitude which the servant of God has to maintain towards the world in which he lives. He must know when to fight it, like David, and when to use it, like Solomon. He must know what in his modern world is represented by Egypt and Kue and the Hittites (1:16–17), and can enrich him, and what is represented by Moab and Zobah and the Philistines (1 Ch. 18:1–3), and would destroy him. He must learn the yet harder task of discerning when Syria is a friend (1:17) and when it is a foe (1 Ch. 18:5–6). His faith is from one point of view a world-affirming one, and from another a world-denying one, and he must understand it in both aspects.

What chiefly distinguishes the two kings, however, is (as we have seen) that David is a man of war and Solomon a man of peace. In due course Solomon's foreign connections caused as much trouble, though in a different way, as David's had done, but for the Chronicler to include such events would confuse the broad picture he wants to paint, so he omits them. For him, Solomon's reign illustrates the saying that 'When a man's ways please the LORD, he makes even his enemies to be at peace with him'.[15] Having sought the Lord, and asked the blessing, Solomon learns to face the world. He sees it clearly for the mixture of good and evil that it is, and from it he learns to draw all the wealth it can afford for his people's benefit as well as his own.

---

[13] Ps. 72:10.    [14] Rev. 21:24, 26.    [15] Pr. 16:7.

## 4. Solomon plans the temple (2:3–18)

We are given a brief heading (2:1–2 summarizes the rest of this chapter, as 1:1 summarized the first one), and then the subject of the temple is taken up again, now to be the centre of attention for no less than seven successive chapters. Here we are concerned with the preliminaries, the laying of plans: not, that is, the detailed drawings, which David had already prepared (1 Ch. 28:11–19), but the logistics of the construction work. Solomon's embarking on the building of this house as the focal point for the meeting of God and man, the place where, in the event, ark and altar will be reunited, is all a part of his establishing of himself as God's king over God's people.

The project is seen as a whole; not for nothing did the earlier history speak of Solomon's 'largeness of mind' (1 Ki. 4:29). His vision encompasses all that needs to be done before construction can start, and all that will follow its completion, the daily worship which is the object of the exercise. Far more is in mind than a mere building, however magnificent: 'with *hymns of praise* These hallowed courts shall ring.'[16] All this is in mind from the outset, and from the correspondence between Solomon and Hiram recorded here we may gather what are the former's preoccupations in his planning.

Hiram, king of Tyre,[17] was well known to have been a friend as well as an ally of David's, and had sent congratulations to David's son at the time of his accession (1 Ki. 5:1). To this man Solomon now sends an outline of his scheme which is at the same time a testimony to his faith. The temple and all that will take place in it we may sum up in the word 'worship', and the letter to Hiram shows the kind of worship towards which Solomon is planning.

First, he has in mind *traditional* worship. To churches which are passing through an 'Athenian' age ('the Athenians … spent their time in nothing except telling or hearing something new'[18]), the word tends to be like a red rag to a bull. Tradition and renewal are thought of as the watchwords of two opposing camps. On this a couple of comments need to be made. The first is that the temple *was* new. Nothing quite like it had ever been seen before. It bore the impress of Solomon's own imagination and of his age and culture.

[16] John Chandler (tr.), *Christ is our corner-stone*.
[17] 'Hiram' is the more familiar, and probably the more correct, spelling of the name, though the Chronicler always uses the form 'Huram'.
[18] Acts 17:21.

The second is that his very concern for tradition was a concern for its renewal. The old was not simply to be ditched and replaced by something different. It was to be taken up again, considered, cleaned and serviced, and brought into use once more. The temple was for incense and showbread and burnt offerings, for the celebration of sabbaths and new moons and appointed feasts, 'as ordained for ever for Israel' (2:4). New buildings, new worshippers, new songs; but all referring, and deferring, to the principles first given to Israel through Moses, and intended to be 'handed down' (which is what 'tradition' means) through all generations. The Chronicler will remind us frequently, with a kind of foreshortening typical of biblical times (and alas untypical of ours), that Moses and David and other great figures of the past are just as real, and should loom just as large, today as in their own time.

Solomon plans too for *spiritual* worship. The danger inherent in building a temple at all lies precisely in this, that it may encourage an unspiritual religion. Many, and more as time went by, must have fallen into the snare. Witness the Samaritan woman's innocent (but deadly) theology: 'Our fathers worshipped on this mountain; and you say that in Jerusalem is the place where men ought to worship' – to which Jesus had to reply, 'Neither on this mountain nor in Jerusalem', but 'in spirit and in truth'.[19] Solomon was not unaware of the danger. But he did not, for all that, give up the project. He saw the temple both for what it was, and for what it was not. Because God is so great, the building and its worship must be as grand as possible (2:5); because he is so great, they cannot possibly be grand enough (2:6). On both counts Solomon would have his people approach God 'in spirit and in truth'. They are to see the temple as a matter of convenience, 'a place to burn incense'; man needs such a prop, because deprived of a place and form of worship he is in the nature of things only too likely not to worship at all.[20] But God is still to be thought of as a Being infinitely too great to be confined within any building. They are on the other hand to see it as an expression, however inadequate, of the greatness they ascribe to God, and that means that nothing but the best is good enough for it.

[19] Jn. 4:20–21, 23–24; and *cf.* p. 74 above.

[20] 'The Church ... provides for a monotony of pardon. It used to be blamed for compelling its members ritually to declare themselves "miserable sinners" day by day, but it knew very well that if they did not do it ritually they would not do it at all' (Charles Williams, *The Image of the City*, Oxford University Press, 1958, p. 140).

This brings us to the final consideration: that it is to be *quality* worship. Now the world outside is to be laid under contribution, and Hiram of Tyre becomes involved. The actual making of everything that will form a part of temple worship is remarkable for the skill devoted to it, Solomon's homeborn craftsmen being directed by the brilliant man of mixed race, Huram-abi, and for the variety of it (2:7, 13–14); for its scope and quantity (2:9), and for the efficiency with which the huge workforce is mobilized (2:17–18). There was more to the enterprise than this, and were we reading the story from another point of view, the king's methods might lead us into other, and darker, trains of thought.[21] But the Chronicler concentrates on the work itself, which was undeniably intended to be of top quality. Rightly so, of course. When, as Solomon points out (2:5–6, and later in 6:18), even the best falls so far short of what God deserves, how can we offer him anything less than the best?

Seeking the Lord and asking for his blessing, drawing from the world around all that it can give towards his prime task, the building of God's house, Solomon establishes himself in his kingdom. It is a magnificent response to the daunting challenge of David's vacant throne. The heathen king of Tyre sets his seal on the man who thus rises to the occasion: 'Blessed be the LORD God of Israel, who made heaven and earth, who has given King David a wise son, endued with discretion and understanding, who will build a temple for the LORD, and a royal palace for himself' (2:12). We cannot tell how far he understood his own words. But they were the plain truth. When any servant of God finds responsibility laid upon him and takes it up as Solomon did, even his unbelieving neighbours will be compelled to speak thus of him, and to give him an accolade which he would never dare to claim, but should yet strive to deserve: 'Because the LORD loves his people he has made you king over them' (2:11).

---

[21] A number of scriptures refer to the question of Canaanites who had survived Israel's conquest of their land (with 2:17–18 compare *e.g.* Dt. 7:2; Jos. 9; Jdg. 1:28). But note also 1 Ki. 5:13 and 12:4, and see Payne, pp. 62, 66.

# 2 Chronicles 3 – 5

## 11.  The building of the temple

Along with many more important qualities, C. H. Spurgeon had the gift of wit, a 'talent to amuse';[1] and he is at his most entertaining in the unlikely context of his own commentary on other men's Bible commentaries,[2] where paragraphs about the authors he regards highly are printed in big bold typeface, and lesser writers are dealt with in smaller print. The comments in tiny type are needless to say the most amusing! But if the size of print indicates the value of the book, what should we make of the fact that some editions of the Bible have the chapters before us in a typeface smaller than usual? Are we to take it that these lists of the buildings and furnishings of the temple are, like the genealogies of 1 Chronicles 1 to 9, in some way of less moment than the rest? Apparently the Chronicler does not think so, or he would have abbreviated or omitted them. Rather, he treats them at some length, and his purpose in doing so is what we now have to explore.

Solomon is still, at any rate to start with, a model of the leader who sets about taking over responsibility among God's people. With chapter 3 he embarks on the task which more than any other will be remembered as his service for God, namely the erection of the temple. From the way the Chronicler describes this, certain lessons may be learned concerning God's doings in the world. Instead of working through the chapters of this section consecutively, we shall consider the passage as a whole, but from three different angles.

### 1.  The devout heart

In one respect, certainly, Solomon's activity in the building of the temple is of real, and not merely academic, interest to all who read of it: it expresses the devotion of his heart. This comes out most clearly, perhaps, if we first set his work in perspective, and only

---

[1] The phrase is Noel Coward's, from his musical *Bitter Sweet*.
[2] Charles H. Spurgeon, *Commenting and Commentaries* (Passmore and Alabaster, 1876).

then go on to consider it in detail, moving on last to look at it in depth.

### a. Solomon's work in perspective

To dip into these chapters at random is to find oneself in the midst of an extraordinary, and not very edifying, miscellany of lamps and lavers, firepans and forks, poles, pillars, and pomegranates. But read the section whole, and read it in context, and these things begin to fall into place. They are not intended as information for the Chronicler's readers, who know already what was included in the making of the temple. They are, rather, a familiar picture set in a new frame. We recall what Solomon has already said concerning the temple, in writing of it to Hiram; it does not exist for its own sake, but for the Lord's, 'for the burning of incense of sweet spices before him, and for the continual offering of the showbread, and for burnt offerings morning and evening' (2:4). The house of God is of value and importance only because of what will happen in it. Chapters 3 to 5 restate this at length. They consist of a series of 'when' clauses, leading up to the great 'then' statement of 5:13–14: *when* the last stone was laid, and the last panel fixed; *when* each lampstand was completed and erected, and each table finished and placed; *when* every golden firepan and every bronze fork was ready; *when* the whole assembly of Israel was gathered, and the priests sanctified, and the musicians marshalled; '*when the song was raised ... in praise to the* LORD', then '*the house ... was filled with a cloud ... for the glory of the* LORD *filled the house of God.*' Nothing like it had happened since Moses' tent of meeting was completed, and similarly filled with the glory of God, at Sinai.[3] The object of the whole array was to provide the right setting for this tremendous event.

On its publication many years ago, a fine series of travel books[4] was hailed as an 'ecstatic inventory' of everything worth seeing in England. The same words might describe this catalogue of all that contributed to the splendours of that day. It is not a mere list, but a worthy setting contrived by a devout heart.

### b. Solomon's work in detail

Now that we have seen to what the 'ecstatic inventory' is leading up, we are in a position to return to the beginning of chapter 3, and to

---

[3] Ex. 40:34.
[4] Arthur Mee (ed.), *The King's England* (Hodder & Stoughton, various dates).

follow the Chronicler as he takes us on a guided tour of the temple.

We enter, naturally, by the lofty porch or 'vestibule' (3:4). Moving into the building proper we find ourselves at one end of the rectangular 'nave', the 'holy place' (3:5). Ahead of us is the square, windowless, 'most holy place' (3:8), and could we enter it we should find there the two cherubim, each more than twice the height of a man (1 Ki. 6:23), standing side by side and wing-tip to wing-tip, with their outer wings touching the sides of the great room to right and left (3:10-13); under them the ark of the covenant will be placed on the day of the dedication. Between us and that inner sanctuary, however, hangs the richly embroidered curtain known as the 'veil' (3:14). So we turn and make our way out of the building, noting as we pass between them the two free-standing pillars Jachin and Boaz (3:15-17).

Now we are standing before the temple looking out over its courtyard. Largest and most prominent of all its installations is the bronze altar, a square structure of astonishing size, as wide as the temple building itself and as high as the cherubim within (4:1). Half as wide and half as high, but still second only to the altar in impressiveness, is the circular basin called the 'sea', for the priests' ritual washing; it stands a little to one side (4:2-5, 6b, 10). Along each side of the courtyard stand five smaller basins, or 'lavers', for use in connection with sacrifices (4:6). Having had our attention drawn to such furniture, we are reminded of items already set up in the holy place, and turning to look back inside we note again, in rows of five on each side, the lampstands and the tables (4:7, 8a). Nor should we fail to observe the kind of thing that might be thought either too obvious or too unimportant to mention – in the one case, the bronze doors and the courtyard enclosure, and in the other, the pots, shovels, and basins (4:9, 11).

Thus far our preview. On the day itself, we have the privilege of seeing all this, together with the rest of the treasure amassed for the enriching of God's house (5:1), made the setting for an assembly which will surpass every such event that the Chronicler has yet described. Whether or not Solomon knows that today the glory of the Lord will fill his house, he summons a vast gathering in the Lord's honour – *everyone* is there (notice the word 'all' in 5:2-4, 11, 12)! – and knows that for the glory of this God, every detail of the preparation has been worthwhile.

*c. Solomon's work in depth*

What underlies it all? What deep inner truths are expressed by Solomon's achievement? We are not here moving into the realms of type and symbol, and asking about the theological truth which might be signified by the structure in its parts or as a whole. The New Testament tells us that it does have such significance; that it is 'a copy and shadow of the heavenly sanctuary'; that already, in the making of the tabernacle, this had been implicit in the fact that Moses was copying what he had seen when he had met God on Mount Sinai; that the rituals also of tabernacle and temple were highly symbolic; and that 'had we but world enough, and time' we could develop the theme at length and in detail.[5] But this is not our interest at present. We are asking a simpler question: what did it all signify as a task undertaken for God by his servant?

One thing that stands out is the extravagance of the work. The sheer quantity of the materials that have gone into it! And nothing but the best! The whole interior of the sanctuary, and practically everything in it, covered with gold – fine gold, pure gold, solid gold[6] – and the walls encrusted with gems (3:6), while the amount of bronze employed is past reckoning (4:18). The temple and its contents are as extravagant in size and decoration as they are in the cost and quantity of materials. Solomon gives free rein to his vision, and while his aesthetic taste might not be ours there is no denying the richness of it.

The incredible detail tells us also of his thoroughness. The Chronicler does not need to reproduce the full length of the Samuel/Kings account (1 Ki. 6 – 7) in order to indicate this. Instead, he inserts a telling little statistic of his own: that Solomon has accounted even for the nails which fix the panels of gold in place (3:9). In a lesser man such attention to detail might show a mean spirit. But in Solomon it is allied to the broadest sweep of vision. The large and the small are equally his concern, extravagance and thoroughness admirably combined.[7]

---

[5] Heb. 8:5 (and *cf.* 9:24); 9:8–9; 9:1–5. The quotation is from Andrew Marvell, *To his Coy Mistress.*

[6] A variety of terms used in 3:4–6; 4:20–22.

[7] *Cf.* Ian MacDonald, in a centenary pamphlet on the Scottish architect Charles Rennie Mackintosh: 'His range was tremendously wide – when he designed a house he provided not only the structure but also the furniture, both fitted and movable ... He thought out everything, right down to the very clocks and cutlery ... This was not a dissipation of his energies, as he was able to tackle with complete mastery whatever he set himself to do.'

And it *is* surely Solomon himself who sees to the nails. His involvement with every aspect of the work is another feature of the story. Huram, that is Huram-abi the master craftsman (as distinct from his namesake the king of Tyre), is the maker of practically everything in the temple except the actual buildings (4:11–16). And yet the phrase 'he made', figuring again and again in these chapters, refers back not to Huram-abi but to Solomon (3:1–2). There is no contradiction here; bricklayer, site manager, architect, and sponsor might each in different ways be said to have 'built' a particular edifice. The point is made quite plainly here with regard to the bronze-work, which 'Huram-abi made … for King Solomon', and which in another sense 'Solomon made' (4:16–18). What does come across from the way the two makers identify with each other is Solomon's deep involvement with every part of the project.

Looking under the surface, then, not for the theological meaning of the temple and its furniture but for what it tells us about its maker, we see the devotion of a heart seeking to serve God with all its powers. At the dedication service we might well hear him leading the great congregation in some Hebrew equivalent of a latter-day Christian hymn:

> Yea, we know that thou rejoicest
> O'er each work of thine;
> Thou didst ears and hands and voices
> For thy praise design;
> Craftsman's art and music's measure
> For thy pleasure
> All combine.
>
> In thy house, great God, we offer
> Of thine own to thee,
> And for thine acceptance proffer,
> All unworthily,
> Hearts and minds and hands and voices,
> In our choicest
> Psalmody.[8]

## 2. The discerning mind

Already the blessing of wisdom, asked and obtained in 1:7–13,

[8] Francis Pott, *Angel voices, ever singing.*

begins to show itself in one particular way as Solomon applies his mind to the temple project.

The Chronicler is sometimes said to have an inordinate affection for the temple. But the high regard in which he certainly holds it needs to be analysed and understood. As we have observed, he actually dwells far less on the making of it than his source-book does; in chapters 3 and 4 he rewrites 1 Kings 6 and 7 in such a way as to cut them to less than half their original length. He will be quite prepared in due course to describe the temple's desecration at the hands of Manasseh (33:1–9), its plundering by Nebuchadnezzar (36:7, 18) and its eventual burning (36:19), seeing them as tragic events, it is true, but not as the end of the world. He[9] records the proposal that another house of God should be built, after the exile, sponsored by Cyrus of Persia (36:23), which will in the event differ in various respects from the first one. In other words, he is not attached to Solomon's temple for its own sake. He sees it in the long perspective of history, and compares it with what has gone before and what will come after. In this he is no doubt thinking himself into Solomon's thoughts, as the narratives help us to see what they were.

The two most meaningful items in the whole complex of buildings provide us with examples of the kind of regard which the Chronicler, and the king, had for these things. One is the huge bronze altar of sacrifice in the court before the holy place; the other is the ark, relatively insignificant in size but of even greater importance, in the inner sanctuary beyond the holy place.

*a. The altar*

With respect to the altar, the Chronicler – and clearly therefore, in the way he tells the story, Solomon also – relates it explicitly to its past. The narrative is at pains to point out that Solomon's temple is the successor to Moses' tabernacle. We do not know how much of the original sanctuary had survived the years between. The ark had, of course. Though Solomon does not mention this himself in so many words, the whole scheme had arisen from David's desire 'to build a house of rest for the ark of the covenant of the LORD' (1 Ch. 28:2). That is to say, the temple was to be the new home of the old ark. But the altar had survived too; and there is in that a

---

[9] Unless, that is, his work actually ends at 36:21. See Williamson, pp. 5–11, 419.

double fascination. We have been told in fact that both 'the tent ... which Moses the servant of the LORD had made in the wilderness' and 'the bronze altar that Bezalel the son of Uri, son of Hur, had made' were still in existence, at Gibeon, and it was there that Solomon had gone to seek the Lord (1:3–6). Yet in spite of the hallowed antiquity of these historic things, there was no question of the site of Mount Moriah being prepared as a place for the reverent rehousing of *them*. As the temple is intended to replace the tabernacle, so the new altar is intended to replace the old one. What is more, Solomon clearly feels under no obligation to keep to the original specifications of the altar. Bezalel's was five cubits square and three high;[10] Solomon's will be twenty square and ten high (4:1). In effect, he pensions off the venerable but no doubt by this time slightly battered relic, and does not even set up a replica in its place. Yet there is no hint that this cavalier treatment of the old altar meets with God's disapproval. It would appear that there is nothing sacrosanct about either a particular altar or a particular blueprint for one.[11] In short, the pattern which Moses was shown on Sinai was presumably not for this or that altar, but simply for *an* altar. The practice of true religion requires that there be a place of sacrifice; that is the principle, and the believer of every age has to understand what it must mean for him. Moses had one altar, Solomon another, the Chronicler and his contemporaries a third, and in our New Testament days 'we have an altar' which is different again.[12]

### b. The ark

With respect to the altar the Chronicler looked back to the tabernacle; with respect to the ark he looks forward to his own time, to the second temple. For here is a fact more startling still: if the original altar was superseded by others, at some stage the original ark disappeared altogether! Whatever may be meant by the curious little aside in 5:9b, that the poles on which the ark was carried to its new home 'are there to this day',[13] in the temple known to the Chronicler's time there was no ark. The builders of that second temple had done what they could to reproduce something of the

---

[10] Ex. 38:1–2.

[11] The altar in Ezekiel's vision is different again (Ezk. 43:13–17).

[12] Heb. 13:10.

[13] 'This may be seen as a survival from an older source when the ark still existed' (it appears in 1 Ki. 8:8), 'or better may be regarded as equivalent to "in perpetuity"' (Ackroyd, p. 110).

'former glory',[14] but the splendours of Solomon's work were beyond them, and there was, literally, an emptiness at the heart of it. The Chronicler's sermon, of course, was even better served by the disappearance of the ark than by the replacement of the altar: that really did underline his point that in the last analysis the sign was not nearly so important as the thing signified.

But granted that the ark was understood in this way by the Chronicler, who had years of hindsight, could it have been understood so by Solomon?

Yes, I think it could. First, because Solomon's chief fame was his wisdom (9:22–23), a wisdom given him by the God of the heavenly patterns. Secondly, because he must have realized that there was no intrinsic reason why, if Moses' altar was dispensable, Moses' ark should not be equally dispensable. Thirdly, because the idea that the temple was to be primarily a home for the ark was David's, not Solomon's (1 Ch. 17:1; 28:2), and when Solomon outlines *his* view of what the temple is for he does not even mention the ark (2:4).

Certainly with respect to the altar, therefore, and in all probability with respect to the ark also, we can see the operation of Solomon's discerning mind. The temple will be his first and most concrete piece of work for God, and in it we see him distinguishing between what is important and what is less important. The similarities between his work and his predecessors' show us what he regards as obligatory, and the differences show what he regards as optional. He is under obligation to go back beyond David's detailed plans (1 Ch. 28:11ff.) to Moses' scheme for the contents and the disposition of the sanctuary.[15] Its location on Mount Moriah (3:1) even connects its essential meaning with the experience of Abraham[16]. These connections are the vital tie-rods running through Old Testament theology as a whole, and uniting it eventually with the New Testament also. They are the inner principles. As to shapes and sizes, quantities and materials, however, Solomon sits loose to tradition; not to the instructions received through his father for what is right for their times, but to the forms of worship that had been reckoned right in other times. Principles matter. Forms do not matter, except insofar as they rightly express the principles. The wisdom to discern between them is a gift greatly to be coveted.

[14] Hg. 2:3.    [15] With chapters 3–4, *cf.* Ex. 25ff. and 36ff.
[16] Gn. 22.

## 3. The divine spirit

There is something else, and something rather different, that we may be intended to see in Solomon's building of the house of God.

This or that Old Testament character is sometimes described as a 'type' of Christ. Because of various similarities such persons are thought to foreshadow him, or (reversing the metaphor) to shed light on him. Both David and Solomon could be seen in this way, David as the greatest king of Israel[17] and Solomon as the prince of peace.[18] But typology is a study fraught with perils, and we need to be careful about it. What can be said with certainty about these two supposed 'types' is somewhat as follows.

### a. The great days

The period described in these chapters might be called the great days of Israel. At every period in the history of his people God has a plan for them, for the framework of their life. In the tenth century BC it was that they should constitute a political entity, that is, that they should be a nation. As a nation he caused them to be governed in a particular way, and Israel began a period of several hundred years in which she was an oriental monarchy. The Davidic kingdom was God's chosen plan for that time, and as it came minted fresh from his hand it was an ideal which he intended David's successors to strive to maintain.

Solomon is from one point of view the first of those successors. But it is perhaps more important to see him as being himself a part of the ideal. It was over the very matter dealt with in our present section, the building of the house of God, that David came to see that his own reign, characterized as it was by strife, could not in itself be the complete foundation of the coming centuries of the Israelite monarchy; for that the Jerusalem temple had to be built, as a focal point for Israel's faith, and for *that* a period of settling would be needed. His son's reign would provide the necessary time of peace: first David's sword, then Solomon's sceptre.

While therefore Solomon is no superhuman figure, and his working out of his own obedient service to God does stand as an example to others, he is also more than a mere example. He is himself part of the 'great days'. He and David must be seen together as a joint ideal, an embodiment of principles. This view of their two

---

[17] *Cf.* Jn. 12:13.    [18] *Cf.* Is. 9:6.

consecutive reigns is so much in line with the Chronicler's whole philosophy of history, the bringing out of its permanent principles, that we should not be surprised at his playing down of their sins and failings, and even of their ordinary humanity. For him they always, as it were, wear their official hats. It is almost by accident that we have seen something of the heart and mind of Solomon as a fellow-believer and fellow-servant with us. That kind of sermon arises more naturally from the story of his successors than from his own story.

### b. The dull days

As time passed, that embodiment of an ideal receded. No longer present before the eyes of Israel, nor even a vivid memory of the immediate past, but distant and unattainable, were the twin reigns from which the last great era of their national life was dated. For the Chronicler and his readers, not even the monarchy remained. Theirs were dull days. The Chronicler preached his sermons nevertheless: the Davidic kingdom was still a picture of how God loved his people, how they could come to him in repentance, faith, worship, how he would govern them in justice and mercy; principles, principles. With his text drawn from a world so remote, he had to take all the more seriously the preacher's ultimate task, application; and he did so, insisting that against all appearances the great days of the kingdom really did have lessons for his own changed world. But all the same the meaning of David and Solomon for the dull days after the exile was not an easy one to understand or apply. They formed as it were a king-shaped blank, around which the godly life was to be constructed.

But though the Chronicler's contemporaries would not witness it, another age was coming, our own New Testament age; 'since God had foreseen something better for us, that apart from us they should not be made perfect'.[19] Our days would be the last days.

### c. The last days

In them, God has, as always, a plan for the life of his people. Still it is a pattern which fits into place around the same key shape of the king. But for us in these last days the central space has been miraculously filled. 'There is another king, Jesus,[20] 'descended

[19] Heb. 11:40.    [20] Acts 17:7.

from David according to the flesh and designated Son of God in power according to the Spirit of holiness by his resurrection from the dead',[21] and once again all the ideals have been, literally, embodied. The study of typology is an approach to the Bible that can readily be abused. But nothing could be more biblical than to hold that the Davidic monarchy is a type of the rule of Christ. One is a pattern of the other, and each demonstrates at its own level how the life of the people of God is to be fostered and governed. With the coming of Jesus 'the kingdom of God is at hand' again, and what is more, it is 'the kingdom of our father David that is coming'.[22] And it is only a step from saying that one kingdom is a type of the other, each demonstrating at its own level how the people of God should be ruled, to saying that one king is a type of the other.

Can we really say, though, that David is personally a type of Christ, as in their various ways Adam and Melchizedek and Moses are?[23] Yes, in a sense. Even so, the pattern of the divine kingship was only half realized in David. He is the man of war, who fights and overcomes his people's foes. But it is not for the man of war to build the temple; that belongs to the time of peace, and to his successor Solomon, the man of peace (1 Ch. 22:8–9).[24]

As we saw when the Chronicler first set before us these two panels of the picture, the difference between them is not intended as a moral judgment, but as a statement of the fitness of things. There is more to it than that, however. For if we allow ourselves to think at all in terms of repeated patterns and of the typology of Scripture, this is not only how things had to happen at the time, but also how they were going to happen afterwards. In the events of those two successive reigns we see reflected as in 'a distant mirror'[25] other events a thousand years later; and I find it hard not to believe that the coincidence is intended, and that one sequence really is a reflection of the other. In the glass of the Old Testament we see enemies defeated, and David completing *his* task, then Solomon beginning his reign of peace and embarking on *his* task. And turning to the New Testament 'original'? A 'David' whose work is

---

[21] Rom. 1:3–4.

[22] Mk. 1:15; 11:10.

[23] Rom. 5:14; Heb. 7:3; 3:2.

[24] See above, pp. 93–94.

[25] Barbara Tuchman's book *A Distant Mirror: The Calamitous Fourteenth Century* (Knopf, 1978), is a brilliant history of the fourteenth century in Europe, an age which she sees as an instructive reflection of our own.

the winning of a glorious victory which brings freedom and security to the people of God, followed by a 'Solomon' whose work is the building of a magnificent temple which actually is the people of God.

If in these two successive rulers of Old Testament Israel, David and Solomon, it is right to see types of the two successive Paracletes of New Testament Israel, the Son of God and the Spirit of God,[26] then Solomon is more than an example to us of the devout heart and the discerning mind. He also stands for the divine Spirit, and it is the Spirit's work that we may see typified in the making of the temple. He sees to the choosing and shaping and fitting into place of every stone in the structure. He sees to the making and disposing of every vessel. He sees to the cutting and polishing and setting of every gem. Stones, vessels, gems, are all of course biblical metaphors of the people of God and their service for him.[27] All these tasks, understood in detail and undertaken with loving, unerring, care, are his work, and he will do it. 'David' has won the victory and ushered in the peace, so 'Solomon's' whole attention can be devoted now to this; until the day when, to use the words of the first and last verses of 2 Chronicles 5, all his work for the house of the Lord is finished, and the glory of the Lord fills it.

# 2 Chronicles 6 – 7

# 12.  The dedication prayer

Where exactly is the God in whose honour the temple has been built?

'Is God everywhere?' says the child.

'Yes, dear,' says its unsuspecting teacher.

---

[26] Jesus Christ the 'advocate', 1 Jn. 2:1 RSV, the Holy Spirit the 'counsellor', Jn. 14:16 RSV (both words translating *paraklētos*).

[27] 1 Pet. 2:5; 2 Tim. 2:20–21; 1 Cor. 3:12. The AV rendering of Mal. 3:17, 'they shall be mine ... my jewels', is unforgettable, but (sadly) inaccurate.

'Is he in my inkwell, then?' (I heard this story in the days when schoolchildren still used pens with nibs, and their desks had inkwells let into them.)

Hesitation, then: 'Yes, dear.'

Whereupon the child blocks the top of the inkwell with its thumb, and exclaims triumphantly: 'Got him, then!'

Well, almost the first words of Solomon at the temple's dedication ceremony are to the effect that God is in this building; and in one story as in the other it is not quite as simple as it looks to explain in what senses the statement is, and is not, true. The temple is intended to be a place for God 'to dwell in for ever' (6:2), and if we ask a reason for the curious linking of this verse with the previous one, the Lord's own declaration 'that he would dwell in thick darkness',[1] it may not be altogether frivolous – in fact it may be the truest answer – to point to the windowless room at the heart of the temple. In the Most Holy Place, especially when it was 'filled with a cloud' (5:13), Solomon, like Moses, had a physical representation of the spiritual truth whose pattern they had both been shown. Solomon is perfectly aware of the ambiguity about the darkness where God is. While his preface to the ceremony calls the temple God's dwelling-place, his prayer states eight times over that God actually dwells in heaven (6:21, 23, 25, 27, 30, 33, 35, 39).

Still, in some real though secondary sense God is indeed 'in the inkwell'. 'I have built thee an exalted house, a place for thee to dwell in for ever' (6:2). The bald declaration that 'this is where he is' needs to be earthed, however, if it is to be real in human experience. One way of doing this is to think of it, as we have already done, in terms of the ark and the altar. These are both to the fore at the dedication service. The sanctuary is at one and the same time a place where Solomon has 'set the ark, in which is the covenant of the LORD which he made with the people of Israel' (6:11), and the 'house of sacrifice' for which this ceremony will be 'the dedication of the altar' (7:12, 9).

But there is another way of explaining in practical terms that 'this is where God may be found'. The words 'Heaven and the highest heaven cannot contain thee', near the beginning of Solomon's prayer (6:18), echo his message to Hiram much earlier, and in that he goes on to say: 'Who am I to build a house for him, except as a place to burn incense before him?' (2:6). Incense is understood in both Old

[1] 6:1 relates to Ex. 20:21.

Testament and New as a symbol for prayer,[2] and 'house of prayer' will become a classical description of the temple.[3] So here it is the part of the ceremony devoted to prayer that the records describe at greatest length. To think of the temple as the place of ark and altar, the place where grace reaches down and faith responds, is to begin to understand the 'how' of the encounter between God and man; to think of it as the place of incense, the place of prayer, is to begin to grasp the 'what' of that encounter, which is, in a word, communication. Nor is it communication in one direction only; and so in these chapters Solomon's speaking to God is followed by God's speaking to Solomon.

The king's first words, however, are addressed to the vast congregation that has gathered. They are both an introduction to his long prayer and a comment on what has taken place already in 5:2–14. In them we see something more of him himself on this great occasion as the one who is to lead his people in prayer.

## 1. The one who prays (6:3–11)

He is Solomon the pastor, first and foremost. Even before the ceremony began it was seen to be a national occasion; but David's assemblies of 1 Chronicles 23 and 28 had been that, without having quite the special character of this one. Solomon has called this assembly for no mundane purpose, but for an encounter with God, and he intends not only to bless the Lord (6:4) but to bless his people (6:3). For a leader thus concerned for the welfare of those in his charge, the regular biblical metaphor is that of the shepherd. In speaking to David, God had already referred to 'the judges of Israel, whom I commanded to shepherd my people' (1 Ch. 17:6).[4] He went on immediately to remind David: 'I took you from the pasture, from following the sheep, that you should be prince over my people Israel' (1 Ch. 17:7). The parallel in the Psalms spells out the implication: 'He chose David his servant, and took him from the sheepfolds; from tending the ewes that had young he brought him to

---

[2] Ps. 141:2; Rev. 5:8.      u23 Is. 56:7; Mt. 21:13 and parallels.

[4] Before the time of the judges, Moses and Joshua had exercised shepherd-care (Nu. 27:17; Is. 63:11), and after the monarchy the heathen king Cyrus would be given the same title (Is. 44:28). Leaders who fail to fulfil this responsibility are denounced as false shepherds in Ezk. 34 and in Je. 23:1–4; 25:32–38, and here in Chronicles the defeat of Israel at Ramoth-Gilead is described as the scattering of a shepherdless flock (2 Ch. 18:16; see below, pp. 186).

be the shepherd of Jacob his people, of Israel his inheritance'.[5] The ideal of the pastor, or shepherd, will stand before each of David's successors, and we shall be seeing how each in turn either strove towards it or rejected it. Here is the first of the line, showing his pastoral heart in every paragraph of his great prayer, with at its outset as proper a summary of it as could be desired: 'the king faced about, and blessed all the assembly of Israel' (6:3).

It was, we should understand, a delegated care. Only two psalms later than the one just quoted, not David but the Lord himself is spoken of as the 'Shepherd of Israel'.[6] It is he who through his viceroys is caring for his people. In this lies the reassuring message for the Chronicler's readers: although the monarchy was perhaps the period when God's pastoral care could best be seen exercised in this way, it was there before the kings began, and still there after the kings had ended. Every generation of God's people would be able not only to sing 'The LORD is my shepherd'[7] but also to find in experience that he would raise up an unfailing succession of under-shepherds.

Here in 2 Chronicles 6 and 7 Solomon is the representative of that line of pastors. He is also, by the same token, Solomon the intercessor. The rest of chapter 6 makes this plain. We call it 'Solomon's *prayer* at the dedication of the temple', but there is more than one form of prayer, and what we have here is primarily and distinctively intercession. This, too, is contained in embryo in his opening words. The fact that he 'blesses' the people implies not only that he cares for their welfare with a pastor's care, but that for all his own enormous gifts it is God's power that he calls into action on their behalf. No doubt he is, as God's servant so often is, the answer to his own prayer. But having in the first instance taken his people's needs to God in prayer, when he asked in 1:10 for the gift of wisdom ('for who can rule this thy people, that is so great?'), he does not then rely on the gift once given, but here again – and, we may presume, often in the coming days – asks that *God* will bless them. More of this in a moment: the prayer is largely about it.

He is, further, a theologian. This not in some daunting academic sense, but as any man or woman of prayer must be a theologian: must know, that is, something of God and his workings. Solomon here declares his grasp of what God has been about in the

---

[5] Ps. 78:71.    [6] Ps. 80:1.    [7] Ps. 23:1.

establishing of the kingdom, and of himself as its present ruler. He understands 'the covenant of the LORD which he made with the people of Israel' (6:11). He understands the exodus from Egypt as the starting-point of that covenant's operation, in its present form (6:5), although the exodus will henceforth be less spoken of as the renewed covenant of the monarchy comes to the fore. He understands the cardinal truths about God which are expressed in the vivid metaphors 'mouth' and 'hand', the mouth that promises and the hand that fulfils (6:4).[8] And he understands the 'theology of Now', relating these things to the present experience of God's people. All this he grasps, as fully as the gift of God enables him, and sets it forth to his people.

He is, finally and fascinatingly, a type. In what has been said so far, he is an example to the rest of us of the man who in prayer undertakes responsibility for his fellows. But he is more than that, and his words indicate it. God's people are for the present time to be constituted a political kingdom, which will express in human terms the eternal kingdom of God. The early Hebrew monarchy is an incarnation of that spiritual reality. Its first two reigns (we exclude always the reign of Saul) are the two complementary halves of the model. In each case God speaks, then acts, to set up the double prototype. When David the warrior conquers Jerusalem, 'the LORD ... with his hand has fulfilled what he promised with his mouth' (6:4); when Solomon the peacemaker builds the temple there, 'the LORD has fulfilled his promise which he made' (6:10).

If the analogy suggested earlier[9] is right, and Solomon, 'risen in the place of David', pictures for us the one whom the last king of David's line promises as 'another Counsellor'[10] to guide his people when he is gone, then to see Solomon as the one who prays is illuminating indeed. 'For we do not know how to pray as we ought, but the Spirit himself intercedes for us ... The Spirit intercedes for the saints according to the will of God.'[11] We shall take all the more seriously, therefore, the prayer that follows, since it is prayed by one who, with the wisdom of God himself, knows what intercession really is.

[8] It is a great loss when modern translators discard these concrete images in favour of abstractions. So 'With his hand has fulfilled what he promised with his mouth' (RSV) is reduced to 'Has kept the promise he made' (GNB). This supposedly in the name of intelligibility!

[9] See above, pp. 141–142.

[10] Jn. 14:16.

[11] Rom. 8:26–27.

## 2. The approach to prayer (6:12–21)

The specially-built platform (6:13) is not mentioned in Samuel/ Kings; the Chronicler inserted it from some other source, helping us to visualize Solomon speaking from a vantage-point from which he could be seen and heard by all. But the one who is really uplifted in this chapter, most of all in this paragraph of it, is God himself. Solomon's approach to prayer is first to exalt the Lord, the God of Israel.

God is primary (6:14–15), the unique, covenant-keeping, loving, speaking-with-the-mouth and fulfilling-with-the-hand God: he comes first. This approach to intercession is well seen in that traditional form of prayer which we call the 'collect', in which before we ask God for anything we remind ourselves of his character. 'Almighty God, to whom all hearts are open, all desires known, and from whom no secrets are hidden ...' 'O God, the author of peace and lover of concord ...' 'O God, the source of all good desires, all right judgements, and all just works ...'[12] Faith in who and what he is, however elementary and uninformed, must precede the asking of anything. 'Whoever would draw near to God must believe that he exists and that he rewards those who seek him.'[13] Here prayer begins.

Secondly, God is holy (6:16–17). The promise to David, 'There shall never fail you a man ... upon the throne of Israel,' is here followed by the condition 'if only your sons take heed ... to walk in my law'. When it was first made to David no conditions were attached (1 Ch. 17:11–14). We cannot here go into the relation between the conditional and unconditional promises of God, except to note what actually happens in the case of the Israelite monarchy: at one level, disobedience does cause the line of kings to come to an end, but at another level it cannot affect the continuance of the true kingdom: again the theme of what is and is not. The point here, though, is that as Solomon accepts the condition, seeking to walk like his father in the law of God, he is recognizing that the God who promises the blessing is a God who requires righteousness in his servants, because he is himself righteous. The ultimate blessing may be ours unconditionally, but a whole series of blessings along the road will depend on whether or not we are taking heed to our way and seeking to be holy as he is holy.

[12] *The Alternative Service Book 1980* of the Church of England: collects from Holy Communion, Morning Prayer, and Evening Prayer respectively.
[13] Heb. 11:6.

Then, God is transcendent: 'Heaven and the highest heaven cannot contain thee; how much less this house which I have built' (6:18). If it was folly to imagine that even the 'house in its former glory'[14] could contain God, how much more ridiculous it is to scale him down to our later and lesser 'temples'. To borrow J. B. Phillips' famous title, we are always in danger of making our God too small. The greater we realize he is, the more we shall bring to him in intercession, and the more we shall expect from him.

But the God who is so high above our imaginings is also, in the good sense of the word, a condescending God (6:19–21). It is a very human attitude which is expressed in the word 'Yet' at the beginning of 6:19. The discoveries of science daily increase our knowledge of things both incredibly large and incredibly small, yet many people seem to think that God cannot be equally interested in both at once, and assume perhaps naturally that he favours the big rather than the little. 'Creatures of a minute historical period – for what is 5000 years in the setting of all time? – and of a minute corner of a single galaxy, how dare we presume to say that one of us is the unique and pre-existing Son of the Universal God? It is a view which has always seemed to me to show an astounding lack of humility in a religion which has made humility one of its primary virtues.'[15] Against that attitude we might say, not 'Although heaven cannot contain you, yet hear us', but 'Because you are so great, therefore hear us.' Solomon expects the eyes of this great God to be open day and night, and his ears to hear every prayer not only of Solomon's own but of all Israel's.

The obvious danger in our telling God things in prayer is that we may come, perhaps without realizing it, to the foolishness of assuming that he needs the information. But when the telling is by way of a reminder to us ourselves, and an expression of how we see God, it is not only proper, but the right approach to prayer.

## 3. The model of prayer (6:22–42)

A model for intercessory prayer, that is. There is more to prayer than this, to be sure, but in these verses Solomon is interceding for his people, and there is much to be learnt from his wisdom in the matter.

[14] Hg. 2:3.
[15] Philip Toynbee, reviewing A. M. Ramsey's *God, Christ and the World*, in *Frontier*, May 1969.

The form common to the seven petitions in the passage that follows is: 'If this, or this, or this happens, and your people pray, then hear from heaven, and act.' The thought is slightly unusual in being not just a prayer to be answered, but a prayer for another prayer to be answered. A consideration of other features common to all the intercessions, however, yields more substantial results.

A point so obvious that it might be overlooked is that they *are* intercessions, rather than petitions, if we define these words as 'prayer for others' and 'prayer for oneself'. We have overheard Solomon's petitions about his own needs back in chapter 1. The rightness of the relation between him and God is at this point taken for granted. His great concern here is his people. The heart of the pastor, the shepherd-king, is taken up with the needs of his flock.

Like the true shepherd, he has a broad overview of those needs. His intercessions range widely, and enter imaginatively into a variety of situations. They go even beyond Israel, to ask for blessing on the 'foreigner' who seeks God. He looks into the future and sees dire possibilities of many kinds, and some good ones too, and brings them all before the Lord in prayer. As the Chronicler records the far-sighted words, most, if not all, of them have in the intervening centuries become realities instead of possibilities. There has been a frequent and urgent relevance about Solomon's prayer that his people's prayer will be heard.

Implicit too in all this is the corporate nature of the king's requests. It is not just that his attention turns deliberately away from his own individual needs to those of others. He seems also to concentrate less on *their* individual needs than on their situation as a people, their social and national relationships. None is seen in isolation; even the singulars, 'a man' and 'a foreigner' (6:22, 32), quickly give way to plurals.

Related to all these features – intercession for others, for others in many different situations, for others in their relationships – is the fact that it is for 'thy people Israel'. The prayer itself accepts the possibility that Israel may one day mean the people but no longer the land (6:36). The Chronicler has seen that day come, and knows that Israel no longer means the kingdom either. But do these intercessions hold good? The message of Chronicles is that under a variety of forms God's people are bound into a unity across all the ages; there is 'one church, one faith, one Lord'; and the Israel of God (a Pauline phrase which would surely have won the Chronicler's approval)[16] will always be finding equivalents for the situations about which Solomon prays.

Two things, therefore, happen as the years go by and Solomon's dedication prayer becomes a text for sermons. One is that the possibilities turn into realities, the hypothetical into the actual. The day comes when the intercessor prays, not 'If such-and-such happens …', but 'Since such-and-such is happening …'. So it is in the exile, and in the Chronicler's world after the exile. The spirit of Solomon's prayer takes on a new reality in the great intercessions of Nehemiah[17] and Daniel.[18]

The other development is that the realities take new forms, as Israel itself is transformed into the world-wide church of Christ. The call for righteous dealing among God's people takes on a new dimension. Defeat, drought, and famine can all be understood (and prayed about) in a new sense. Something new is meant by the stranger who 'comes from a far country for the sake of thy great name', and the warriors who 'go out to battle' also for the sake of that name; for these too we learn to intercede. And it will always be part of the 'one faith' of God's church that sin leads to captivity, while repentance leads to restoration. All come within the scope of the intercessor who kneels where Solomon knelt in the house of prayer.

## 4. The vindication of prayer (7:1–22)

The ceremony is no religious exercise for its own sake. Prayer looms large in the account, and intercessory prayer at that; the worshippers therefore cannot get away with a merely human performance. Much of the church's activity, it is cynically said, would carry on regardless even if the Holy Spirit were departed, or God were dead. But the kind of service described here is plainly nonsensical unless God is as really present as the human participants. The assembly of Israel is not simply processing, or singing, or talking, or dancing. It is asking for something, and it wants an answer. Will its faith be vindicated?

God has indeed been present, he has heard, and he answers twice, once immediately and again later. There and then, 'fire came down from heaven and consumed the burnt offering and the sacrifices, and

---

[16] Gal. 6:16.   [17] Neh. 1:4–11.   [18] Dn. 9:3–19.

the glory of the LORD filled the temple' (7:1). The glory has been mentioned already, in 5:14; the answer to prayer was the fire. God had answered in this spectacular way before in his people's history, when Moses first set up the altar in the wilderness,[19] and when David set one up on this very site, while it was still the threshing-floor of Ornan the Jebusite (1 Ch. 21:26). It would happen again, in a time of crucial decision for Israel, at Elijah's altar on Mount Carmel (1 Ki. 18:38). To speak of the fire from heaven as a 'subjective' answer to prayer is perhaps not quite accurate; the fire was real enough, and the offerings were actually consumed.[20] But it was subjective in that the senses and the emotions responded to it. It was immediate, it caught the imagination, it would haunt the memory. We ourselves can hear across the centuries the huge collective gasp as the vast assembly 'saw the fire come down and the glory of the LORD upon the temple' (7:3). Since God has given man this kind of awareness, and himself makes use of it, we should be wrong to discount the importance of emotional response. But it is to be noted that *all* saw the fire and the glory, and bowed and worshipped, and so the snare of individual emotionalism is avoided – it was not only I who saw the fire, you saw it too. And it is further to be noted that God backed up his immediate answer by another, later, one of a different kind: 'Then the LORD appeared to Solomon in the night and said to him ...' (7:12).

'Objective' may seem an inapt word for this (since it is a dream),[21] as 'subjective' may have seemed an inapt word for the previous answer (since there was real fire). But the dream came with words, and the words have not died as the fire died. It might almost be said that 7:14, another famous text which we owe to the Chronicler,[22] has sometimes been made to live in a way that was not intended; there is no modern nation, however much it may need to repent, which God will address as 'my people who are called by my name'. But the principles live, and it is a case of working out in each age what is meant by the land of God's people being blasted or healed, as the case may be.

The main point, however, in the context is that God's answer to

[19] Lv. 9:24.

[20] How wide of the mark were the old-fashioned 'explanations' which dismissed these miracles as trickery! The very question at issue every time was whether or not the God of Israel was a reality in the life of his people. In either case a contrived 'miracle' would have been pointless.

[21] The Chronicler does not call it a dream; but see 1 Ki. 3:5 and 9:2.

[22] The parallel passage, 1 Ki. 9:1-9, does not contain it.

Solomon's intercession has taken the form of words that engage the mind as well as fire that thrills the soul. Although much briefer than Solomon's intercession, the second answer to it follows its line of thought closely. The petition with which Solomon opened and closed, that God's eyes would be open and his ears attentive to prayer offered in the temple (6:20, 40), is replied to almost word for word (7:15). But with certain necessary extra emphases, the general sequence also is the same. Trouble arises from sin, humble penitence leads to restoration. These, as well as being the fundamental principles of history which underlie all the Chronicler's work, are the substance both of Solomon's request and of God's reply.

It is pleasant to think that a specific prayer is answered specifically, and that perhaps we can expect this God to give similar close attention to our own listed intercessions. Before we jump to conclusions, though, we need to recall what was truly the order of events. There was more to it than chapter 7 following chapter 6. The great intercession itself had followed 1:7–13, the promise of wisdom. That is to say, it was not simply that God gave what Solomon asked; it was that Solomon asked what in the first place God wanted him to ask. We might have known that Solomon would have his prayer answered, because he had previously been given the word and wisdom of God. His was the kind of intercession that gets results. If I may once more suggest him as a type, he pictures the one who 'intercedes for the saints according to the will of God',[23] for he alone 'comprehends the thoughts of God'.[24] But when we regard him not as a type but as an example, he kneels on his platform on the great day of dedication to show *us* the way of true intercession before God. 'This is the confidence which we have in him, that if we ask anything according to his will he hears us. And if we know that he hears us in whatever we ask, we know that we have obtained the requests made of him.'[25] May we not only sense the fire and the glory, but rest confident in the word which guarantees us our answers because it has taught us our requests.

---

[23] Rom. 8:27.
[24] 1 Cor. 2:11.
[25] 1 Jn. 5:14–15.

# 2 Chronicles 8 – 9

## 13.  The greatness of Solomon

The Chronicler's role of preacher is one which has seldom been far
from our minds. This passage in particular, the chapters with which
he completes his account of the reign of Solomon, is worth
considering as an example of his preaching skills. He takes the basic
Samuel/Kings narrative (1 Ki. 9:10 – 10:29), makes a text of it,
and constructs a sermon on it: with what results, we shall see.

### 1.  The text of the sermon

Solomon's story ends, in the Chronicler's version, with 2 Chronicles
8 and 9, which cover four main subjects. In a fashion we have
noticed elsewhere, they overlap and interweave to some extent. They
are Solomon's power (8:1–10), his worship (8:11–16), his riches
(8:17–18; 9:9–28), and his wisdom (9:1–12). The most obvious
adaptation that has been made of the older history is that practically
the whole of 1 Kings 11 has been left out. We know by now the sort
of portrait which the Chronicler wants to paint of the first two great
kings of Israel; he was not so selective with Saul, nor will he be with
the later kings, but this confirms the view that for him David and
Solomon are intended as a kind of double ideal, the original twofold
picture of God's true kingship. It is not surprising then that just as
the unhappinesses of David's last days did not figure at the end of
1 Chronicles, so the follies of Solomon's do not figure here. That he
'loved many foreign women' who in the latter part of his reign
'turned away his heart after other gods' (1 Ki. 11:1, 4), and that he
made lasting enemies – Hadad, Rezon, Jeroboam – from quite an
early stage in his reign (1 Ki. 11:14–40), are facts which the reader
is aware of. The Chronicler knows that he knows, and deliberately
leaves them aside in order to concentrate on the greatness of the
man, ending his reign, like his father's, at a high point.

The curious paragraph which begins chapter 8, about a gift of
cities' from Hiram to Solomon, shows this process taken to an
extreme. It appears to be not just a selection from, but an actual

reversal of, the equivalent passage in Samuel/Kings (1 Ki. 9:10–14). The commentaries discuss whether the two can be harmonized, the group of villages being an unattractive gift from Solomon first, duly returned to him and then refurbished by him; whether the Chronicler is simply contradicting Samuel/Kings; or whether he was working from a problematic source text. The difference, whatever lies behind it, is that the earlier story shows Solomon being mean, and the later one shows him being constructive. He was no doubt both, and we note which aspect is important for the Chronicler.

We shall see the same emphasis throughout these chapters, together with a feature less obvious but equally important. The spotlight which is turned on Solomon illuminates his people also. His achievements cannot help but reflect on their quality of life.

### a. Solomon's power (8:1–10)

Whatever may be the facts behind 8:1–2, and however the territory spoken of in these verses relates to that which Solomon had given to Hiram, he is here seen as Solomon the builder, and his building activities are now directly concerned with his people's welfare. He builds the Lord's house, he builds his own house, and he builds homes for the people. So his reconstruction work in these northern towns sees Israelite citizens housed and settled.

Next, what seems to be a military campaign (8:3). Though Solomon's reign was characteristically a time of peace, it did nonetheless have its occasional alarums and excursions, and it suits the Chronicler's theme in this passage to refer to one of them. The verse is an enigma, having no equivalent in 1 Kings 9, and bracketing as a single place the names of Hamath, which had been friendly to David, and Zobah, which had been an enemy (1 Ch. 18:9–10). Again, commentators find problems enough to grapple with, but agree that the Chronicler is at any rate conveying the idea of military consolidation on what is traditionally regarded as Israel's frontier. As Solomon's people are settled, so they are also guarded.

Then they are provided for as he builds store-cities (8:4, 6a), defended by his fortifying of places like the two Beth-horons (8:5), and armed, by the setting up among them of a series of garrison towns (8:6).

A note of his policy towards the surviving non-Israelite population of the land rounds off the section, and, like the rest of it, indicates the benefits that Israel enjoys by virtue of the king's power: the Canaanite remnants provide forced labour, but not so his own people. His rule, then, means his people's security and independence.

### b. Solomon's worship (8:11-16)

The two verses on which this passage is based (1 Ki. 9:24-25) are here expanded considerably. In addition, they also bore little relation to each other previously; the Chronicler's extra words here bind the two statements together, and, as with the rewriting of the note about Hiram's towns (8:1-2), make them serve his own special purpose. The reason that his Egyptian queen moves house is explained as a religious one, less perhaps for the sake of the purity of the ark and its surroundings than for the sake of her own safety. We remember Uzzah (1 Ch. 13:9-14), and before him the Philistines and the men of Beth-shemesh (1 Sa. 5 - 6). The holiness of the ark and of everything connected with it[1] leads naturally to Solomon's general religious practice. The offerings (8:12), the festivals (8:13), the ministries of priests and Levites (8:14), and all his regulations concerning these things (8:15), in short 'all the work of Solomon' for 'the house of the LORD' (8:16), everything is brought together in this brief but comprehensive paragraph.

And where does the spotlight focus? *Solomon* offered the offerings, *Solomon* appointed the priestly divisions, the regulations were what *the king* had commanded, all was 'the work of *Solomon*'. The Chronicler does remind us that all was also 'according to the commandment of Moses' and 'according to the ordinance of David'. But this in no way detracts from Solomon's exalted position in the Chronicler's scheme of things; on the contrary, it shows us with what lofty company he is to be ranked.

Yet here too he is not to be thought of apart from his people. The whole religious system takes for granted the worshipping *community*. Solomon may seem to be the moving spirit behind all that happens, but it is no solitary hobby. Israel joins him in offerings, feasts, and praises, and by this means seeks to cultivate nationally a right relationship with its God. Solomon's worship means his people's righteousness.

---

[1] 'Everything', *etc*, rather than 'the places to which the ark ... has come'; see Williamson, p. 231, on 8:11.

*c.   Solomon's riches (8:17–18; 9:9–28)*

The Chronicler follows his source-book closely in this section. As in 1 Kings 9:26 – 10:29, the structure is interesting. There are four brief references to the influx of gold from foreign sources into Solomon's treasury. Between the first and second (8:17–18 and 9:10–11) and again between third and fourth (9:13–14 and 9:21), are framed two memorable pictures.[2] The earlier is the story of the visit of the queen of Sheba (9:12, her return home, does fall just outside the frame), and we shall consider that in a moment under the heading of Solomon's wisdom. The other is an account of the uses to which the imported gold was put.

There is something exotic about the four framing paragraphs. Israel was never much of a seafaring nation, as is perhaps hinted by Hiram's sending 'servants familiar with the sea' (8:18) to accompany Solomon's on these voyages, and Eloth must have seemed to most Israelites to be itself the end of the world, rather than a gateway to places still more remote.[3] 'Gold from Ophir' was legendary,[4] though Ophir's whereabouts are not known. It came too, along with silver, from the kings of Arabia, and although 'ships of Tarshish' can mean simply long-distance traders, it was part of the spectacular cargo of 'gold, silver, ivory, apes, and peacocks'[5] which came every three years, or so the Chronicler understood, apparently from Tarshish (Spain) itself.

What did he do with it all, once the temple's requirements had been met? The passage 9:15–20 tells us. He made for his own house the unique chryselephantine throne. He had all his drinking vessels made of gold; no doubt we may visualize every set of tableware in the palace as being solid gold. Finally, as though almost at a loss to know what to do next, he began making shields, large and small, for display, not defence, and hung them in their hundreds in the House of the Forest of Lebanon. Yet this is not a picture of personal ostentation. We should not forget, and the Chronicler has not forgotten, the verses which he adapted from his present source in 1 Kings 10 to place at the very beginning of his account of Solomon's reign: 'The king made silver and gold as common in

---

[2]   I am tempted to the frivolous comment 'a pair of gold-framed spectacles'!

[3]   See below, pp. 223–224.

[4]   *Cf.* 'Gold of Parvaim' (3:6). The name Ophir may not have been used in Solomon's time. It may be an 'anachronism' in the sense that 'darics' are (see on 1 Ch. 29:7, p. 113).

[5]   Whether the last word really means peacocks is not known. A (slightly) less colourful suggestion is 'baboons'.

Jerusalem as stone' (1:15). The original version, mentioning only silver and cedar, reads better here (9:27) as some uses of the gold have just been specified. But the point is clear, and is the same as that in the accounts of Solomon's power and worship: in the summary of the whole, the paragraph 9:22–28, the one mention of his huge income is to the effect that it enriched Jerusalem also. His riches mean his people's wealth.

### d. Solomon's wisdom (9:1–12)

The previous section includes and is interwoven with the celebrated story of the visit of the queen of Sheba. Williamson speaks of its 'universal fascination, attested by its constant reuse and amplification in a wide variety of later texts and works of art'.[6] The person of the glamorous visitor must not be allowed to distract us from the reasons for her coming. She had heard of his achievements and of his wisdom, and came to 'test him with hard questions' (9:5, 1 NIV). When she did come, she found the experience literally breathtaking (9:4). What she saw of Solomon in all his glory and wisdom was far greater even than the reports she had heard, reports which had themselves been so unbelievable as to move her to undertake the journey for herself.

But more important was her considered comment in 9:7–8. When we recall how closely linked to Solomon's power, worship, and riches are his people's security, righteousness, and wealth, we shall not be surprised at the judgment of the queen of Sheba (who, for all her admiration for Solomon, must herself have been quite a remarkable lady): that his wisdom means his people's welfare. 'Happy are your wives! Happy are these your servants, who continually stand before you and hear your wisdom! Blessed be the LORD your God, who has delighted in you and set you on his throne as king for the LORD your God! Because your God loved Israel and would establish them for ever, he has made you king over them, that you may execute justice and righteousness.'

So at the end of his sermon text on the reign of Solomon the Chronicler is able to balance with this second comment from a perceptive onlooker the first one which he had quoted near the beginning. The verdict of the queen of Sheba is that of the king of Tyre: *'Because the LORD loves his people* he has made you king over them' (2:11).

[6] Williamson, p. 233.

## 2. The preaching of the sermon

With all this as his text, the Chronicler now has to preach his sermon, and the ultimate question, as with every good sermon, is how it is to be applied. It is easy enough to spiritualize the story for a Christian audience, to multiply the 'types' and make Solomon speak New Testament language. But honest exegesis must make us think twice. Before we see what Chronicles is saying to us, we have to see what it was saying to its first readers, as a matter not simply of priority but of necessity. We cannot find our application till we have found theirs.

But the task is not as hard as it sounds. What we have to do is to put ourselves in their shoes. And although in many ways our situation is very different, in the way that matters most we actually *are* in their shoes. As if we were ourselves Israel after the exile, the Chronicler's audience in Persian Jerusalem, let us consider what we may be supposed to learn from this Solomon.

### a. The imitation of Solomon

Are we to imitate him? It is all very well for the Chronicler to proclaim him as an ideal. But what does that mean? What are we supposed to do about it? It is the valid aim of one kind of preaching to move its hearers to an admiration of the works and character of God; but it would seem strange if that were the only or the main object of this sermon. Are we simply to admire what God achieved in the acts of this man? Or if he is an ideal, is he meant to be the kind of ideal we should strive towards?

But then the question arises as to whether we *can* imitate him. His circumstances, his privileges, his resources, all sorts of factors combined with his character and his godliness to make him the great man that he was. Those external helps we lack, and the lack of them makes Solomon for us the kind of ideal which inspires despair rather than determination. Think of the greatness that has been paraded before us. Is wisdom like his a thing to be striven for? There have been great men in our day (we are, remember, Israelites of the Chronicler's time), men like Ezra the scribe, instructed themselves and instructors of others in the wisdom of God, and wisdom as such is without doubt a noble thing to seek. But – and it is a big 'but' – the wisdom of Solomon was in a class by itself. As an example to the ordinary person who lacks wisdom,[7] to encourage him to ask God

---

[7] Jas. 1:5 will say this, long after our time!

for it with the assurance of getting it *as Solomon did*, the great king is not quite believable.

Or are riches like his a thing to be aimed at? There are those who tell us that a sure sign of God's favour is that one's standard of living improves. If we really trust the Lord, they say, our bank balance will show it. True, when we returned from exile we did experience something of the sort: God's hand was upon us not only in the royal decree that opened the way but in the unexpectedly lavish gifts, in cash and kind, which financed it. But surely that does not justify a striving for wealth, and surely, apart from the rights and wrongs of the matter, it would in any case be just ludicrous to strive for wealth *like Solomon's*.

Or is the worship of Solomon's temple a thing to be aimed at? Are we told about its lavishness so that we, in fourth-century Jerusalem, may be as lavish as possible with what we contribute to worship in God's house? We are doing our best in the present building, and trying to recapture something of the splendour of those services in the old temple. But costs are up, and manpower is down, and the choir is not what it was, and we just don't get the congregations these days. To set before us Solomon's style of worship as an example is if anything positively discouraging, rather than the reverse.

As for Solomon's power, in what way can that possibly be an ideal to strive towards? Even more than the other aspects of his greatness, that is laughably irrelevant in our present situation as subjects of the Persian empire. There may be a few of us who have opportunities to get into positions of influence in our world, but in *that* world, 500 years ago, the people of God were a nation, an empire! There is just no way that Solomon's kind of power can be a realistic aim for us, and it is no good preaching sermons that try to persuade us otherwise.

The question may even arise, over and above all this, as to whether we *should* try to imitate Solomon at all. Is it not the poor rather than the rich, the simple rather than the clever, who are dear to the heart of God? Do we not already know what in many years' time the New Testament will teach our descendants, that he puts down the mighty from their thrones, and exalts those of low degree, filling the hungry with good things and sending the rich away empty; that he chooses 'what is foolish in the world to shame the wise,' 'what is weak in the world to shame the strong,' and 'what is low and despised in the world, even things that are not, to bring to nothing things that are'?[8] The practice of preaching good characters in Bible history as examples to imitate, just as bad ones show us evils to avoid, comes to a confused halt before such an outrageously successful figure as the Solomon of Chronicles. To take his power, glory, wealth, and wisdom as a serious object for imitation would make for the worst kind of triumphalism, and we must have grave doubts as to whether we should so regard him at all.

The Chronicler has, we may be sure, thought through all these questions, and felt the force of them. Yet with all the greater conviction, with if possible even more vivid pointing and stronger lighting, does he portray the greatness of Solomon, rewriting the older history till he has produced a personage who is simply not imitable – who is almost, dare one say it, superhuman.

With what object?

### b.  The acceptance of Solomon?

He preaches a sermon on Solomon to those whose power is small, whose worship is poverty-stricken, whose riches are scanty, and whose wisdom is little. In every respect the great king is a contrast to the book's readers, and such a contrast as places him beyond imitation. But they may see themselves in the king's *subjects*, who have also been in view throughout the story of his reign as the beneficiaries of his rule. 'Greatness', he says, 'belongs to the one who sits on the throne. His people are needy. But his greatness meets their needs.' That is the heart of the message. For the throne is not Solomon's but God's, and the throne of God stands for ever. The throne is there, whether his people see it visible and tangible in gold and ivory and are subjects of an independent monarchy centred round it, or whether they are vassals of a foreign empire with the golden chair long since destroyed, or whether they have ceased to be a political entity altogether and have suffered 'a sea-change Into something rich and strange',[9] a world-wide community that knows no frontiers, membership of which depends no longer on human birth. In every age the throne is there, and is to be occupied by the one of God's choice. David and Solomon occupy it in their day, not blamelessly, but sufficiently well under God for it to be possible to derive from their reigns a blueprint for the future. Twenty kings in turn follow them on the Jerusalem throne, some with great success

---

[8]  *Cf.* Lk. 1:52–53; 1 Cor. 1:27–28.

[9]  Shakespeare, *The Tempest*, I.ii.394.

and some with none in their vocation to embody the rule of God. But during that time, and afterwards, when Israel lies captive in another land, there are glimpses of the Lord 'sitting upon a throne, high and lifted up',[10] and of the Most High ruling the kingdom of men.[11] Then for a period, the Chronicler's period, the 'throne' again means men of God's choice governing in Jerusalem – Zerubbabel, Nehemiah, and their successors – even though they are not kings, and Israel is no longer a monarchy. The sermon is not telling them or the people they govern to try to reproduce the brilliance of the reign of Solomon. It is telling them that where the life of God's people is directed by the one of God's choice, there his blessing will follow. This can be their present experience. And they may also look ahead to a greater outworking of the principle. As scriptures old and new will remind them, 'The sceptre shall not depart from Judah, nor the ruler's staff from between his feet, until he comes to whom it belongs; and to him shall be the obedience of the peoples';[12] 'For to us a child is born, to us a son is given; and the government will be upon his shoulder, and his name will be called "Wonderful Counsellor, Mighty God, Everlasting Father, Prince of Peace"'.[13]

This is the message which the Chronicler proclaims to all the ages. Where God's throne is occupied by the one to whom it rightly belongs, there all the needs of his people are met, and they find the realm of blessing. They may feel feeble and insecure, but there they will find his mighty power. Their relationships with God may be far from right, but there they will find true worship. Their lives may be lives of emptiness and poverty, but there they will find the unsearchable riches of Christ. Their minds may be dulled and perplexed, perverse and foolish, but there they will find the very wisdom of God. To that place the people of God must come.

And where is it to be found? We may let that enlightened lady the queen of Sheba have the last word. She is reported in 1 Kings 10:9 as saying to Solomon: 'The LORD your God ... has delighted in you and set you on the throne of Israel.' The Chronicler's version puts his sermon in a nutshell: 'The LORD your God ... has delighted in you and set you on *his* throne as king *for the LORD your God*' (9:8). Solomon is only the temporary occupant. It is the Lord's throne, and today we rejoice to submit to the last and greatest of the rulers of God's choice. Where Christ by his Holy Spirit is enthroned in the

---

[10] Is. 6:1.    [11] Dn. 4:17, 25, 32.
[12] Gn. 49:10.    [13] Is. 9:6.

hearts of his people, there the blessings are poured out. So we are back after all with the types. 'The queen of the South will arise at the judgment with the men of this generation and condemn them; for she came from the ends of the earth' to see the power of Solomon, to share his worship, to marvel at his riches, and to hear his wisdom, 'and behold, something greater than Solomon is here'.[14]

[14] Lk. 11:31.

# Part Four
# THE KINGS
# (2 Chronicles 10 – 36)

## 2 Chronicles 10 – 13

## 14. Rehoboam and Abijah: the kingdom divided

After his father's forty-year reign (1 Ch. 29:27), Solomon too ruled Israel for forty years (9:30), and was then succeeded by his son Rehoboam. Within days, so the record seems to say, the glorious kingdom had fallen apart. 1 Kings 12:1–19 tells the sorry tale clearly enough, and the Chronicler reproduces it almost word for word. From now on, however, precisely because of the break-up of the Israelite nation into two kingdoms, north and south, he will be treating the older narrative with a new kind of freedom, concentrating almost wholly on the story of the southern kingdom, amplifying it from other sources, and simply ignoring the history of the north, except where it relates directly to events in the south. He even stops short of the verse which, by telling us that Jeroboam became first king of the northern kingdom (1 Ki. 12:20), would

# Chronology of

| | | |
|---|---|---|
| | ?? 1050 BC | Saul |
| | 1011 | David |
| | 971 | Solomon |
| Jeroboam I | 931 | Rehoboam |
| | 913 | Abijah |
| | 911 | |
| | 910 | Asa |
| Baasha | 909 | |
| | 886 | |
| Omri | 885 | |
| Ahab | 874 | |
| | 873 | Jehoshaphat |
| | 870 | |
| Ahaziah | 853 | Jehoram |
| | 852 | |
| Jehoram | 848 | Ahaziah |
| | 841 | Athaliah |
| Jehu | 835 | Joash |
| | 814 | |
| Jehoash | 798 | |
| | 796 | Amaziah |
| Jeroboam II | 793 | |
| | 791 | Uzziah |
| | 782 | |
| | 767 | |
| | 753 | |
| | 750 | Jotham |
| | 744 | Ahaz |
| Pekah | 740 | |
| Hoshea | 732 | |
| | 729 | Hezekiah |
| Fall of Samaria: | 722 | |
| the northern kingdom | | |
| exiled to Assyria | | |

# the Hebrew kingdoms

| | | |
|---|---|---|
| Hoshea | 732 BC | Ahaz (sole king) |
| | 729 | Hezekiah |
| Fall of Samaria | 722 | |
| | 716 | |
| | 696 | Manasseh |
| | 687 | |
| | 642 | Amon |
| | 640 | Josiah |
| | 609 | Jehoahaz |
| | | Jehoiakim |
| | | Jehoiachin |
| | 597 | Zedekiah |
| | 587 | Fall of Jerusalem: the southern kingdom exiled to Babylon |

The right-hand side of this chart lists the rulers of the southern kingdom for the whole period of the monarchy. All except Saul and Athaliah are of the family of David, and form what is practically a continuous father-son line of descent. The list of the rulers of the northern kingdom, on the left-hand side, has no such continuity; only the dynasties of Omri and Jehu survive as far as a fourth generation. Kings not mentioned in this book have been omitted from the chart.

Many of the dates have been simplified; it would, for example, be more correct to date the split of the kingdom not in the twelve months which we should call 931· BC, but (because the Hebrew calendar began at a different time of year from ours) in '931/930'. The length of Saul's reign, and hence the date of his accession, are not known. The system of co-regencies, which obtained often in Judah (and once in Israel), is indicated by a dotted line where father and son ruled jointly.

The chart is based on the work of Thiele, as revised in the article 'Chronology of the Old Testament', by K. A. Kitchen and T. C. Mitchell, in IBD.

have rounded off chapter 10; and he then omits nearly two and a half chapters which follow in 1 Kings, describing Jeroboam's reign, although he does give a couple of sidelong references to it (11:14–15; 13:8–9).

It is vastly over-simplifying the matter to say that the Chronicler does this because he considers the north can do no right and the south can do no wrong. The folly by which Rehoboam precipitates the split will be only the first of many wrongs of which the south will be guilty. It is truer to say that the Chronicler concentrates on the kingdom of Judah because there David's throne and Solomon's temple are. But even they possess no magical, automatic powers, no virtue in and of themselves. With his unwearying quest for theological principles, the Chronicler is able to use these first two reigns of the southern kingdom of Judah, Rehoboam's seventeen years and Abijah's three, to demonstrate this crucial point. The point, in fact, was what Rehoboam managed to miss, and what his son, though no paragon of virtue, was able (on one occasion at least) to grasp.

## 1. Rehoboam misses the point

Chapters 10 to 12 cover the story of Rehoboam. If family connections within the house of David could guarantee another forty-year reign of glory, this man would be assured of it. His favourite wife is his cousin Maacah;[1] he has already married another cousin, and her father (Rehoboam's uncle Jerimoth) has previously married *his* cousin (11:18–21), so that for good or ill the family is very thoroughly Davidic. The fact remains that even so classical a pedigree does not in itself guarantee effective leadership of the people of God. What Paul would later say about Israelite religion – 'he is not a real Jew who is one outwardly, nor is true circumcision something external and physical'[2] – had its equivalent in these early days with regard to Israelite royalty.

### a. Missing the point about personal responsibility
Rehoboam comes to the throne a haunted man. Out of the corner of our eye we just glimpse ghosts from the past, whose doings will

---

[1] Perhaps in 11:21 'daughter' means 'granddaughter' (a common Hebrew idiom). This would provide a possible harmonization with 13:2. See p. 178, n. 6.

[2] Rom. 2:28.

affect the history of God's people for centuries to come unless the son of Solomon acts wisely and decisively. In each case we have here only the whisper of a name, a shiver of apprehension; the full stories, all three interconnected, are to be found in 1 Kings 10 and 11.

First Jeroboam the son of Nebat comes back to haunt the new king (10:2). This man is solid enough, of course, and no phantom. It is the shadow of the past, Jeroboam's record in the days of Solomon, which should alert Rehoboam to trouble ahead: brilliant man, demon for work, sense of destiny, fallen foul of the authorities, many years abroad, everything is in the dossier (1 Ki. 11:26–40).

Then there is Solomon himself, Rehoboam's dead father, with another reminder of the past. In the official portrait the Chronicler has deliberately emphasized the great king's good qualities, but he is well aware that Solomon was not perfect, and the hints of 'hard service' (10:4) and 'forced labour' (10:18) suggest that there is another side to the picture.

And Ahijah the Shilonite – do you recall the name? We have just seen it in Chronicles in a list of sources for the history of Solomon (9:29). But Ahijah, who was a prophet, figures in a more sinister context, the story of 1 Kings 11 to which we have already referred in speaking of Jeroboam. The Chronicler does not re-tell that story, but the shadow of it falls across the encounter at Shechem (10:15). Jeroboam surely sees in his mind's eye the prophet's cloak torn in twelve pieces, and ten of them given to him; and now is the time for the prophecy to come true. So behind Jeroboam looms Ahijah, and behind Ahijah looms Solomon again, because the unspoken reason for the prophet's 'word' in 10:15 is the multiplied sin to which the aged king was tempted by his pagan wives (1 Ki. 11:1–13).

Now Rehoboam could quite plausibly have said that the ghosts were too much for him, that there was no way the disaster at Shechem could have been avoided. Solomon *had* sinned, Ahijah *had* prophesied, and Jeroboam was right there with a sense of the inevitability of the moment. But Rehoboam still had the responsibility of trying. He should have done what he could, whatever the consequences: *fiat iustitia, ruat coelum* – let justice be done though the heavens fall. And he did nothing. Indeed, he did worse than nothing. The account is before us, of bad advice followed and a harsh answer given, and it was 'when all Israel saw that the king did not hearken to them' (10:16) – when *he* failed at the point of testing – that the kingdom was torn apart, never to be reunited.

Let us make no mistake about it. Whatever the Chronicler has said about Davidic monarchy as the embodiment on earth of the rule of God over his people, he is now saying equally clearly that the first public act of the first successor of David and Solomon is a catastrophe which will resound down the ages.

### b. Missing the point about faithful service

The reign was not the period of unrelieved gloom that one might suppose from the brief summary in 1 Kings 14:21–31. After mentioning Rehoboam's abortive attempt to regain the northern tribes by force (11:1–4), the Chronicler turns from the Samuel/Kings material to a source of his own, which provides more heartening information, at any rate about Rehoboam's first three years. Three paragraphs deal with a programme of fortifications (11:5–12), an upsurge of religious life (11:13–17), and details of the royal family (11:18–23), all typical signs in Chronicles of blessing and success.

Without a map, we might be tempted to think that the fortifying of the towns listed in 11:6–10 was a task which would have been unnecessary had Rehoboam not himself brought into existence an enemy state on his northern frontier. But in fact that seems to be the one border on which these places are *not* located. A curve of strong, well-equipped fortresses swinging round from east to west, *south* of his remaining territory, argues a strategic mind, and it is possible (though there may be other reasons for this) that the lack of fortifications along the north – a kind of 'forty-ninth parallel' – may show a refusal to regard his northern neighbour as an enemy, and even to hope for eventual reunification.

Religious life in the south was greatly strengthened, oddly enough, by Jeroboam, who in this overreached himself. The very policy by which he hoped to cut the ties of loyalty between his own northern tribes and the temple in the south, the setting up of 'the calves which he had made' (11:15) as his own representation of the Lord who had brought Israel out of Egypt (1 Ki. 12:25–33),[3] rebounded against him. Sincere worshippers of Yahweh flocked to the south, some by compulsion but many by choice (11:14–17). Till then, the hope of the faithful must have been that, as with many churchmen in modern Ireland, they might continue to see themselves as members of a single church covering the whole

[3] *Cf*. Ex. 32:4.

country, and so far as possible ignore the frontier. But the result was more like that in seventeenth-century France, where after the revocation of the Edict of Nantes, which had granted toleration to Protestants, the departure of the persecuted Huguenots impoverished the country while enriching its neighbours.

With regard to Rehoboam's family, its obvious inbreeding is probably meant not as a fault but as a positive virtue, remembering the ancient traditions of Israel[4] and the recent follies of Solomon (1 Ki. 11:1–8). In this the son showed himself wiser than the father. The tone of this paragraph, like that of the previous two, is encouraging, and although it is possible to translate 11:23b in a way less complimentary to Rehoboam, it is more of a piece with the rest of the section if we take it as it stands in the RSV.[5]

But pride goes before a fall, 12:1 seems to say. For all the injection of spirituality by the influx from the north of 'those who had set their hearts to seek the LORD' (11:16), in a time of ease the attractions of the old paganism reasserted themselves. That, according to the parallel passage (1 Ki. 14:22–24), was the substance of the southern kingdom's unfaithfulness. The upshot was a second disaster, with the country invaded, its fortifications overrun, its treasures looted, and its people in some measure subjected to a foreign power (12:2–9).

Again the mercy of God supervenes, through the message of his prophet Shemaiah. The sequence of events is already familiar from the Book of Judges, and will become equally familiar in Chronicles: trouble, conviction, repentance, restoration. 'The LORD is righteous,' the king and his princes confess (12:6) – that is, he is right and we have been wrong. So Rehoboam's second failure is followed by a second reprieve.

Not all is gloom in the south, then. The curious observation 'Conditions were good in Judah' (12:12) should be read 'There were still some good things in Judah';[6] as in Sardis in New Testament days there are 'still a few ... who have not soiled their garments'.[7] Small thanks to Rehoboam, though. There have been ups as well as

---

[4] *I.e.*, warnings against intermarriage with outsiders, as early as the days of the patriarchs (Gn. 24:3–4; 28:1–2); though the Chronicler has already planted early in his narrative the seeds of a different outlook (see above, pp. 000, 000).

[5] 'He consulted the many gods of his wives' (JB); 'he ... procured wives for [his sons]' (RSV).

[6] So Williamson, p. 248; *cf.* RV, NIV. In this verse AV has an even more commonplace modernity about it than RSV – 'In Judah things went well'!

[7] Rev. 3:4.

downs, but the fact of the matter is that he has not been a good king. He has missed the point that his people will not be blessed automatically just because he happens to be a scion of the house of David; his own faithful service is also required. The inclusion of favourable items in chapters 11 and 12 serves only to stress by contrast that in the end the Chronicler has to concur with the verdict of Samuel/Kings: a regrettable reign.

Again, it is important to hear just what the Chronicler is saying. His condemnation is of Rehoboam personally, in a way that the earlier historian's was not. There, 'Judah did what was evil in the sight of the LORD' (1 Ki. 14:22); here, it was Rehoboam who 'did evil, for he did not set his heart to seek the LORD' (12:14). And this is surprising in the writer who is sometimes said to revere the house of David as the sole channel of God's righteous government of his people. For he tells us plainly that *the king is wrong*. The chosen ruler in the line of David has been a failure. So wrong is he, that the revolt of the ten tribes against his authority is regarded as 'a turn of affairs brought about by God' (10:15), and the forcible reassertion of his rule over them is actually forbidden: 'this thing is from me' (11:4). Rehoboam is wrong, and the north is right to reject him. So much for the 'divine right of kings' in ancient Israel!

## 2. Abijah grasps the point

Rehoboam's son 'walked in all the sins which his father did before him' says the older history (1 Ki. 15:3), dismissing Abijah in a scant eight verses. One of the few things it does tell us is that there was war between him and Jeroboam, who still ruled the northern kingdom (1 Ki. 15:7). The Chronicler has information from another source about one such time of hostilities. In the course of it the southerners captured some northern territory, the first of several fluctuations in the frontier which took place during the sporadic warfare of the years that followed (*cf.* 15:8; 16:1–6; 17:2); and at the time of the crucial battle in the campaign, the Chronicler has a remarkable speech made by this otherwise undistinguished ruler, which shows a grasp of spiritual principles totally lacking in his father. Coggins calls it his 'Sermon on the Mount'![8]

[8] Coggins, p. 193.

*a.  Grasping the point about God*

The Chronicler records this speech (13:4–12) presumably because it expresses his own views of Israel's situation at the time. It is to be read therefore in the light of what he has just been saying about the rights and wrongs of the kingdom's division under Rehoboam. If this is so, then what Abijah seems to have understood about the workings of God is, in a phrase, that he will not be trapped in his own system.

Remember how things were seventeen years ago, he says, and contrast that with the way they are now. It ought to be clearly recognized, as a basic fact, that the kingship over Israel belongs primarily to the Lord, and then by delegation to the house of David. Under the third of the dynasty, Rehoboam, the system went awry. Jeroboam rebelled against him, 'certain worthless scoundrels' gathered round him and persuaded him to make the unwise answer of 10:14,[9] and he himself 'was young and irresolute'. This was not how the system was intended to work. In the circumstances, God authorized the separation of the northern tribes, and forbade their forcible reunion (10:15; 11:4). But Rehoboam's weakness was an abnormality in the system. The norm is for the Davidic king to be strong, and so I am (says Abijah) – not perhaps in numbers, but in resolution and wisdom. Now once again you can see unmistakably 'the kingdom of the LORD in the hand of the sons of David' (13:8). With the fourth king of the dynasty· normality has returned. Rehoboam was not a true Davidic king; the north seceded; and God said, 'Let them go.' I am a true Davidic king; the north should reconsider; and God is saying, 'Let them come back.' At each point there is the chance of a fresh start. God is not trapped in his own system; you were subjects of Rehoboam, but God did not hold you to that when Rehoboam failed; you became subjects of Jeroboam, but God does not expect you to hold to *that* when there is a true king in the south again.

This brings us immediately to one of the most debated matters in the book.

---

[9] So 13:6f. should be understood: 'Jeroboam … rebelled against his lord', Rehoboam; the 'scoundrels', the younger advisers of 10:8–11, 'gathered about him', Rehoboam (this is not the rallying of the northerners round Jeroboam), and *persuaded* him, he being 'young and irresolute' and unable to 'withstand them'. 'Persuaded', not 'defied' (RSV) or 'opposed' (NIV); see Williamson, pp. 252f.

### b. Grasping the point about Israel

The meaning of the name 'Israel' is clear enough in Samuel/Kings. Once the nation has divided, the ten northern tribes form the kingdom of Israel, while the two southern ones are the kingdom of Judah. In Chronicles the question is much more difficult. Some would go almost so far as to say that the situation is exactly reversed: 'Israel' is the people of God, God's true people are those who stand by the Davidic monarchy, therefore Israel is really the south! The answer is not so simple.

How does the Chronicler use the name?

Israel's princes humble themselves when Egypt invades: that Israel is southern (12:6). Israel is in rebellion against the house of David: that Israel is northern (10:19). 'All Israel' goes along with Rehoboam in forsaking the law of the Lord (12:1) – that must mean the south; but earlier, priests and Levites have fled *to* the south *from* 'all Israel' (11:13), which there must mean the north. Rehoboam rules 'the people of Israel' who live in the south (10:17), but his minister Hadoram is stoned to death by 'the people of Israel' who live in the north (10:18). In other words, as Williamson says, 'both north and south may legitimately be called "Israel"'.[10] The northern tribes did not forfeit the name when the nation split; the secession was not their fault.

And here Abijah distinguishes two kinds of responsibility, and in doing so shows that he has grasped the point about Israel. He declares that it was Rehoboam, not Israel, who caused the division in the first place, and clearly it is now Jeroboam, not Israel, who is determined to perpetuate it. If blame is to be allocated for the sorry state in which Israel finds itself politically, the rulers, not the people, are the culprits. This does not mean that the people of Israel have no responsibility; rather, that they have one of a different kind. So Abijah, although he begins with the words 'Hear me, O Jeroboam and all Israel' (13:4), ignores the northern leader from then on (even talking about him as though he were not there), and addresses himself altogether to the 'sons of Israel'. The rulers are responsible for ruling; the people are responsible for discerning between proper and improper rule, and for accepting the one and rejecting the other. The laity are expected to submit to the Lord's authority as it is delegated through his chosen leaders. But they are

---

[10] Williamson, p. 239, on 10:3. See further in this exposition pp. 204–205

not expected to swallow uncomplainingly any sort of rule which is foisted upon them by a loud voice, a forceful personality, or even a seemingly legitimate claim. God's people need to learn this lesson as much in the life of today's church as ever they did: 'I speak as to sensible men; judge for yourselves what I say.'[11]

### c. Grasping the point about throne and temple

However we look at it, this is the nub of the Chronicler's teaching. David's throne and Solomon's temple together are the core of the faith and life of Israel. Apart from them there is no salvation. The amount of space and of loving care he devotes to the twin subjects have indicated how fundamental they are to the Chronicler's thought: royal power and priestly worship, both centred in Jerusalem. We have seen, moreover, how in the ages of preparation for the monarchy the themes of kingship and priesthood were already there in embryo. As the rest of the history unfolds we shall continue to hear the recall to the faith represented by the symbols of throne and temple.

But – 'symbols'? Is not the Chronicler's attachment to the things themselves? If so, the consequences are serious. If so, the message of the Chronicler for us will be of academic interest only, since neither throne nor temple exists any longer. It even becomes doubtful if he had very much to say to his own generation, which although it had a temple had no throne.

If, on the other hand, he has a message for all time, it must concern not only the sign, but the thing signified; not only the throne and the temple, but what they mean. And if that is so, we shall not be surprised to find that it emerges already in his depictions of the people of Israel and their rulers in the days when the signs, the throne and the temple themselves, still existed.

This, I believe, is what we do find. We have already seen how Abijah recognized his father's failure. Even though 'the LORD God of Israel gave the kingship over Israel for ever to David and his sons by a covenant of salt' (13:5),[12] it was perfectly possible for one of those sons to forfeit the greater part of his kingdom, and for God to ratify the right of the breakaway state to exist. The Davidic king, and the godly government which the Davidic king was supposed to stand

[11] 1 Cor. 10:15.
[12] 'The term "covenant of salt" is obscure ... but evidently means the covenant is eternal' (McConville, p. 163).

for, might or might not coincide. If they did, as Abijah believed they did in his case, then it was of course the duty of God's people to recognize them. But if they did not, as had happened with Rehoboam the 'young and irresolute' and most un-David-like, then God's people were not bound to allegiance to the Jerusalem throne.

The same must I think be said about the temple, though many commentators will disagree. Abijah is recalling northern Israel to loyalty to Davidic rule, which he understands is at present embodied in himself. At the same time he is recalling it to an observance of the historic faith of Israel; and that means, *at present*, worship in the Jerusalem temple. That too had gone by the board in his father's reign, and (apparently) been restored in his own, according to the contrasting verses 12:1, 'Rehoboam ... forsook the law of the LORD', and 13:10, 'But as for us ... we have not forsaken him'. The restored faith, like the restored rule, did in practice centre on Jerusalem, and involved the daily offerings, the showbread, the lampstand, in a word the temple (13:11). *But it might not always be so.* The northerners are not recalled to the Jerusalem temple as such, and the inadequacy of their present religion is said to lie in areas other than their failure to worship in that particular place (13:9). What if one day there is no temple to worship in anyway? Concerning the throne, the Chronicler's generation has already had to ask the equivalent question.

Abijah, even if he 'walked in all the sins which his father did before him' (1 Ki. 15:3), in this inspired moment grasped the truth. What matters is the *kind* of godly government seen in the Davidic kings when they are what they should be, and the *kind* of godly worship seen in Solomon's temple when it operates as it ought. Leaders who encourage devotion to the principles, and people who seek it, however changed the circumstances, are those who can truly say with this otherwise nondescript king, 'We keep the charge of the LORD our God' (13:11).

# 2 Chronicles 14 – 16

## 15.  Asa: the basic pattern

'Abijah slept with his fathers ... and Asa his son reigned in his stead
... and Asa did what was good and right in the eyes of the LORD his
God' (14:1–2). Here is a new thing; and although it may seem
strange to say so, what we should first note about Asa is that he is
*real*. It needs to be said for two reasons. He is a real person as
distinct from the personages ideal or illustrative which the
Chronicler has made of David, Solomon, Rehoboam, and Abijah
(real though they also were), and he is a real person as distinct from
the semi-fictional character which some commentators would make
him out to be.

David and Solomon were portrayed selectively, to give a picture
of the fundamental ideals of God's rule over his people. The next
two kings were not particularly shining examples of how the
principles were to be put into practice, but some events in their
reigns did help to clarify important aspects of the matter. So it is
time now for us to see how the Davidic kingship, God's delegated
leadership, will work in the hands of plain, well-meaning,
God-fearing human beings. We need examples of the working out
of the principles with real people, of how leaders should exercise true
leadership and how those who are led can discern it. Asa is just such
a real person.

The other reason for stressing his reality is that, as has been said
frequently, the Chronicler's purpose is served only by realities. It is
one thing to select and rearrange your facts in order to stress the
chief characteristics of your subject (especially if your readers know
what you are leaving out); this the Chronicler unashamedly does. It
is quite another thing to alter and even to invent facts to create an
effect which the actual history would not warrant. We need make no
judgment about the honesty or otherwise of such so-called
'theological creativity'. What is striking about it is its pointlessness.
If God did not in fact do such-and-such a thing, what sort of lesson
about him do we learn from a fictional statement that he did?

For these reasons the following exposition takes chapters 14 to 16 to be serious history, and begins with a comment on how the Chronicler planned his narrative, before going on to consider the content of each of the three chapters in turn.

## 1. The plan of the Chronicler

Unless the reader stays resolutely on the surface, he will find only just under it a series of considerable problems about the dating of events in Asa's reign. The apparent order of things is as follows. Asa comes to the throne, and there is ten years' 'rest' (14:1); an Ethiopian invasion is defeated, and there are great celebrations in the fifteenth year of his reign (14:9 – 15:10); there is no more war till his thirty-fifth year (15:19); his northern neighbour Baasha attacks him in his thirty-sixth year (16:1); he is ill 'in the thirty-ninth year of his reign', and dies in the forty-first (16:12–13).

The problems turn largely, though not wholly, on the two verses 15:19 and 16:1. The Chronicler's account seems to be inaccurate, because by Asa's thirty-sixth year Baasha had already been dead for ten years (1 Ki. 16:6, 8). It seems to be inconsistent, because when 15:19 says (as it does say)[1] that 'there was no war' till Asa's thirty-fifth year, it ignores the Ethiopian attack which the Chronicler himself mentioned in 14:9, to say nothing of the repeated statement in Samuel/Kings that 'there was war between Asa and Baasha king of Israel all their days' (1 Ki. 15:16, 32). And it seems to be tendentious, because of the Chronicler's supposed disapproval of the Samuel/Kings story as it stood ('Asa, a good man, cursed with war and disease? Unthinkable!'), and his insertion of extra material to account for these woes.

If however we start with the assumption that the Chronicler really is concerned to record facts, there are just two problems, one major and one minor, to grapple with, and then we shall be in a position to outline the dating of Asa's reign as perhaps it actually was.

The major problem concerns the 'thirty-fifth' and 'thirty-sixth' years of 15:19 and 16:1. If they really are years 'of the reign of Asa', there is a conflict with all the other relevant facts, as we have seen (and as the Chronicler and his readers must themselves have seen). The suggestion of Thiele and others is that they actually mean Years 35 and 36 *since the split of the kingdom*,[2] and 15:19 is in effect saying

---

[1] The word 'more' is not there in the original. Several English versions have inserted it presumably to try to 'correct' the inconsistency.

[2] Thiele, p. 60. For these dates in our reckoning, see the chart on pp. 164–165.

that 'there was no war in the reign of Asa till Year 35 of the kingdom', *i.e.* of the kingdom of Judah. If this is so, and if the minor problem – whether there was war with Baasha before then – is answered by the realization that the two kingdoms were in a perpetual state of 'cold war', which did not actually flare into open conflict till the events of 16:1, then the Chronicler's plan of the reign is this. Rehoboam reigned for seventeen years, and Abijah for three, so it was in Year 20 of the kingdom that Asa became king, and ten years of peace ensued (14:1). The events of 14:1–8 either belong to that period, or are a general description of the whole reign. The Ethiopian invasion (14:9) was Asa's first real war, in Year 35, and it is to this that 15:19 refers; it led to victory for Judah, and a great celebration followed, which 15:10 dates in precisely that year, the fifteenth of Asa's reign. Meanwhile the 'cold war' with Baasha was hotting up, as Asa's annexation of some Ephraimite hill towns perhaps indicates (15:8), and mass defections from north to south after the victory of Year 35 led to Baasha's attempt in Year 36 (16:1) to put a stop to this unwelcome process. Asa had then been king for sixteen years. It was a long time after this, 'in the thirty-ninth year of his reign' (Year 59), that he contracted his fatal disease, dying two years later (16:12–13).

It will be seen that this narrative does not readily fit the simplified view which the Chronicler is often said to hold, that trouble is the direct result of sin and that virtue or repentance brings immediate blessing, very much better than did the 'unimproved' version of the story in Samuel/Kings.[3] What the Chronicler has achieved is the double aim of showing on the one hand that life is in practice a little more complicated than this, and on the other that this is nevertheless the way that life does turn out in the end. His supposed doctrine of 'immediate retribution' and its converse, not so different (when one thinks about it) from the doctrine of Job's comforters, is in fact almost precisely the opposite of what he actually teaches; as we shall see when we come to consider the prophecy of Azariah in chapter 15.[4]

Meanwhile let us see how the story of this good-hearted, far from perfect, very human king begins.

[3] We should beware of the circular arguing by which the evidence is said to give rise to a theory, and then the theory is used to discount whatever in the evidence does not suit it. Where one does not fit the other, the proper course is not to discard the evidence but to change the theory.

[4] See below, p. 182.

## 2. The heart of the king (14:1–15)

It was in Asa's heart that he should be a good ruler of the people of God. The notion that evil begets only evil must at some point give way to the interference of grace, or the consequences would be unthinkable. And we find that the retribution theory does not in the event commit the Chronicler to rewrite history in such a way that bad fathers regularly produce bad sons.[5] Asa's desire to do 'what was good and right' (14:2) is unlikely to have been inherited from his grandfather or his father, by what Samuel/Kings says about them. If we may infer that after Abijah's short reign Asa came to the throne while still a minor, with the queen mother Maacah still much in evidence,[6] she can have had no good influence on the boy either (15:16). But wherever it came from, the desire was there, and we shall now see in chapter 14 how it worked out.

First, Asa's object. He aims to discharge properly the responsibility of leadership that has come to him with, in his father's words, 'the kingdom of the LORD in the hand of the sons of David' (13:8). Kingship and priesthood are separate functions, but he is in a sense responsible for both. He is concerned that his people should worship rightly, as well as that they should be governed rightly. So with the first in mind he deals with the various abuses that have crept into Judah's religion over the years (14:3–5). Some of these will be frank innovations of the kind brought in by Solomon's pagan wives: another faith, the worship of another god, raising the spectre of doubt about the uniqueness of Israel's Yahweh, in whom alone (our fathers would have said) is salvation; but Ashtoreth, Milcom, it's all the same thing really, we're all going the same way, aren't we? Other abuses will be the attractive but poisonous preoccupations of the old local Canaanite beliefs, no doubt dressed up these days with Israelite terminology (such a lovely pillar where we worship, you just feel Yahweh must be there). It is Asa's task as leader of his people to see that both foreign infection and home-grown folk religion are recognized for what they are, and that the true faith of Israel is practised in its purity. The Chronicler places this

[5] See below, pp. 206–207.

[6] This is presumably the Maacah who had been Rehoboam's favourite wife (11:20–22), who was queen mother in the short reign of her son Abijah ('Micaiah' in 13:2 must be the 'Maacah' of 11:20, 22 and 1 Ki. 15:2),and who continued to hold that influential position for the first part of her grandson's reign. 'Mother' (15:16) can of course in Hebrew idiom mean any female ancestor, just as 'father' can mean any male ancestor; 'children' can mean 'descendants', and so forth. See pp. 31, 46 n. 9, 201.

thoroughgoing reform at the head of Asa's achievements, so it is fair to assume that the non-removal of high places mentioned in 1 Kings 15:14 refers to the northern (Israelite) territories which the Chronicler also mentions later (15:8, 17).

Then Asa is concerned for his people's political security, so we have a description of the building, fortifying, and arming of strategic towns (14:6–7). We are not to take this to indicate a lack of faith and a resort to unspiritual means of defence; it is clear in the sequel that Asa puts no ultimate trust in human armour. Rather the opportunity to build such defences is itself seen as a reward for godliness. At all events his care for his people is as practical as it is spiritual. The Davidic kingdom is already, only twenty years after the death of Solomon, in greatly reduced circumstances; but in a situation far different from that of his great-grandfather, Asa seeks nevertheless to reproduce the quality of faith and life that belonged to the glorious past.

The military aspect of this is seen not only in the fortifying of his frontiers, but in the raising of a respectable army of 580 units,[7] both heavy and light (14:8). This note of his armed strength leads into the next paragraph. All these preparations, spiritual and secular, are shortly to be put to the test. The first major military challenge of Asa's career will be the invasion of his country by an Egyptian army (14:9ff.). Before we move on to that, we should look again at the opening verses of the chapter to understand what lay behind the young king's aims.

This was, in a word, faith. Glibly said, easily dismissed; to be understood therefore more fully as a right relationship with Yahweh, the Lord, the covenant God. Knowing and trusting him is the basis of all that Asa does. He can speak to his people of 'the LORD his God' (14:2), of 'the LORD, the God of their fathers' (14:4), and of 'the LORD our God' (14:7). Each phrase has its implications. There is the individual knowledge of the Lord in Asa's own experience, for he is a real flesh-and-blood human being, not to be taken as a type or a fictional character or a cardboard cut-out illustration: a person called Asa once really lived, and had a personal faith in Yahweh *his* God. It should not need to be said (but it probably does) that the first necessity in one called to be a leader among God's people is this individual relationship with God. It needs to be said in the same breath that to require of all believers a stereotyped conversion

[7] See above, p. 38 n. 14.

experience is precisely what is *not* implied in the expression 'the Lord his God'. God may have brought me to that faith by a very different route from the one by which he has brought you. The vital thing is that each of us should be able to say, like Thomas, 'My Lord and my God.'[8]

If faith is purely individual, though, it runs the risk of being too private and subjective. We know that Asa has not fallen into this trap when we hear him speak to his people of 'the LORD, the God of their fathers'. His is historical as well as individual faith. The newly-awakened have a way of saying, 'Why have I not seen this before?' which is natural and true. They also have a way of saying, 'Why has nobody seen this before?' which is understandable but foolish. New enthusiasm lays itself open to excesses, follies, downright sins, if it assumes that 'We were the first that ever burst Into that silent sea',[9] and is not humble enough to check its findings against the historic faith of the church. But to know 'the LORD, the God of our fathers' does more than restrain: it strengthens and inspires.

> We come unto our fathers' God:
>     Their Rock is our Salvation:
> The eternal arms, their dear abode,
>     We make our habitation;
> We bring thee, Lord, the praise they brought,
> We seek thee as thy saints have sought
>     In every generation.

As individual faith reflects the Chronicler's concern to illustrate truth by real living examples, so historical faith is of a piece with his whole concept of the regularity of God's dealings with his people. The God of that generation is the God of this one. We are all part of the same continuum.

> The fire divine, their steps that led,
>     Still goeth bright before us;
> The heavenly shield around them spread
>     Is still high holden o'er us;
> The grace those sinners that subdued,
> The strength those weaklings that renewed,
>     Doth vanquish, doth restore, us.[10]

[8] Jn. 20:28.       [9] Coleridge, *The Rime of the Ancient Mariner*, part II.
[10] Thomas H. Gill, *We come unto our fathers' God.*

It should, finally, be a corporate faith. It will not always be so; we shall see this most clearly in the reign of the last of the 'sons of David' who was worthy of the name, three centuries after this time, when the leader could not carry his people with him but pressed on regardless.[11] But happy the man who knows himself to be part of a community of believers, who are together willing to move forward in God's service, and to whom he can speak of 'the Lord *our* God'.

Having considered Asa's aims and the faith that lay behind them, we see in the rest of the chapter the vindication of his policy. Virtue does not necessarily lead to peace, nor must trouble always be due to sin. This good man's praiseworthy aims and sound convictions led to both peace and war in turn, and each is stressed. 'In his days ... rest'; 'the kingdom had rest under him'; 'the land had rest. He had no war in those years, for the LORD gave him peace' (14:1, 5, 6). But then 'Zerah the Ethiopian came', bringing against Asa's 300 heavily-armed and 280 lightly-armed units an army of 1,000 units.[12] Whatever the actual numbers were, the odds, like those in the battle between Abijah and Jeroboam (13:3), were such as to provide a real test of Asa's faith in his God, his fathers' God, and his people's God. His faith is expressed in 14:11. The first sentence is difficult: JB's suggestion is 'No one but you can stand up for the powerless against the powerful.' The second is another of the gems in which Chronicles is so rich, most familiar perhaps in the AV: 'We rest on thee, and in thy name we go.' (How many who have sung the hymn based on these words know where they come from?) The third sums up the confidence of the Lord's people: when they find themselves in such a conflict, it is not simply a case of two opposed armies, but of God versus man. Certainty of this kind may not be easily come by, but it brings with it the heady awareness that one greater than the king has taken over as 'commander of the army':[13] 'The LORD defeated the Ethiopians', 'the fear of the LORD was upon them', 'they were broken before the LORD and his army' (14:12, 14, 13). Thus Asa's aims and his faith are vindicated.

And to him on his return from the victory the Lord's word comes.

[11] See below, pp. 269–270.

[12] See again p. 38 n. 14. 'Million' (14:9 RSV) is as misleading in its way as GNB's '2,400 kilometres' and '60 metres' for the 12,000 stadia and 144 cubits of Rev. 21:16–17. In each case the computation of a total in a way that satisfies the modern mind misses the point of the original figures.

[13] Jos. 5:14.

### 3. The word of the Lord (15:1–19)

It comes clear, powerful, and true, for though the mouth is the mouth of Azariah ben Oded, the voice is the voice of the Spirit of God. And it is simple. The gist of it is 15:2b: 'If you seek him, he will be found by you, but if you forsake him, he will forsake you.' Yet not so simple, when you recall that in the previous chapter the 'seeking', Asa's obedience (14:2), did not result in the 'finding', his triumph (14:12), without the trauma of the Egyptian assault coming between. But whether the incidents the Chronicler chooses to recount illustrate the principle in its basic clarity, or with the more usual complications of ordinary life, as here, he is demonstrating constantly 'the fundamental correspondence between an action and its outcome.'[14]

To the returning king the word of the Lord is brought by his prophet. As with nearly every one of the sons of David, these chapters are a portrait of the man rather than an account of his reign. His character and achievements are the subject of 14:1–8. His faith has been tested and proved in the Egyptian war in 14:9–15. True, the message is intended for his whole nation, but it is addressed in the first instance to the king himself (15:2).

There is more to Azariah's word than exhortations or the proclaiming of spiritual principles. The bulk of it is an unusual passage about the experience of Israel. It is thought by some to be 'prophecy' (15:8) in the sense of prediction, so that it should really read 'Israel will be without the true God', and so on, and looks ahead to the time of the exile. But in fact it probably looks back to the period of the judges, described in Scripture in similar terms, a sequence in which first sin is punished by God 'with every sort of distress' (15:6) and then repentance leads his people back to him and out of distress (15:4).

As a result of the prophet's message, a major religious reform takes place (15:8–19). Asa initiates it, but the multitude he gathers around him is fully involved too. They represent the true Israel, not only southerners but also many from the north who recognize what God is doing (15:9). Even that formidable woman Maacah is dealt with, says the Chronicler, as if to impress us with Asa's courage

---

[14] Brevard Childs, *Introduction to the Old Testament as Scripture* (SCM, 1979), p. 655. *Cf.* also McConville, p. 16 (on the Chronicler's simplifying of the account of the fall of the house of Saul): 'How often a real nexus of cause and effect is veiled from general observation by a host of attendant circumstances!'

(15:16)! But the main impression of this latter half of chapter 15 is that 'all Judah rejoiced ... they had sworn with all their heart, and had sought [the LORD] with their whole desire' (15:15).

It is surely no accident that the word of the Lord is shown as an individual message spoken primarily to Asa himself, appealing to the historical deeds of God among his people, and aiming at a corporate response from them. Just as chapter 14 made plain, it is Asa's God, his fathers' God, and his people's God who is speaking by the Spirit through the prophet. The truth of that chapter is underlined in this. How close to the Chronicler's heart is the need for repetition in the teaching of the divine message of history! It is exactly what we might expect in a preacher who sees so clearly the unity of God's people down the ages, the constancy of God himself, and the regularity of the dealings of the one with the other. 'One church, one faith, one Lord.'

## 4. The voice of the world (16:1–14)

We have already considered the problem of 16:1, the dating of Baasha's attack on Asa.[15] Of much greater consequence for the message of the book is the problem of 16:2–3. How could it be that as a way of coping with this threat from his northern neighbour 'Asa took silver and gold from the treasures of the house of the LORD and the king's house, and sent them to Ben-hadad king of Syria, ... saying, "Let there be a league between me and you"'? Such policies are typical of the rulers of this world, who do not know and therefore cannot trust God. But how could such a favoured leader, whose own heart had from the outset told him the right way, and who had heard the word of the Lord explicitly confirm it, now when confronted by a new crisis listen instead to the voice of the world? How could it happen?

Perhaps it is after all no problem. We have only to look into our own experience to see how readily such a thing can happen. It is not hard both to acknowledge the authority of the Lord's word and in practice to heed another voice whose suggestions sound more attractive, prudent, or effective.

We may observe in this chapter both the subtlety and the strength of the worldly-wise proposal that slips into Asa's mind. His important frontier town of Ramah is captured and fortified against

[15] See above, pp. 176–177.

him by his enemy the king of Israel (16:1). He decides therefore to make an alliance with the Syrian king Ben-hadad, who will then put pressure on Baasha's northern border and draw Israel's forces away from the southern one. What makes the scheme so subtly attractive is first that Asa has the wherewithal to carry it through; there is plenty of 'silver and gold' in 'the treasures of the house of the LORD' (16:2), and Asa has no difficulty in finding the financial inducement to offer to Ben-hadad. Secondly he has a precedent for it: 'Let there be a league between me and you, *as between my father and your father*' (16:3). Apparently Abijah too had no qualms about being in league with the Syrians of Damascus. Indeed, Asa may be looking back even to the political manoeuvrings of David and Solomon themselves to justify his action. Thirdly, the subtlest danger in this policy is that it actually succeeds! The temple treasures are raided to provide the cash which is then sent to Syria, the Syrians respond by attacking Israel from the north, and the threat to the southern kingdom is removed. Whereupon Asa 'carried away the stones of Ramah and its timber, with which Baasha had been building, and with them he built Geba and Mizpah' (16:6). So the voice of the world tells Asa that such things are possible, that they have been done before, and that they work. What it does not tell him is that they are wrong. The stones of Ramah, like the stones of Jerusalem many years after,[16] might have told the truth about the matter; but as on that later occasion, such a miracle was not needed, for God sent his prophet Hanani with a word of rebuke for the king.

In this, ironically, we see the strength of the worldly wisdom that had taken hold of Asa's mind. The prophet's message brought him conviction about his unbelief: he 'relied on the king of Syria, and did not rely on the LORD' (16:7), so that he achieved what he thought a good result (the dismantling of Ramah, 16:6) but missed what God intended as a better one (a defeat not of Israel but of Syria, 16:7b). It brought him a reminder of his own experience of the Lord's power, when at the time of the Egyptian invasion he *had* 'relied on the Lord' and had been given the victory. It brought him a further revelation of God's greatness, in another of the book's memorable verses: 'The eyes of the LORD run to and fro throughout the whole earth, to show his might in behalf of those whose heart is blameless toward him' (16:9). There had been no need for Asa to trust his own political wit, since God oversees the movements and destinies of nations, and

[16] Lk. 19:37–40.

the first necessity in leadership is to keep in tune with him.

And because of all this, sadly, we see how strong was the voice of the world. For even these great prophetic words went unheeded. Asa, addressed directly and rebuked for his lack of faith, reacted with anger, and imprisoned Hanani. He went further, and ill-treated others besides, presumably for expressing indignation and sympathy with the prophet. And when in due course he was stricken with disease, this man who had been so firm a believer and whose faith had been so signally rewarded 'did not seek the LORD, but sought help from physicians' (16:10, 12). By then no doubt he was scarcely on speaking terms with the Lord.

There then is the story of one responsible believer, with his successes and his failures. For all the defects of character that emerged in the later part of his reign, his people recognized his stature, and gave him a magnificent funeral (16:14). He was the first successor of David and Solomon to be thought worthy of such honour. The lessons of his reign are simple. The Chronicler has outlined them before, and will do so again, and the repetition is itself another lesson: 'To write the same things to you is not irksome to me, and is safe for you', agrees the apostle Paul.[17] When Asa trusted the Lord he was strong; when he did not, he was weak. The Lord's blessing is for those who put their trust in their covenant-keeping God, and when they fail to rely on him there are consequences which, apart from his undeserved mercy, they will certainly suffer.

[17] Phil. 3:1.

# 16. Jehoshaphat: the pastor in his weakness

At a dramatic juncture in the reign of Jehoshaphat, a word from the Lord comes to him and his fellow-monarch Ahab as they are preparing for a joint military campaign. The prophet Micaiah, foreseeing the defeat of the combined armies of north and south, declares: 'I saw all Israel scattered upon the mountains, as sheep that have no shepherd' (18:16). If Israel is the flock, her kings are the shepherds. This graphic picture, appearing frequently in the Old Testament prophets[1] and already noted in connection with the reigns of David and Solomon,[2] is one which becomes increasingly meaningful as the story of the kings of Judah proceeds. David and Solomon represent, in the setting of a monarchy of the ancient Near East, the ideal government of God's people. Behind and above them is the eternal reign of God which on their own level they embody. Long after them, in the days of the monarchy visible only to the eye of prophecy, will appear on earth 'the kingdom of our Lord and of his Christ'.[3] At every point between, the people of God are charged to see that, however their circumstances may change, they are rightly governed according to the same principles. It is in this way that the figure of the shepherd, the pastor, helps towards an understanding of the Chronicler's preaching of history. The kings are a succession of shepherds whose function is to care for the sheep, and who therefore, being men 'of like nature with ourselves',[4] stand as examples to every other pastor appointed over the flock of God. Each king, if he was faithful to his calling, 'served God's purpose in his own generation',[5] and in the framework of an oriental monarchy he was called to do what, in a wide variety of situations, all responsible leaders of the church are called to do.

The model can of course be misleading. It can seem to justify a

---

[1] *E.g.* Je. 2:8 RV mg., JB; 50:6; Ezk. 34; Mi. 5:5; Zc. 10:3.
[2] See above, pp. 144–145.
[3] Rev. 11:15.     [4] Jas. 5:17.
[5] Acts 13:36 NIV, concerning David.

style of leadership in the Christian church which aims to be autocratic, or omnicompetent, or both; and in many a congregation that is what has emerged in practice – all the power, or all the jobs, have been gathered into the hands of a monarchical leader. We need in this respect to remember two things.

On the one hand, monarchy was an intrinsic part of the political mould into which, for that limited period, God cast the life of his people.[6] The days of the Hebrew kingdoms are long gone, and we should not be surprised to find that he has changed, not the principle, but the form which expresses it; thus the New Testament clearly envisages plural and corporate leadership in the church, rather than the 'one-man band'. Indeed even the Israelite kings knew something about shared ministry, consulting with advisers, and prophets, and their own sons as co-regents, and we shall learn from them some thoroughly New Testament lessons on the subject.[7]

On the other hand, Christian shepherding functions at many different levels: some pastor small groups, some pastor groups of groups, some pastor pastors. One result of this is that a perfectly proper church structure may sometimes look rather like the Old Testament 'pyramid' with the king at its apex. Indeed even the New Testament church combined shared leadership with an 'overseeing of overseers' by such men as Timothy and Titus.

But the principle should be clear. We are not talking about either democracy in the one case or authoritarianism in the other. It is God who exercises the rule and delegates the responsibility, and who expects a leadership among his people which is neither dictatorial nor boneless.

So it is with the matter of pastoral leadership in mind that we come now to the account of the reign of Jehoshaphat. It might fairly be said that this fine man is one of the Chronicler's favourite characters, judging by the space devoted to him. Samuel/Kings gives a bare outline of his reign (1 Ki. 15:24; 22:41–50), and adds to it the story of the alliance with Ahab mentioned above (1 Ki. 22:1-40). The Chronicler expands that one chapter into four, and in giving a fuller portrait of Jehoshaphat he brings out an aspect of the king's personality which may take us rather by surprise. The lasting impression we are given of Jehoshaphat is not that he was a great man, though he was; nor that he was a good man, though he

[6] See above, p. 42 n. 4.
[7] *E.g.* from Uzziah (see below, pp. 220ff.).

was that also. It is that here we are shown the shepherd of the people of God in his weakness.

This is not at the outset an obvious feature. The Chronicler begins in chapter 17 on a very positive note. Here and in part of chapter 19 we discern one of three strands which are intertwined to make up the story of Jehoshaphat.

## 1. A basis of pastoral care (17:1–19; 19:4–11)

These two lengthy passages, inserted into the Samuel/Kings outline from another source, show us Jehoshaphat's activity as a shepherd of his people. They give the lie to the suggestion that the Chronicler favours a kind of 'quietist' religion, which expects God to act while we look on passively and do nothing. In fact he is all for *both* trust *and* action. He has quoted in exactly this sense the famous words of Jehoshaphat's father Asa: '*We rest* on thee, and in thy name *we go*' (14:11 AV). He will tell Jehoshaphat's own story to the same effect. In due course we shall discover this man's quiet reliance on the grace and power of God; but that is only half his faith. The other half is here: it is a faith which is 'active along with his works', and 'completed by works'.[8] He sees that grace operates through nature, and the God who governs Judah expects to do so through his human viceroy.

First Jehoshaphat cultivates his own relationship with God. 'He walked in the earlier ways of his father', and 'sought the God of his father and walked in his commandments', and 'his heart was courageous in the ways of the LORD' (17:3, 4, 6). This personal devotion is the prime requirement for a basis of pastoral care. In a letter which is basically about pastoral care for others, Paul urges Timothy 'Take heed to *yourself*'.[9]

But then that spiritual activity flows out in practical work for the welfare of his people. We see his military activity, as he rings his country with fortifications (17:2) and sets up in addition a standing army against time of need (17:13b–19). He is concerned for the safety and protection of his people.

Alongside the military system he sets up a judicial one. We find judges appointed throughout the land, appeal courts at Jerusalem, and eminent men as chief justices in matters both religious and

[8] Jas. 2:22.
[9] 1 Tim. 4:16.

188

secular (19:5ff., 8ff., 11). The king riding out himself 'among the people, from Beer-sheba to the hill country of Ephraim', and himself commissioning judges 'city by city' (19:4–5), shows a personal and active involvement in the whole system of justice not unlike that of Samuel, years earlier, with his annual circuit round the cities of Israel (1 Sa. 7:15–17).

Over and above all this, Jehoshaphat is interested in his people's spiritual well-being too. He roots out the unworthy, destructive things in popular religion (17:6) and sets up a nationwide programme of education based on 'the book of the law of the LORD' (17:7–9). This raises an interesting question about the application of the Chronicler's 'sermon'. If we are meant to take a good king like Jehoshaphat as a model of pastoral care and leadership, we shall need to think of the equivalents in church life today of the armies and lawcourts with which he guarded and governed the people of God. But supposing that the military and judicial systems in the model, in Bible times, stand for something different in 'real life', in our time, what are we to make of the religious system? Does that also stand for something different? Is the whole thing merely a kind of allegory? No, not at all. Once again we are made to realize that God is illustrating his principles by depicting the lives and experiences of real people. We have to discern what has and what has not changed between then and now. We are not expected to copy Israelite warfare; for that we have to find an analogy. With regard to the administration of justice, the change of key will be a more subtle transposition. And with regard to worship, we may say that allowing for certain vital differences theirs is a direct model for ours. Indeed, when we come to consider Jehoshaphat himself, we shall be right to see him (as I have said earlier) as 'a man of like nature with ourselves', and an example which scarcely needs translating between that world and this.

Already in fact his shepherding of his people can be seen as a pattern for all pastoral leadership. His personal devotion is at the heart of it, and that works outwards in all kinds of practical consideration for the well-being of those committed to his charge. But it needs to be stressed that this is simply a *basis* of pastoral care. It could, of course, be taken as an ideal, a goal towards which every responsible Christian leader should strive. When in the reigns of his son and grandson, men looked back to the days of Jehoshaphat, he must have seemed a paragon indeed. But, in a strange sense, to see his pastorate as an ideal to aim at is too easy a lesson. The sort of activity described in these paragraphs should be thought of not as a goal but as a starting-point. It should be possible to take such shepherding for granted. The leaders of God's flock should take it as read that they will walk in the commandments of the God of their fathers, and lay themselves out to protect and provide for those committed to them. There should be no question of their needing to work *towards* the achievement of such things; it is with these that they *begin*. The detailed, wide-ranging, exercise of kingship described in these paragraphs is the very basis of pastoral care.

With this understood, and laid as a foundation, the Chronicler is now ready to re-tell at length the story of the ill-fated expedition to Ramoth-gilead, from 1 Kings 22. This narrative, though admittedly a long one, was almost the only material with which the older historian had fleshed out the bare bones of his Jehoshaphat section. The Chronicler, having established Jehoshaphat as a great king, lifts the story bodily from Samuel/Kings, tidies it up a little here and there, adds a significant footnote, and incorporates it as his own chapter 18. For it illustrates well how the best of leaders may have an Achilles' heel.

## 2. A peril of pastoral care (18:1–34; 19:1–3; 20:35–37)

The king of Judah pays a state visit to the king of Israel. In the course of a lavish banquet Ahab broaches a subject dear to his heart – the recapture of an Israelite town, Ramoth in Gilead, which has for too long been occupied by his and Jehoshaphat's common enemy, the king of Syria. Will Jehoshaphat join him in the enterprise? Yes, he will; provided there is a word from the Lord to confirm that it is the right thing to do. The prophets of Israel duly prophesy (with visual aids to drive the point home, so to speak – 18:10!) what Ahab wants to hear. Jehoshaphat, however blinded by charity, does find it odd that there should be such a chorus of truth in Samaria, and asks for a second opinion. So the one genuine truth-teller in the city is brought forward, Ahab's conscience, Micaiah the son of Imlah.

If this were not Jehoshaphat's story, it would be Micaiah's. He is a man of the word, and we hear him proclaim it fearlessly. First the flat refusal to speak anything but what God has said. Then the mocking echo of the false prophets: 'Go up and triumph' (18:14). Then the real truth: 'Israel scattered ... as sheep that have no shepherd' (18:16). Last, the awesome revelation: the deliberate sending by the Lord of lying prophecy, to make Ahab set out for a battle in which he will be destroyed.

And so they went to war: and Ahab disguised himself as a commoner, while Jehoshaphat rode forth as a king; but all availed nothing, not even though the Syrians, ordered to attack Ahab only, missed the right king and pursued the wrong one. For the enemy realized his error (God was protecting his servant), and turned back from Jehoshaphat; but 'a certain man drew his bow at a venture' (18:33), and the random shot struck Ahab through a gap in his armour. For all his wickedness, he was a brave man: propped in his chariot, he faced his enemies till sunset, and then died.

But Scripture tells the story better – read it again for yourself! Just one notable thing the Chronicler adds to the Samuel/Kings account. Jehoshaphat escaped from the scene of battle, and got safely home to Jerusalem. 'But Jehu the son of Hanani the seer went out to meet him, and said to Jehoshaphat, "Should you help the wicked and love those who hate the LORD?"' (19:2).

Jehoshaphat's weakness – and this the Chronicler sets before us as a peril of pastoral leadership – was an inability to say no. 'Fatal inability' is a cliché, but in a literal sense it almost *was* fatal. When you come to think of it, it was the other side of the splendid qualities which made him a good shepherd of his people: so kind, so large-hearted, so concerned for everyone, so willing to help. Ahab's invitation to Samaria, therefore, is accepted. Ahab's suggestion about Ramoth-gilead is accepted. But Jehoshaphat should have said no. 'Ahab ... induced him to go' (18:2) would be better translated 'Ahab *se*duced him'.

Here is a danger to beware of. In the story it is clearly a *persistent* peril. I have not yet drawn attention to the statement which the Chronicler adds at the beginning of chapter 18: 'Jehoshaphat had great riches and honour', and yet, having no need to do so, 'he made a marriage alliance with Ahab'. He married his son Jehoram to Ahab's daughter Athaliah (*cf.* 21:5f. with 22:1f.), a union from which nothing but evil would come. There the theme is introduced. If it was Ahab who proposed the marriage, and not Jehoshaphat (it is hard to believe *that* of him), then there had already been an occasion when he should have said no, and instead said yes. The Chronicler then develops the theme through all the rest of the chapter. Finally, to ensure that we shall not miss it, he adds yet another example at

191

the end of chapter 20. After the thrilling events of that chapter, which we shall come to shortly, and after many blessings poured out by God upon his servant, '... Jehoshaphat king of Judah joined with Ahaziah king of Israel, who did wickedly' (20:35). First a marriage alliance, then a military alliance, and now, as if he has still not learnt his lesson, a commercial alliance: he and Ahaziah build a fleet of merchant ships at Ezion-geber. Yet another prophet, Eliezer the son of Dodavahu, comes to rebuke him, and the ships are wrecked. I am not sure, however, that it is exactly a case of persistent refusal to learn a lesson. For at no point is Jehoshaphat forsaken by God. The Lord is there to rescue him from the results of his folly at Ramoth-gilead, and to discipline him at Ezion-geber (18:31; 20:37). It seems more likely that his constant danger of being taken in by a succession of plausible crocodiles[10] is simply a part of his character, one of the defects of his qualities. You do not grow out of this sort of thing, you are not freed from it, because it is an intrinsic part of you. What you must do is to recognize it and be constantly on your guard against it. As with Paul's thorn in the flesh, you may claim not deliverance but victory.

The Ramoth-gilead campaign makes it clear also that this was a *subtle* peril. On this side is Ahab, who does after all rule part of God's land and part of God's people, and is actually known as the king of 'Israel'. It is in a sense accurate for one king to say to the other, 'I am as you are, my people as your people' (18:3). The unity of all Israel is indeed one of the Chronicler's own dearest visions, and he could well sympathize with Jehoshaphat's desire to break down 'the dividing wall of hostility'[11] and to take steps to re-integrate the divided nation. On the other side is Syria. Both kings regard Syria as an enemy. Furthermore, Ramoth-gilead does lie within traditional Israelite territory, and the integrity of Israel would seem to demand not only that the two kings get together but that they reach out also to regain their own lost property.

No doubt there was a like plausibility about the marriage proposal of 18:1 and the trade agreement of 20:35–36. Every such scheme could be made to appear, by those who knew Jehoshaphat's weakness, as a worthwhile venture which would, in one way or another, be of benefit to the people of God. In each case Jehoshaphat

---

[10] Concerning the crocodile: 'How cheerfully he seems to grin, How neatly spread his claws, And welcomes little fishes in With gently smiling jaws!' (Lewis Carroll, *Alice in Wonderland*, chapter 2).

[11] Eph. 2:14.

needed the discernment and the toughness to see where the 'good' was the enemy of the best, and to say no to it.

The narrative of chapter 18 shows too that Jehoshaphat's weakness led him into *increasing* peril. As the spikes of the lobster pot point inwards, so that it is simple for the lobster to slip past them into the pot, but far more difficult for it to get out, so his circumstances make it increasingly hard for him to draw back. Though he protests friendship, he holds back from going with Ahab unless there is a prophet to say he may. No problem, however – here are 400 of them! But, he asks, holding back still, is there a *proper* prophet? Slide in a little further, Jehoshaphat, we have one of those too ... But (hesitating yet) this prophet says clearly that the plan is doomed! Yet the king is next to be seen, slipping further down into trouble, before the walls of Ramoth-gilead. Whether he baulked at the extraordinary plan that he should dress as king while Ahab went in disguise, we do not know; but by the time the battle began he was in so far that there was no getting out, and it was only the mercy of God which rescued him at the last. The fact was, he should never have gone to Samaria in the first place.

The weakness of Jehoshaphat, then, is a perilous thing. It is actually related to his excellence as a shepherd. He cares; if he is to be a good pastor, he cannot afford to be hard-hearted. His troubles begin when he is not sufficiently hard-headed. If he cares without discernment, he will be imposed upon, misled, and eventually rendered useless by his own charity. What he needs is steel in the soul. A clear grasp of his own gifts and calling, the courage of his own convictions, 'a godly fear, A quick-discerning eye, ... A spirit still prepared And armed with jealous care',[12] the Lord's own toughness, and the precious ability to say no.

And yet from another point of view this particular weakness can be seen, in the example before us, as a positive virtue. Indeed it is even more than that.

### 3. An essential of pastoral care (20:1–30)

In chapter 20 the Chronicler matches the Samuel/Kings story with another, from a source of his own, almost as long and told with equal vividness. The personal care that Jehoshaphat has invested in

---

[12] Charles Wesley, *Jesus, my strength, my hope.*

the welfare of the nation is here seen to pay dividends. When he travelled round his kingdom fortifying towns, appointing judges, and setting up religious education courses, he was becoming personally known to his people and storing up a fund of goodwill among them.

When therefore invasion threatens, and he is told 'A great multitude is coming against you' (20:2), he finds that he does not stand alone. The response to his call to prayer and fasting is universal: 'from all the cities of Judah' they converge on Jerusalem, men, women, and children, to support in the hour of his need and theirs the king they love (20:4, 13).

What is now set out at length is first Jehoshaphat's cry to God and then his answer from God. He 'stood in the assembly of Judah and Jerusalem, in the house of the LORD' (20:5), and prayed a remarkable prayer. It is throughout an appeal to facts. It begins with the facts of the past (20:6–9). It harks back a hundred years to Solomon, whose great prayer in chapter 6 this paragraph is surely intended to recall (with 20:9 cf. 6:28–30), then before that to David, whose words are actually quoted by Jehoshaphat (with 20:6 cf. 1 Ch. 29:11f.). Then our minds are carried back 400 years to the time of Joshua, when God drove out the Canaanites before Israel, and, in the same sentence, a thousand years to the days of Abraham, whose descendants were to be given the land. The anchoring of Jehoshaphat's prayer in that remote point of history is of special interest. There must have been in mind the promises made to Abraham from the very beginning of his walk of faith, that Canaan would belong to his posterity,[13] and the final demonstration of his faith, when he proved his right to be called the Friend of God[14] by his willingness to sacrifice his son – in the very place where Jehoshaphat and his people were now assembled.[15] The basis of the prayer is a conviction that 'our God' and the 'God of our fathers' are one and the same, and that his words and deeds in the past may be appealed to as facts, the like of which his praying people may expect to see repeated in their own time of need.

Again we should note, in passing, that both ends of this thousand-year span are thought of as being equally historical. In the days of Jehoshaphat it is expected that the Lord actually will stand by promises which in the days of Abraham he actually did make.

---

[13] Gn. 12:7; 13:14f.; 15:7, 18ff.; 17:8.     [14] Gn. 22:12; Jas. 2:21–23.
[15] See above, p. 95.

Furthermore, if this is an assumption which the Chronicler includes within the story, as it were, we must surely take it that he is preaching both these actualities to readers who are themselves actual in the same sense – who are part of the same continuum. When in his voyage back through Scripture he makes landfall at Jehoshaphat's Jerusalem and Abraham's Moriah, these are islands in history, as real as the port from which he set out; he has not sailed beyond the rim of the world, out of fact and into myth.

The praying king thus brings together the facts of the past and those of the present (20:10–12). 'Now behold, the men of Ammon and Moab and Mount Seir': Judah, faced with imminent invasion, is in dire need. And here is the nub of Jehoshaphat's prayer, in another of the Chronicler's ever-memorable verses: 'We are powerless against this great multitude that is coming against us. We do not know what to do, but our eyes are upon thee' (20:12). All kinds of 'great multitudes' may come against the servant of God, innumerable cares and troubles, exasperations and dangers. But if they make him realize his helplessness, and that in turn makes him look to his Lord, they may yet be a cause for gratitude.

> Glory to thee for strength withheld,
>     For want and weakness known,
> For fear that drives me to thyself
>     For what is most my own. [16]

The answer to Jehoshaphat's cry has in part reached him already, in the united community which has come to surround him with its love and support: 'All the men of Judah, with their wives and children and little ones' (20:13 NIV). To them is given an inspired message, through an obscure Levite, Jahaziel, in words scarcely less memorable than Jehoshaphat's own: 'The battle is not yours but God's ... You will not need to fight in this battle; take your position, stand still, and see the victory of the LORD' (20:14–17). The Chronicler recounts the unforgettable sequel: how panic turned to praise, how the army marched out like a festive procession with a choir as vanguard and a psalm for battle-cry, how 'when Judah came to the watch-tower of the wilderness' they found that their enemies had already destroyed one another, and how they came back rejoicing and hugely enriched (20:18–30). Again, read the splendid story in the Chronicler's own words.

[16] Anna L. Waring, *My heart is resting, O my God*

It has been the church's experience again and again that in the event fear and danger disperse like the morning mist, as in this instance the threat to God's people evaporated before their eyes. But it does not happen always, or automatically. These chapters make three simple but necessary points concerning the man for whom God brought about such a deliverance. First, his trust, which is a joyful and whole-hearted belief in what God has said, and which in the strength of that word accepts with praise a seemingly impossible situation. 'Believe in the LORD your God, and you will be established; believe his prophets, and you will succeed' (20:20) – a constant theme of the Chronicler's, emerging here also. Secondly, his diligence: trust is not for him the quietism which sits and does nothing, expecting the Lord to get on with the job. On the contrary, chapters 17 and 19 have shown how exceedingly active he has been in fulfilling his responsibilities, and in this chapter too he rises 'early in the morning' (20:20) to lead his people out on the new enterprise. Thirdly (and this surely is the distinctive feature of the portrait of Jehoshaphat), his weakness. The very thing which when he was not aware of it could constitute a real peril, leading him along disastrous paths, was actually, when he recognized it, an essential part of his role as pastor. 'We are powerless against this great multitude ... We do not know what to do' (20:12). When he was not only weak, but aware that he was weak, then he had no resource but to throw himself on the mercy of God. And God did not fail him. It is at Wits' End Corner that you meet the miracles, says the Psalmist;[17] and the Lord proclaims the same truth to his New Testament people – 'My grace is sufficient for you, for my power is made perfect in weakness'.[18]

[17] Ps. 107:27–28.
[18] 2 Cor. 12:9.

# 2 Chronicles 21 – 22

## 17.  Jehoram, Ahaziah, Athaliah: near-disaster

As we have seen, the thought of the king as pastor is not one which emerges only in the reign of Jehoshaphat. It had been present from the start of the monarchy, with David as its most noted example. The divine kingship, delegated by God to this line of human kings, included the concept of the Lord as Shepherd of Israel,[1] delegating his pastoral work likewise, and calling David 'from the sheepfolds … to be the shepherd of Jacob his people, of Israel his inheritance'.[2] God is the supreme Shepherd-King: each ruler of the house of David is in his turn the deputy shepherd-king. In Judah the pastoral care of God's people is inseparable from the role of king, which is why the stories of these men teach such relevant lessons for Christian leadership.[3]

But not much pastoring is done in the brief period covered by the two chapters that follow. Jehoshaphat's son, grandson, and daughter-in-law occupy the throne successively, and far from caring for the kingdom, they contrive in less than fifteen years to bring it to the brink of ruin.

At this point, about the middle of the ninth century BC, the story of the Israelite kings becomes in one respect very confusing. It would be less so if we knew the Chronicler's account only, and if he followed his usual practice of virtually ignoring the affairs of the northern kingdom. But he begins to refer to the north as well as the south just at a time when the same royal names seem to become fashionable in both. Each kingdom is ruled by both an Ahaziah and a Jehoram. In fact, the reason for this doubling up of names has something to do with the reason for the Chronicler's referring to the north at all. More of that in due course. For the moment a simplified family tree may help to set names and relationships in order.

---

[1] Ps. 80:1.
[2] Ps. 78:70f.
[3] See above, pp. 144–145, 186.

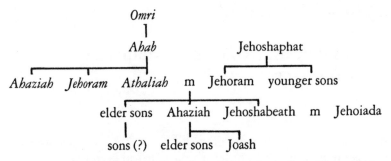

In this table the names of northerners are in italics. Though the Chronicler mentions all five of them, he does so only with regard to their connections with the south; that is still his main subject, and our present chapters cover the next three reigns in the southern kingdom, in each of which it skirted the edge of disaster. After we have surveyed each reign in turn, we shall consider the reasons for this.

## 1. Three reigns of near-disaster

In Judah, there had been a co-regency for a few years before Jehoshaphat's death; he and his son Jehoram had reigned jointly, as the older history indicates.[4] Ahab of Israel had died at the beginning of that period, and the northern throne had been occupied by his two sons in turn, first Ahaziah and then the other Jehoram. The three southern reigns with which we are now dealing begin at the death of Jehoshaphat, when our Jehoram becomes sole king of Judah, reigning for eight more years in Jerusalem, while Jehoram of Israel reigns in Samaria. Jehoram of Judah dies before his namesake, and is succeeded by his youngest son, the other Ahaziah. After a brief and inglorious reign of a single year, Ahaziah of Judah is murdered, along with Jehoram of Israel, by Jehu, usurper of the latter's throne; and for the next six years Judah is ruled by a woman, Athaliah, wife of Jehoram and mother of Ahaziah and now queen in her own right.

### a. Jehoram (21:1–20)

On this occasion it is Samuel/Kings which gives a rather bare account of the reign, and the Chronicler who fills it out with

[4] 2 Ki. 8:16 RV, RSV mg., NIV.

considerable vivid detail. The outline in the older book (2 Ki. 8:16–24) gives us Jehoram's age at his accession, the length of his reign, the fact that he was a bad king, cross-references to other histories, and a note of his death. It tells us also that his wickedness was a northern infection, due to his having married Ahab's daughter; that the Lord refrained from destroying Judah on his account only because of the divine promises to David; and that there was a successful revolt against his authority by peoples long subject to Judah, in the course of which he only just managed to escape with his life.

To this the Chronicler adds some thought-provoking extras. Following a tradition which had a long pedigree, but which was scarcely appropriate among the people of God,[5] Jehoram murdered his brothers when he ascended the throne. It may be that his needing to be 'established' (21:4) implies that his succession did not go undisputed.[6] That may have accounted for the massacre, but it did not excuse it. Then, like Jehoram's brand of politics, the Lord's patience also is more clearly spelt out: it is 'the house of David' which he will not destroy, 'because of the covenant which he had made with David' (21:7). Thirdly, it is made clear that the wickedness of Jehoram is not a private but a public thing. He sets up pagan 'high places' and leads his people astray (21:11).

As a result of all this, the Chronicler continues, a remarkable thing happens. A letter proclaiming God's judgment comes to Jehoram from Elijah the prophet. The judgment follows two parallel lines of crime, sentence, and punishment. On the one hand, the king has made Judah sin; therefore the people will suffer; in due course enemies invade the country. On the other hand, the king has committed multiple murder; therefore he himself will die an unpleasant death; in due course a fatal disease takes hold of him (21:12–19). What is remarkable about this is not so much the prophecy of doom and its fulfilment, as the fact that it comes in 'a letter ... from Elijah' (21:12). Some have reckoned that Elijah must have been dead by this time, so that the letter was either written prophetically before the sins of Jehoram were ripe to receive it, or (still more startling) sent supernaturally from heaven! It is a sufficiently arresting thought that, whether or not Elijah was still alive, his message should have come in written form, since he is

[5] Cf. Jdg. 9:1–6.
[6] Cf. Solomon's accession, 1:1; 1 Ki. 1.

nowhere else portrayed as one of the 'writing prophets'; and that Jehoram should thus be addressed by a man who was throughout the rest of his ministry a prophet to the northern kingdom, and whose name indeed appears in this one place alone in the books of Chronicles, as against sixty-five occurrences in the books of Kings.

The account ends with the terrible words recorded in 21:20 about Jehoram's death: 'He departed with no one's regret.' It could be that the phrase (literally 'without desire') has to do with the absence of cross-references like those we find at the end of most other reigns, for instance 'the rest of the acts of Jehoshaphat ... are written in the chronicles of Jehu' (20:34), as if here the Chronicler is saying 'No one will want any more information about this unpleasant man'.[7] But neither epitaph –'No one is interested', or 'No one is sorry' – is worthy of a shepherd-king of the people of God.

## b. Ahaziah (22:1–9)

The involvement of the people of Jerusalem in Ahaziah's accession may imply, like Jehoram's needing to establish himself,[8] that the transfer of power was not altogether smooth. With Ahaziah's being the youngest son of the dead king,[9] and with the formidable presence of the queen-mother Athaliah in the background, whether working for her son (22:3) or for herself (22:10), it would not be surprising if there were clashes of interest. Once on the throne, Ahaziah was able in the course of a reign which lasted only one year to establish a reputation for wickedness in no way inferior to his father's. It was not simply that 'the way of the house of Ahab' (2 Ki. 8:27) was his pattern, says the Chronicler; he was personally tutored in that way by his mother and her relatives and advisers from the north (22:3–4).

One particularly horrible feature disfigures this whole period, and may be noted here, as all its occurrences cluster round the life of Ahaziah. We have already noted that as a teenager at the time of his father's accession he must have known of the murder of his six uncles, a deed by which Jehoram no doubt hoped either to gain the wealth left to them by their father Jehoshaphat, or more probably to secure the throne for himself. Ahaziah then lost all his brothers, in the Philistine-Arab invasion described in 21:16–17. At the time of his own death at the hands of Jehu, the 'sons of Ahaziah's brothers',

---

[7] So Ackroyd, p. 155.

[8] See above, p. 199, on 21:4.

[9] 'Forty-two' is a misreading for 'twenty-two'; see 2 Ki. 8:26.

or his 'kinsmen' (22:8; 2 Ki. 10:13), met the same fate. And 'when Athaliah the mother of Ahaziah saw that her son was dead' (22:10), the unnatural woman set about destroying all her own grandsons, the heirs to the throne, to take it for herself.

Jehoram's crime, as we have seen, is perhaps more shocking than surprising. But when we see the Lord of history allowing the same sort of thing to happen four times over in the space of a few years among his own chosen people, we may begin to wonder whether there is something more here than meets the eye. Our attention may be drawn not just to the historical parallel at Ophrah, long before,[10] but to the theological parallel at Bethlehem, long after.[11] To this too we shall return.

### c. Athaliah (22:10–12)

What more colourful story-book character is there than the Wicked Queen? Here is one in real life. Indeed the author of Kings, writing the history of both nations, has not one but two to present to his readers, Jezebel in the north and her daughter Athaliah in the south. The Chronicler, concentrating on the southern kingdom, refers only to the latter. Although in Samuel/Kings she is sketched much more briefly and simply than her flamboyant mother, the short account of her six-year reign (2 Ki. 11:1–3) is enough to make the Chronicler's point for him, and he reproduces it practically unchanged.

I have called the two women mother and daughter. Some commentators take in the narrow modern sense the description of Athaliah as 'the daughter of Omri' (22:2 RV), which would make her the *sister* of Ahab and sister-in-law of Jezebel. The genealogy suggested above takes the marriage alliance arranged between the two royal families (18:1) to be the union of Jehoshaphat's son Jehoram with the daughter of Ahab (21:6), and the *daughter* in question to be Athaliah, to whom in due course Ahaziah was born (22:2). She was thus in our terms 'the granddaughter of Omri'.[12]

As if it were not enough for her to have had four successive northern kings as her grandfather, father, and brothers, and three successive southern kings as her father-in-law, husband, and son, this extraordinary person murdered all those of her own flesh and blood who might possibly lay claim to the throne, in order to become reigning monarch herself. Although the baby Joash,

[10] Jdg. 9:1–6    [11] Mt. 2:13–18.
[12] So RSV interprets 'daughter' in 22:2. See above, p. 178 n. 6.

presumably her youngest grandson, escaped the slaughter, there was 'no one able to rule the kingdom' (22:9) or to dispute her right to it.

Her reign of wickedness was no doubt within the plan of God. For the long account of the bloodthirsty exploits of Jehu the son of Nimshi (2 Ki. 9 – 10), although relating mostly to the northern kingdom, is not altogether ignored by the Chronicler. This was the one 'whom the LORD had anointed to destroy the house of Ahab' (22:7). He was not a man to do things by halves, and his violence knew no bounds. He was quite prepared to kill not only Jehoram of Israel, and his relatives, but Ahaziah of Judah, and his. Yet the crucial link between the two houses, Athaliah, sister of Jehoram and mother of Ahaziah, not even Jehu managed to destroy. 'Executing judgment upon the house Ahab', he stopped short of 'that wicked woman' (22:8; 24:7), and for six years she was allowed to tyrannize Judah before the judgment of God removed her. On that day – we shall read about it in our next section – thirteen years of misrule came to an end, and 'all the people of the land rejoiced' (23:21).

There is scarcely another single reign in 300 years of Judah's history which is not in itself longer than these three put together. But though the period they cover is so comparatively short, it sees the fortunes of God's people take a rapid and almost disastrous downward turn. We have now to ask what were the reasons for this ruinous slide.

## 2.   Three reasons for near-disaster

'The downfall of Ahaziah' was 'ordained by God' (22:7). The word translated 'downfall' (*tᵉbûsat*) is very unusual, and it may just be that the Chronicler originally used a slightly different one meaning 'a turn of affairs' (*tᵉsubbat*) – as when God brought about a 'turn over' in the kingdom from Saul to David, or from Rehoboam to Jeroboam (1 Ch. 10:14; 2 Ch. 10:15). However that may be, 'downfall' certainly expresses the trend throughout the reigns of Jehoram, Ahaziah, and Athaliah, and God was behind it (21:12–15, 16, 18; 22:7). Even in his statement that the Lord would never finally break his promise to David, the Chronicler indicates the divine displeasure: 21:7 says that the Lord would not actually *destroy* the house of David, implying that he would nevertheless teach it a very sharp lesson.

There are also three reasons on the human level, however, for

Judah's moral and spiritual decline, which emerge as the Chronicler recounts the story. Under God, three causes for it are discernible.

### a. Foreign influence

We must never imagine that the 'exclusiveness' of God's people in Bible times has anything to do with modern racism. The instances in the early genealogies of outsiders brought into the circle of blessing will give the lie to the notion that Israel was prejudiced against 'the Gentiles' as such (cf. 1 Ch. 2:1–4; 4:17).[13] Conversely, the two men regularly denounced as pernicious influences on later generations of the Israelite monarchy, Jeroboam the son of Nebat and Ahab the son of Omri, were themselves true-born Israelites. No; when we see Old Testament Israel on its guard against foreigners, what is feared is not alien blood but alien spirituality.

The Chronicler rarely goes beyond the bounds of Judah. Ahab is one of the few kings of Israel that he mentions, and Ahab's wickedness is described in the most general terms: he hates the Lord, does what is evil in the sight of the Lord, leads Israel into unfaithfulness, and so on (19:2; 21:6, 13). Behind this, and well known of course to the Chronicler and his readers, is the detailed Samuel/Kings account, nearly seven chapters long (1 Ki. 16–22). Almost the first comment made there on Ahab is that his sins were even graver than those of Jeroboam, for 'he took to wife Jezebel the daughter of Ethbaal king of the Sidonians' (1 Ki. 16:31). Glamorous the seafaring Phoenicians may have been, with their rich and powerful city-states, Tyre and Sidon in Palestine and Carthage in North Africa; they were pagan nonetheless, and Jezebel's religious background together with her own powerful personality brought about a great revival in Israel of the old Canaanite Baal-worship (1 Ki. 16:31–33; 21:25–26). This is what the Chronicler means when he speaks of Ahab leading Israel, who had once been wedded to the Lord, to prostitute herself (21:13 RV, NIV).

So our author has no need to go even as far as the Phoenicians of Sidon to find the baleful foreign influence which is now contaminating the family of Jehoshaphat. The northern kingdom itself has become so disfigured by alien ideas as to be barely recognizable. That is the source of the infection.

This is in fact a part of the Chronicler's underlying theology. It emerges in a curious use of words, in a view of the relationship

[13] See above, pp. 30, 34.

between north and south, and in a choice of events included in this particular narrative.

Here again we note the seeming confusion about the use of the terms 'Judah' and 'Israel' in Chronicles.[14] At the beginning of the account of Jehoram's reign, for example, 'Judah' in 21:3 and 'Israel' in 21:6 clearly mean the southern and northern kingdoms respectively. This is the standard usage of Samuel/Kings. But it must be princes of Judah who in 21:4 are called 'princes of Israel', and the late king of Judah is himself referred to (according to the better reading) as 'king of Israel' (21:2 RV, NIV). Are these merely slips of the pen? Hardly, for we have seen in the reign of Abijah that the Chronicler is quite prepared to use the name 'Israel' in more senses than one. On the geographical and political level, Israel simply means the northern kingdom, as Judah is the southern. But on the spiritual level, where the true people of God are normally – but not necessarily – to be found in the southern kingdom, while an alien spirit is abroad in the north, we have to discern between two other uses. In 21:2 Jehoshaphat, king of Judah, is a real 'king of *Israel*', the true people of God, being himself 'an Israelite indeed, in whom is no guile'.[15] But the other sense is intended when we are told that his successors walk 'in the way of the kings of *Israel*'. Here, Israel stands for all that is false, rebellious, and (paradoxically) non-Israelite: the northern kingdom at its typical worst.

This is the 'foreign influence' which helps to push Judah on the downward path. The Chronicler emphasizes it by pointing out the links between the two royal houses, as he describes the three successive southern rulers. Jehoram 'walked in the way of the kings of Israel ... for the daughter of Ahab was his wife' (21:6). Ahaziah 'walked in the ways of the house of Ahab, for his mother was his counsellor in doing wickedly' (22:3). And the third in the sequence, Athaliah, was herself that daughter, wife, and mother. The very confusion of names with which our study of this section began[16] tells the same tale. We cannot know if either of the Ahaziahs or Jehorams was actually named after the other, but all the signs are of a close relationship of that kind between the families. The frequent comings and goings between the two capitals no doubt originated in Jehoshaphat's desire to think the best of his neighbour, to foster the unity of the two nations, and to overlook inconvenient differences.

---

[14] *Cf.* p. 172. above.    [15] Jn. 1:47.
[16] See above, pp. 197–198.

Subsequent events showed the perils of goodwill without discernment.

The point is punched home by the unexpected appearance of the name of Elijah, in connection with the warning message that was sent to Jehoram. What makes it unexpected is that, as we have noted and as Samuel/Kings tells us at length, Elijah's work as a prophet was practically all related to the northern kingdom, and might be thought therefore to lie outside the purview of Chronicles. That however is exactly why he comes in here. It is to 'Israel' in the sense of the renegade faithless north that Elijah is sent; so that when we ask why the king of the south should need to hear the stern words of an Elijah, it is because the infection of Ahab is turning Jehoram too into a 'northern' kind of king. Historically, he and his father were both kings of Judah; spiritually, both were 'kings of Israel', though in opposite ways – Jehoshaphat as a ruler of the true people of God, and Jehoram as a convert to the falsehoods of Samaria.

### b.  Family inheritance

We should do well not to underestimate the power of the kind of temptation that comes from the house of Ahab – plausible, talking our own language, related to our interests. It would have been pleasant to read that Jehoram had been armed against it by his godly upbringing. Godly it was; men said of Jehoshaphat his father that he 'sought the LORD with all his heart' (22:9), and the Lord himself held up his ways as a model his son should have copied (21:12). But it was not sufficient to keep Jehoram from falling; and once he had fallen, there was little hope for his son Ahaziah, while as for Athaliah, she was bad from the start. Sad to say, the influence of Jehoshaphat was not simply inadequate to keep his son straight. It was actually exerted – with the best of intentions; that was just the trouble! – to the young man's disadvantage. We are certainly meant to see a direct connection between Jehoshaphat's fraternizings with the house of Ahab[17] and the ruinous events of the next three reigns, and none of those contacts was more far-reaching in its evil effects than the occasion when 'he made a marriage alliance with Ahab' (18:1). That was presumably the well-meaning scheme which brought the infamous Athaliah, and with her 'the way of the kings of Israel', into the heart of the kingdom of Judah, to everyone's cost.

We may think of her as the channel of the foreign influence which

[17] See above, pp. 197–198.

was to do so much damage in the south. But her marriage to Jehoram was also a standing witness to the legacy which was being passed down to the sons of Jehoshaphat – namely, their father's weakness. For thirteen years after his death,[18] the follies of that good king would bear fruit in the machinations of this wicked queen. The inheritance was to play no small part in the disasters that followed. So when Athaliah, seeing 'that her son was dead, ... destroyed all the royal family' (22:10) to usurp the throne herself, the divine justice was at work 'visiting the iniquity of the fathers upon the children and the children's children, to the third and the fourth generation'.[19]

There is another side to the Lord's character, however, as it is known from that ancient revelation in the days of the exodus. He is also, in the previous verse, described as 'a God merciful and gracious'. It is not to be thought that the grace of God is powerless to prevent the consequences of Jehoshaphat's sin, nor that they are bound to follow on, whatever his descendants may do. Jehoram's and Ahaziah's personal responsibility is as much a factor in the downward slide of Judah as Jehoshaphat's legacy or Ahab's influence.

### c. Personal responsibility

There is comfort here for parents who are conscious of having made mistakes in bringing up their children – still more, therefore, for parents who so far as they know have done their best for children who nevertheless turn out badly. It is perhaps no less hard, but it is hard in a less crushing way, to know that sons grown to adulthood must answer to God for themselves. 'What do you mean by repeating this proverb concerning the land of Israel, "The fathers have eaten sour grapes, and the children's teeth are set on edge"? ... Behold, all souls are mine; the soul of the father as well as the soul of the son is mine: the soul that sins shall die.'[20]

This is the lesson which godly Thomas Fuller found in the sequence of reigns from Rehoboam to Jehoram. He is commenting

---

[18] The three reigns do not, as might be thought, add up to 16 calendar years (8+1+7). Because of the inclusive system of reckoning used, 848–841 (Jehoram) is counted as 8 years, 841 is counted again for Ahaziah, and 841–835 (Athaliah) includes that year yet again, giving her 7 years (officially; 6 effectively, as in 22:12) – a total of 16 regnal years, but 13 calendar years. See Thiele, p. 67.

[19] Ex. 34:7.

[20] Ezk. 18:2–4.

on the kings as they appear in 'the book of the genealogy of Jesus Christ', in Matthew 1. 'Lord, I find the genealogy of my Saviour strangely chequered with four remarkable changes in four generations. Rehoboam begat Abia: a bad father begat a bad son. Abia begat Asa: a bad father and a good son. Asa begat Jehoshaphat: a good father and a good son. Jehoshaphat begat Joram: a good father and a bad son. I see, Lord, from hence that my father's piety cannot be entailed: that is bad news for me. But I see also that actual impiety is not hereditary: that is good news for my son.'[21]

'So each of us shall give account of himself to God.'[22] True, the foreign influence which surrounded the throne of Judah in those difficult days was an entanglement from which anyone would have found it hard to break free. True, the family inheritance could not be denied, and there were effects from the past which were bound to linger. Yet having allowed for all that, there is still a personal responsibility which none of these rulers can evade.

Behind all these human reasons for the disastrous events of the period, the fact remains that it is God who punishes and God who preserves. In the last analysis he is the Lord of history. To read four times over of wholesale slaughter in the royal family, survived each time by one single heir to the throne, cannot help recalling the massacre of the children of Bethlehem, from which the infant king Jesus miraculously escaped. Not only the preservation of the one, but also, in a profound and mysterious way, the reduction of the many, are the work of God. The fulfilment of the pattern is that last drastic pruning of the stem of Jesse, when the true Israel is reduced to one single fragile human life. It is the inscrutable will of God that this should happen, and that that individual should survive. The vine which is Israel has become the vine which is Jesus, and the reason that only those who abide in him are branches of the vine is simply this – that he is the only vine for them to be branches of. Such, in New Testament terms, is 'the covenant which he had made with David'.[23]

[21] Thomas Fuller (1608–1662), *Gnomologia*. See p. 178.
[22] Rom. 14:12.
[23] 21:7; *cf.* Jn. 15:1–6.

# 2 Chronicles 23 – 25

## 18.   Joash and Amaziah: covenant, justice, mercy

In contrast to the rapid changes of the period of which we have just been reading, the next seventy years of the history of the kingdom of Judah cover only two reigns, those of Joash (835–796) and Amaziah (796–767). The pace of the narrative is therefore not quite so breathless. Nevertheless as told by the Chronicler, who fills out the Samuel/Kings framework considerably, it is a stirring, eventful, untidy story, very human in its lights and shadows. Neither of these two men, of course, provides in himself an ideal of kingship; we should not expect to find that in any of the successors of David and Solomon. Nor do we find here the whole-hearted following of that ancient ideal, as an example to follow, or even the whole-hearted rejection of it, as a warning to note. Joash and Amaziah are sometimes obedient and sometimes not, capable of both wisdom and folly, a mixture of good and bad – in a word, typically human. But perhaps the very humanness of the story is meant to point us to the divine principles which are at work behind it. Certainly it tells us as much about God and his ways as it does about this disappointing father and his unsatisfactory son.

Our chapters tell of the child-king Joash, of his protector and guide the high priest Jehoiada, and of the deposing of his grandmother Athaliah from the throne she had usurped. They show Joash's godliness, while Jehoiada was still alive, in his care for the temple and its worship. But in the latter part of his long reign he turned away from God, was rebuked by the priest Zechariah, had his critic killed, and himself came to a miserable end after both invasion from beyond his borders and conspiracy at home.

The story of his son is centred around two wars, each preceded by a visit from a prophet. First, Amaziah was warned against hiring Israelite mercenaries for his campaign against Edom. He heeded the warning, and won the victory. But then he turned away from the true faith to false gods, and, deaf to a second prophetic warning, he lost the war which later broke out between Judah and Israel. A long period of captivity in Israel followed, while his son Uzziah ruled Judah for him, and though he eventually came home it was only to fall a victim in the end, like his father, to conspiracy and murder.

Here, as everywhere, God is at work in covenant, in justice, and in mercy. His *covenant* never fails. He has said, 'I will take you for my people, and I will be your God',[1] and he has further said that it is through the house of David that he will rule this people of his for ever (1 Ch. 17:7–14). This is the way the tide is flowing, even when the wind is contrary and the waves seem to move in the opposite direction. His *justice* however is seen in those very fluctuations, when on the surface of history things appear to go against the house of David and the people of Israel. God is then saying: 'If you sin, I will punish you; if you repent, I will forgive you; if you are loyal to me, I will bless you.' By a paradox, it is actually in the variety of his reactions that we see the constancy of his dealings. Finally, all these operations of grace are shot through with his *mercy*. This is seen, not only when he blesses the undeserving, but also when he condemns the wicked, for he does so only after giving them every possible chance to repent.

These three aspects of the way he works are well illustrated in the chapters before us. The greater part of the story shows his justice. His covenant and his mercy provide a prologue and an epilogue to it.

## 1. God keeps his covenant

The notion of 'covenant', a decision binding two or more parties, is basic to chapter 23. Jehoiada the priest, who with his wife Jehoshabeath had looked after the little prince for the first six years of his life, now judges that the time is right to reveal Joash as the true king, and covenants are made which bind first the high priest and the commanders (23:1), then the assembly and the king (23:3), and finally, after Athaliah's execution, the king, the priest, and the people (23:16). Not all the translations show it, but the word is the same in each case. Throughout these chapters, indeed, the Chronicler's use of words is precise, and full of significance, as we shall see. Here, the restoration of a son of David to the throne is accompanied by these three covenants, as a sign that *the* covenant, the original one between God and David, cannot be broken. The

[1] Ex. 6:7.

importance of this emerges as we look in turn at the three people with whom the events of chapter 23 are chiefly concerned.

### a. Athaliah

We have already surveyed briefly the years during which Athaliah ruled, as if they constituted a proper 'reign' on a par with those of the other rulers of Judah. But they should probably not be so regarded. Although Joash's reign is reckoned to begin only when Athaliah dies, hers is not described with the usual brief summary (as in, for example, 24:1–2); she was after all no descendant of David, and Jehoiada can speak of Joash as the true 'king' even while she is still alive (23:7). She had usurped the throne, and it is as a usurper that we must think of her now.

We may regard her with a sneaking admiration for the bold, brave woman she undoubtedly was: 'they made way for her' (23:15 RV) as she left the holy place where she knew they would not execute her, and walked proudly out to her doom. She was nonetheless a bad woman too. Her cry of 'Treason!' at the uncovering of the plot against her has many overtones. From her point of view, Jehoiada might indeed be called a traitor. As head of the church, so to speak, he must have been at least formally the colleague of the one who was head of the state, and in that sense he had betrayed her.

At another level, she was herself the traitor. She had betrayed the calling of God's people to be a special people, distinguished from all others by a life lived in loyalty to God under the rule of godly monarchs. In a word, she had betrayed the covenant.

How total was her treason is shown by yet another aspect of her cry. For she had done more than merely introduce to the southern kingdom from her northern background the practice of false religion. Judah's whole way of thinking had been infected by 'northernness'. As McConville points out, the deeper irony of the cry of 'treason' was that 'by Athaliah's own standards there *can* be no treason ... For her, power is rightly held by those who can hold it (the morality, incidentally, of the most respectable modern diplomacy).'[2] So the distinction between north and south is being blurred; the true Israelite tradition, preserved till now in the Davidic south, would never have thought this way.

We know there were many in Judah still faithful to the covenant. But insofar as the ruler has taken the nation with her, it is far gone

---

[2] McConville, p. 206.

in unfaithfulness. In the days of Saul, Israel was so dominated by the Philistines that it was happy to be so, seemed to have lost all taste for distinctiveness, and had practically forfeited its place in the covenant. That historical pattern seems to be repeating itself here. Through the process begun by Jehoshaphat's fateful alliance with Ahab, Judah has become so 'Israelite' in the bad sense that it has almost ceased to be 'Israelite' in the good sense.

### b. Jehoiada

The high priest may have betrayed Athaliah, but he is no traitor to the covenant. Some have thought that his prominence in the story has to do with a shift of emphasis from kingship to priesthood related to the situation in the Chronicler's own day when there were no kings, but only priests. In my view, we should surely see his greatness rather as that of the king-maker, exercising his authority for the restoration of the true line of David.[3] He knows that just as the young king is still alive though hidden in the temple precincts, so behind the scenes the covenant is still a living reality. Athaliah has struck, very effectively, at the earthly kingdom. But she cannot destroy the true kingdom. She may have perverted both Judah's practice of religion and its inner ways of thinking, but the covenant relationship is a deeper thing yet, and is not so easily shaken. It is in fact rooted in the faithfulness of God, and will outlast all the disloyalties of men. With the proclamation of Joash as king the real Israel is once more revealed. The Chronicler brings this out in the way he rewrites the opening of the story (23:1–3; cf. 2 Ki. 11:4). Jehoiada calls together not just the temple guard, but the leading Levites; this is not just a palace intrigue, but the act of the whole popular assembly; Joash is not just the late king's son, but is already himself the king; and these are not just the words of the high priest – this is what the Lord has spoken. A great weight of authority declares that the covenant is to be betrayed no longer. No wonder that this part of the story, which begins with Jehoiada the maker of covenants, ends with his being honoured in death with a burial among the kings of the covenant people (24:16).

### c. Joash

Compared with Jehoiada the priest and Athaliah the queen, the small boy now anointed king may seem an insignificant figure. But

[3] Cf. Williamson, pp. 313f.

211

not in terms of the covenant. Both by his descent and by his very youth he shows how the Lord keeps covenant with his people.

First, Joash is a son of David. We have noted how Judah's situation here in the ninth century resembles that of the reign of Saul two hundred years earlier. Now, as then, ways of thinking which are foreign to the true faith of Israel have infected its body politic, and its ruler, far from guiding it back into the right paths, is an outstanding example of the same disloyalty. Such destructive rule God will himself destroy, and set up in its place the rule of the house of David, through which he has covenanted to bless his people. Thus Saul was replaced, and thus Athaliah has now been replaced. Joash, child though he is, stands in the line of the covenant kings.

And his tender years are themselves another aspect of the covenant. For while the Chronicler merely alludes to the incident, his readers know well what lay behind the public anointing of Joash's ancestor David. When after Saul's unfaithfulness 'the LORD slew him, and turned the kingdom over to David the son of Jesse', and the elders of Israel 'anointed David king over Israel', it was 'according to the word of the LORD by Samuel' (1 Ch. 10:14; 11:3). It rested, that is, on the events described in 1 Samuel 16: Samuel's visit to Bethlehem, and God's choice through him of the youngest of Jesse's sons, reckoned too insignificant to parade with his brothers before the prophet. So Joash embodies two of the principles of covenant history: he is Davidic, and he is unlikely!

The Chronicler may or may not have foreseen how this double pattern might reach its climax. But I think that had he been able to visit the 'little town of Bethlehem', David's birthplace, on that night centuries later when David's descendants were gathered there for an historic census, and to understand how 'the hopes and fears of all the years'[4] were focused on a·baby lying in a manger there, he would have been awed, but not surprised. Nor would he have been surprised, had he looked even further into the future, to find the same principles well known to the people of the new covenant – to hear them also cry 'Hosanna to the Son of David', and to see how among them also God chooses 'what is weak in the world to shame the strong'.[5]

---

[4] Phillips Brooks, *O little town of Bethlehem*.
[5] Mt. 21:9; 1 Cor. 1:27.

## 2. God administers his justice

In the characters of Joash and Amaziah good and bad are mixed, so that in two successive reigns the Chronicler has the opportunity to show the constancy of God's character by the variety of his dealings. As often, he adds to the Samuel/Kings account extra notes about this (for example 24:24; 25:20). In addition, the narrative itself, as he describes each king in turn declining from a reasonably good start down to a sad end, brings out the same principle; and with these two kings in particular the point is made in yet another way – by the very precise use of words which has already been mentioned.

### a. Joash

Chapter 24, which covers the reign of Joash, deals first with his early devotion to God, and the consequent blessing, and then with his lapse into disloyalty, and the inevitable punishment.

*1. Good beginnings.* The young king, still of course a minor for several years after his anointing, 'did what was right in the eyes of the LORD' (24:2), and his marriages and family are no doubt to be understood as the resultant blessing, as well as the restoration of the royal family decimated in the slaughter of the last three generations. Jehoiada was the guide of Joash's obedience and the instrument of his blessing (24:2–3), and after the high priest's death everything would go wrong. But for the time being matters went well, and the Chronicler's way of saying this is characteristically to deal at length with a thorough renovation of the temple set in hand by the king.

There are curious features in the account of this. Perhaps the simplest way to follow the sequence of events is to put 24:5b–7 in brackets, as it were, so that briefly what happened was this: the restoration scheme was decided on (24:4–5a) and put in hand (24:8–10), gifts were put into the collecting box 'until it was full' (24:10 NIV, NEB) and then stored and in due course distributed as the work proceeded (24:11–13), and money surplus to the needs of the main work went towards the making of 'utensils for the house of the LORD' (24:14).[6] In the verses I have suggested we read as a parenthesis, the phrase 'sons of Athaliah' (24:7) probably means not her actual sons, dead some time before (22:10), but her supporters –

---

[6] The Chronicler no doubt understands 2 Ki. 12:13–14, which some see as a contradictory account, to mean that no money went to this lesser work until, as he says, 'they had finished' the restoration of the house itself.

'Athaliah's people'. We shall consider in a moment why the Chronicler mentions the tardiness of the Levites in carrying out Joash's instructions (24:5b–6). Whatever purpose he may have had in including this, he uses in it a very interesting turn of phrase, which leads us to a brief survey of the careful use of words which characterizes the story of Joash's latter days, and which highlights the justice of God. To this we turn now.[7]

2. *Bad endings.* 'After the death of Jehoiada the princes of Judah came' (24:17), and their influence led Joash into a disastrous change of policy. It was as though Judah, having suffered under Athaliah a repeat of the days of Saul, had enjoyed all too briefly a period of David-and-Solomon blessings before being plunged into a repeat of the follies of Rehoboam (10:6–14). The nation's leaders 'forsook the house of the LORD' (24:18).

'Forsake' is the first of the words which the Chronicler uses with deadly precision to show us the divine justice. (We miss the force of his language by using versions which tend to translate a single Hebrew word by a variety of English 'equivalents'; even the RV is not completely consistent. But probably no version can be.) We might try translating this word, *'āzaḇ*, as 'abandon'. The prophetic message to Joash makes it clear that in God's economy the punishment always fits the crime: he has *abandoned* the Lord, so the Lord has *abandoned* him (24:20). Zechariah's prophecy looks back to the sin – they had indeed *abandoned* the house of the Lord (24:18) – and forward to the punishment, when Joash's large army is defeated by a small Syrian one because he has *abandoned* the Lord (24:24). And in one final chilling phrase Joash's personal guilt is brought home to him (the Chronicler's Hebrew readers would have noted this, though we may miss it), as the Syrians withdraw, literally *abandoning* him to severe wounds and treacherous servants (24:25).

Notice similarly the word 'conspire'. The murder of Zechariah the priest-prophet, the son of Jehoiada, is described in a single verse (24:21). But behind that brief note there must lie a process like that by which in the northern kingdom Jezebel brought about the judicial murder of Naboth (1 Ki. 21:1–14), a protracted, cold-blooded conspiracy which will give to this deed of the once-godly

---

[7] In connection with the word-studies which ensue, *cf.* McConville's remarks on similar usage in the accounts of Asa (pp. 168f.) and Jehoshaphat (p. 187), as well as that of Joash (p. 211).

Joash a deathless infamy.[8] But again the Chronicler is concerned with more than the judgment passed by a later generation. Retribution is personal and exact: Joash and his princes *conspired* against Zechariah (24:21), and so in due time 'his servants *conspired* against him because of the blood of the son of Jehoiada' (24:25). Related directly to this is the third word we should note, again a tit-for-tat repetition in the Hebrew, though not in every English version: Joash *killed* Zechariah (24:22), and was therefore later *killed* by his own servants (24:25). This too is the fate of other leading men of Judah. The princes who led Joash astray (24:17) are duly destroyed (24:23), for destruction is the proper fate for those who turn away from God.[9] The God of Israel is the Lord of life; and to turn from him to the gods of heathendom is to cut oneself off from the source of life.

The fourth and last of these repeated words is the hardest to translate. The harshness of Zechariah's dying prayer, 'May the LORD see and avenge' (24:22), has been compared unfavourably with the forgiving spirit of those of Jesus and of Stephen.[10] But the word 'avenge', *dāraš*, is very important in the context of God's dealings with his people in Chronicles. It may be translated as 'enquire' or 'require'. Perhaps one reason for the Chronicler's inclusion of 24:5b–6 in his account of the collection for the temple restoration, which we noted earlier, is that it dramatized this very word – the Levites had been slow to do what Joash had *required* of them. The root meaning seems to be 'ask' or 'seek'. We have already read of both David and Solomon *seeking* God (1 Ch. 21:30; 2 Ch. 1:5), and before that, of the ark not being *sought* as it should have been (1 Ch. 13:3; 15:13).[11] If you *seek* God, you will find him (1 Ch. 28:9; 2 Ch. 15:2), and this is stated to be the experience of several of the kings of Judah.

There is however a contrast between the use of this word and that of the first three. There are two very different kinds of enquiry. As we have seen, he who abandons is abandoned; he who conspires is conspired against; he who kills is killed. But he who seeks will *not* be sought, while he who does *not* seek *will* be sought. For the Lord's enquiry has a different purpose from ours. Because Saul did not seek him out with desire (1 Ch. 10:13), the Lord sought *him* out with vengeance. Joash, like many another, would find the same principle

---

[8] *Cf.* Lk. 11:51.     [9] As Amaziah also will find; *cf.* 25:16.
[10] Lk. 23:34; Acts 7:60.     [11] See p. 120 n. 3.

at work in later generations. Zechariah's words, though scarcely breathing the spirit of charity, express a stern truth about justice: since the king has not sought out the Lord with desire, let the Lord seek out the king with punishment.

### b. Amaziah

Chapter 25 describes the outworking of the same pattern in the life of Joash's son. Here too there is a period of obedience and blessing to start with, and afterwards one of disobedience and punishment.

1. *Good beginnings.* Though 'not with a blameless heart' (25:2), Amaziah did make a reasonable attempt at godly rule, going back as Joash had done to the teachings of Moses (25:4; cf. 24:9). Having in view a military campaign against Edom, he mustered an army which when raised seemed to him inadequate. We are not given his opponents' numbers for comparison, but his own were smaller than those of Asa's and Jehoshaphat's forces in earlier times (14:8; 17:14ff.), and to supplement them he hired Israelite soldiers from the northern tribe of Ephraim. He was rebuked through the mouth of a prophet, with the message, so often proclaimed to the kings of Judah, that the way to success is through reliance on God. He duly sent the Ephraimites back to Israel and went on without them to win a great victory.

So far, so good. His half-hearted devotion to God peeps through, however, both in the original idea of hiring extra troops and in the very human reaction of 25:9 – 'But what shall we do about the hundred talents which I have given to the army of Israel?' The answer of the prophet is another of the Chronicler's gems, a memorable (and practical) reproof to the tight-fisted: 'The LORD is able to give you much more than this.' Although Amaziah acted on the prophet's words, the seeds of tragedy were already sown, and he would soon reap the harvest.

2. *Bad endings.* He prepared to fight a second war, this time against Israel, where now the throne was occupied by his father's namesake, the other Joash (often in Samuel/Kings called Jehoash). The challenge was accepted, battle was joined, and everything began to go wrong. The causes of the disaster may be sought at several levels. Amaziah's primary aim was no doubt to avenge the looting and murder which his northern territories had suffered at the

hands of the dismissed Ephraimite mercenaries (with 25:13, *cf.* 17:2). The cause of their anger, in turn, was presumably their being baulked of a share in the spoils of the previous war (25:10). Behind that again was Amaziah's folly in hiring them in the first place. That was one chain of causes and effects.

At a deeper level, the cause of his embarking on a war he was bound to lose was his over-confidence after his earlier victory. In the words of his opponent Joash of Israel, 'You say, "See, I have smitten Edom," and your heart has lifted you up in boastfulness' (25:19). The northern king drew a cartoon, as it were, of a thistle challenging a cedar, which depicted the situation graphically.

There is a deeper cause still. At bottom, it is the breakdown in the relationship between Amaziah and God which causes his downfall. The Chronicler is reiterating his constant message. Amaziah had adopted the worship of Edomite gods; we are not told the reason – the obvious point, that the gods of a defeated foe were not worth worshipping, he must have seen and rejected – but the result was that he himself was defeated, not simply by a sequence of military events or by an over-confident character, but by the God he had turned away from (25:14–16, 20). Adept as the Chronicler is at selecting the facts which best teach the lessons, he will not manipulate them. He is quite prepared, for example, to record how the immediate result of Amaziah's obedience to the first prophet was not success but trouble (25:7ff., 13).[12] But the story as a whole shows clearly that he who obeys is blessed and he who rebels is punished. And the Chronicler's use of significant words, though less extensive than in the case of Joash, is equally forceful. The 'counsel' of God, brought by the second prophet, which would lead to blessing, is refused; so Amaziah is left to 'counsel' which will take him in the opposite direction, and destroy him (25:16–17).

So the reigns of these kings illustrate two of the great principles of God's working: his covenant, by which his people as a whole will infallibly be blessed, in spite of the sins of particular individuals, and his justice, by which those individuals who do sin will just as infallibly be punished. But over and above these there is a third principle, and reviewing the careers of Joash and Amaziah we can see God's mercy at work, as well as his covenant and his justice.

---

[12] Other similar instances include that of Asa (14:2, 9).

## 3. God proclaims his mercy

Three times in these chapters a message of mercy is brought by a servant of God. Only one of these men is named (24:20), only one is actually called a prophet (25:15), and all of them – the other is simply 'a man of God' (25:7) – have stern things to say. But they stand in the tradition of the great prophets whose names we do know, and who were all, however doom-laden their words, mouthpieces for the grace of God. The priest with whom God's Spirit clothes himself in order to address Joash (24:20 RSV mg.; *cf.* 1 Ch. 12:18), and the man of God and the prophet who speak to Amaziah, are all in effect saying what is said so often in Chronicles, 'He who seeks the Lord will be blessed, while he who abandons the Lord will be abandoned.' It is a plain statement of fact, and does not need exhortation, pleading, or emotion in order to proclaim the mercy and grace of God to all who will act upon it. Alongside God's covenant with his people as a whole, and the justice which accepts some individuals and rejects others, is the mercy which shapes the operation of both.

Many a prophetic message is recorded in the pages of Chronicles. This is perhaps the right point at which to consider how the succession of messengers fits into the Chronicler's overall view of history.

It has become a commonplace of theology to see Christ himself as prophet, priest, and king; in other words, to regard him as the fulfilment of the threefold function shared out in Old Testament days among many individuals in each of these three categories. All prophets are summed up in his prophetic work, all priests in his priestly office, and all kings in his kingly rule.

The three figures are of prime importance in the Old Testament, and recur through hundreds of years of its history. The title 'the Lord's anointed' can be applied to each of them. What is more, all three look forward to a future glory beyond anything seen in Old Testament times. Moses predicts the eventual coming of a prophet speaking words more divinely powerful than those of any of his predecessors.[13] The Psalmist foretells the setting up of a Melchizedek priesthood, eternal, unlike the mortal and constantly-replaced Aaronic one.[14] David is promised an everlasting throne for

[13] Dt. 18:15ff.
[14] Ps. 110:4.

his offspring.[15] The New Testament sees these visions fulfilled in Christ. He is 'the prophet who is to come into the world',[16] 'a priest for ever, after the order of Melchizedek',[17] and the royal and immortal heir of 'the throne of his father David'.[18]

If then we read back *into* the Old Testament story the pattern that has been derived *from* it, we may well expect to find the Chronicler weaving together an analogous threefold cord. And indeed, as we have seen, prophets are as numerous in his 'sermon' as priests and kings. So has the concept of *twin* poles, priest and king, around which the life of God's people revolves as it were in an elliptical orbit, been an inadequate one? Should we really try to picture the prophet there also, as part of a *triple* centre, without which they cannot be the true Israel? And if so, in what sense are the three, rather than the two, anointed ones to be seen as present realities in our own experience? Should we benefit from Christ's prophetic word in the same sense as we benefit from his priestly ministry and his kingly rule?

The truth is that although the word of prophecy is certainly very much a feature of the Chronicler's story, we have been right to see the two institutions of throne and temple as the core of it. According to the Chronicler, as we long ago came to see, the converse of our being represented to God through the priesthood is his being represented to us through the kingship. It may be startling, but it is a fact, that in this interpretation of history the prophet plays no part in the life of Israel! – no part, that is, *in the life of the people*, as distinct from that of their kings. The ideal king governs the people as they should be governed, and directs every aspect of their lives without the need of reinforcement by the voice of a prophet. In practice, however, none of the kings *was* ideal, not even David or Solomon, for the simple reason that they were real, and therefore sinful, human beings. And (as we realize in looking back over the story) it was to them, and not to the people in general, that the prophets were sent. Had they been mere lay-figures, without human weakness, created by the Chronicler simply to embody ideals and to teach lessons, no prophets need have come into the story at all. But we return yet again to the insistent claim that the story is *both* lesson *and* fact, and that these characters *both* prefigured the Christ *and* were real live factual people themselves.

---

[15] 1 Ch. 17:11ff.    [16] Jn. 6:14.
[17] Heb. 5:6.    [18] Lk. 1:32–33.

219

That is how God works. That is the principle of incarnation. And where it is sinful men who embody the lesson, they themselves will from time to time need to be taught and the prophetic word will come to them. We shall find in due course that Hezekiah, one of the finest of them, will plan the worship of God's house 'according to the commandment of *David*', since this had always been a royal responsibility, 'and of *Gad the king's seer* and of *Nathan the prophet*' (29:25).

So the prophets in Chronicles are there not to guide God's people directly, but to speak to their kings, and to provide yet more backing for the view that fact and not fiction is the Chronicler's stock-in-trade.

It is with all this in mind that we read once again how the Spirit of God clothed himself with Zechariah the priest, to warn King Joash of the folly of forsaking the Lord, and how the unnamed man of God, and after him the prophet, reminded King Amaziah similarly of the perils of disobedience. Each message, though stern, was a message of mercy, because by heeding them the way back to blessing was to be found. It is not without such living words from God, genuinely heard and heeded (or not, as the case may be), that the larger schemes of his justice and his covenant are carried through.

# 2 Chronicles 26

## 19.   Uzziah: the pastor in his strength

In some respects the account of Uzziah's reign reiterates the lessons of those of his father and grandfather. We see in this chapter (26), as in those dealing with Joash (chapter 24) and Amaziah (chapter 25), a good beginning as God's word was heeded and a sad ending when it was rejected. But Uzziah was arguably a greater man than either of his predecessors. At his death, after a long and prosperous reign, the vision given to Isaiah of 'the LORD sitting upon a throne'[1] was among other things a reassurance that the kingdom would still be secure *even though* Uzziah ruled no more. The praiseworthy activities of the greater part of his reign were more wide-ranging than Joash's temple repairs or Amaziah's military campaigns. We may see him as the next ruler of real stature after his great-great-great-grandfather Jehoshaphat a hundred years earlier.

It is in his capacity as a faithful shepherd of the people of God that he stands comparison with Jehoshaphat. There is however an instructive contrast also between the two men. In the account of Jehoshaphat's reign (chapters 17–20) we noted his weakness, a characteristic which for good or ill affected his 'pastorate', that is, his rule as a shepherd-king. The characteristic of Uzziah's rule which is brought out in several ways in the chapter before us is the opposite one – his strength. Three times we are told in so many words that 'he was strong', 'very strong' (26:8, 15, 16). The first two-thirds of the chapter describe what it meant in practice for Judah to have such a pastor: first the keynote of a strong pastorate is struck, and then its source and its distinguishing marks are indicated, while the last part of the story spells out the great danger of such strength. Indeed, Uzziah's very name announces the theme in the chapter's opening verse, for it may be translated 'The Lord my strength'. We should not think of this as a pun or a coincidence; nor should we imagine the Chronicler making the history fit the name, any more than he would have invented the name to fit the history.[2] We know how significant personal names were thought to be in Bible times, and in the providence of God the hope or foresight of those who named this child was borne out by his actual life.

The story of Uzziah, then, teaches lessons concerning strong leadership among the people of God, its blessings and its perils, and is of particular interest to all, even today, who are called to positions of pastoral oversight.

[1] Is. 6:1.

[2] Once in Chronicles (1 Ch. 3:12), and frequently in Samuel/Kings (2 Ki. 15:1, *etc.*), we find the variant 'Azariah'. The roots of the two names differ by only one letter, and they are not unlike in import ('*zz*, strength; '*zr*, help, which is also a theme in the story). The Chronicler may have used 'Uzziah' to distinguish the king from the high priest Azariah (26:17), or else because it made his point so well – 26:8 might be rendered 'Strong-in-the-Lord ... indeed became very strong'.

## 1. The keynote of a strong pastorate (26:1–2)

There are two curious features in the statements with which the Chronicler opens this chapter. Like the Irish preacher, before he begins to speak he has something to say, and the usual introductory formula ('Uzziah was sixteen years old', *etc.*, 26:3–4) is itself introduced by the intriguing notes about Uzziah's being made king by the people, and his annexation and rebuilding of Eloth.

Taken together with the last paragraph of the previous chapter, which ends with the murder of Uzziah's father Amaziah, these two verses might seem to be a straightforward account of how Amaziah at his death was succeeded by his son, then aged sixteen, and how the first notable achievement of the new king was the recapture of the town of Eloth. If that is so, however, 26:2 reads rather oddly, in that Uzziah – still only a teenager – was scarcely likely to have restored Eloth *before* his father died. The fact of the matter is more complicated, and turns on two aspects of the Israelite monarchy which we have already noted.

One is the obvious fact that a nation which is a monarchy has to be ruled by a king! The Chronicler has made it plain long before this that where God's people are truly God's people, it is because they are represented to God by the true priesthood and he is represented to them by the true kingship. By the time of Amaziah it has become unthinkable that Judah could exist without the latter, any more than she could exist without the former. So when 'the king of Israel captured Amaziah' and with his 'hostages ... returned to Samaria' (25:23–24), the people of Judah were faced with an unprecedented problem. In one sense they still had a king: Amaziah was still alive. In another sense they did not, since he was a captive in Samaria, and for all practical purposes the throne was vacant. It was at *this* point (and not at Amaziah's death twenty-five years later) that they decided to set Uzziah on the throne, literally 'in the place of his father' (26:1 NAS).

The other aspect of the monarchy we need to remember is the system of co-regency which often operated in ancient Judah, the crown prince sharing the government with his father for some time before the death of the latter. This is what happened here. Amaziah was a captive in the north for ten years (25:23–24), then returned and reigned over Judah again for another fifteen years, till he was murdered at Lachish (25:25–28). The sixteen-year-old Uzziah had been made regent, as we would say (26:1), *when his father was captured*; after the latter's return, the two ruled jointly for the rest of Amaziah's life; and it was after Amaziah's death, as the Chronicler carefully notes, that Uzziah (now at last sole king) captured Eloth, being already nearly halfway through his total 'reign' of fifty-two years (26:2).

But why this particular note of the capture of Eloth? That is the other curious feature of these opening verses. If 26:1–5 are meant to be a summary of the most important facts about the reign of Uzziah, what is so important about Eloth? The mention of it is particularly strange in view of what the narrative does *not* say. Sherlock Holmes once drew the attention of his friend Dr Watson to 'the curious incident of the dog in the night-time'. But, replied Watson, 'the dog did nothing in the night-time'. 'That was the curious incident', said Holmes.[3] As in the circumstances of that story one would have expected the dog to bark, so in these one would have expected an historian to refer to the most memorable event in Uzziah's reign – an earthquake, notable enough to be recorded by a writer in a different country[4] and by another in a different age, 200 years later.[5] But even that is considered by the Chronicler to be less worthy of mention than the restoration to Judah of the town of Eloth. Why should this be included in the 'headline' to the account of Uzziah?

Its name, 'Elath' in Samuel/Kings (2 Ki. 14:22), persists today as Eilat, the holiday resort on the shores of the Red Sea in the far south of Israel. It has a very long history, since it was a watering-place in a slightly different sense more than 3,000 years ago![6] Archaeology tells us that Solomon developed it as an industrial centre, mining and smelting copper and iron. But it was also from there that he sent out his ships along the great trade routes of the ancient world, as the Chronicler has told us (8:17–18), and its chief importance in the Bible narratives is as a seaport. After Solomon's time it was destroyed; Jehoshaphat re-established it, but his trading venture was unsuccessful (20:35–37); later it was captured by the Edomites, and it was from them that Uzziah took it again – surely because of its strategic position as a gateway to the outside world.

For if there is one thing more than another which the Chronicler tells us about Uzziah in the paragraphs that follow, it is the breadth of his outlook. We are shown the literal, geographical, greatness of

---

[3] Sir Arthur Conan Doyle, *The Memoirs of Sherlock Holmes*: 'Silver Blaze'.
[4] Am. 1:1.     [5] Zc. 14:5.
[6] Elath/Ezion-geber, Nu. 33:35–36; Dt. 2:8.

the kingdom at that time; the long reigns of Uzziah and his contemporary Jeroboam II were a period of expansion for both Israel and Judah. To say therefore, at the beginning of the chapter, that Uzziah reached out to the far south of his territories, and there established at Eloth a port from which his fleets might sail further still, to the horizons of the known world, is to say 'Here is a far-sighted man, a man of vision.'

And that is the keynote of a true, strong pastorate. It is the kind of leadership among the people of God which in New Testament terms is called *episkopē*, 'oversight'. It reminds us how much of a good leader's strength lies in his ability to see further than most of his people – as to the possibilities of the future, further ahead; as to the complexity of the church he serves now, further around; as to the lessons of tradition and history, further back. It emphasizes, incidentally, the value of a full-time ministry in the church, for the understanding both of detail and of broad issues which Uzziah clearly had is not a pastime for evenings only. It shows the courage which is needed by one who will lead his people by 'a way that they know not',[7] and persuade sea-hating Israelites that their own landlubber wisdom might in this instance be depriving them of a good thing.[8] And it highlights the patience which enabled Uzziah to wait – for whatever reason – until his father's death before taking in hand, halfway through his reign, this key enterprise. Mary Tudor, the queen in whose reign England lost possession of the French port of Calais, reckoned that after her death its name would be found written on her heart; here is a king whose acquisition of another seaport in far more distant times has linked its name with his as a permanent memorial of his greatness.

## 2. The source of a strong pastorate (26:3–5)

'He set himself to seek God.' God, of course, was the source of his strength. But let us ask where and how this strong man drew on the divine resources. The Samuel/Kings account gives us a clue, and the Chronicler makes an interesting addition to it. We find, in sum, that Uzziah found his strength in the tradition of his family, in the consecration of his own heart, and in the ministration of his friend.

---

[7] Is. 42:16.

[8] 'The Hebrews betrayed little interest in, or enthusiasm for, the sea' (*IBD*, art. *Sea*). Payne, however, suggests (in connection with Jdg. 5:17) that 'maritime trade' was 'a Canaanite interest adopted on a large scale by Israelites' (p. 6).

### a. The tradition of one's family

It may seem rather a backhanded compliment to say that Uzziah 'did what was right in the eyes of the LORD, according to all that his father Amaziah had done' (24:4). We know that Amaziah, though he began well, made many mistakes along the way and came to a bad end. Is the Chronicler telling us, with his tongue in his cheek, that Uzziah's obedience to the Lord was like his father's, namely, half-hearted and incomplete? For of course in a sense it was, as we have seen; this king repeats the 'good beginning/bad ending' pattern not only of his father but of his grandfather too. However, the Chronicler is after all talking about 'doing *right* in the eyes of the Lord', and Amaziah for all his failures was sometimes capable of doing right. In that, his son followed suit. It was, we must remember, the tradition of the family. Many of David's descendants failed to live up to it, but the standards were never quite forgotten, and the structures which encouraged godliness were never altogether dismantled.

It may sometimes seem, both inside and outside the church, that there are so many things wrong with the situation committed to our care that the only way forward is to make a clean sweep and start afresh. But however much a pastor and leader may want to be a new broom, and brush things not under the carpet but right out of the door, he needs to remember that the old structures did nourish piety as well as hypocrisy. Respect for the experience of the past is a biblical virtue, and it is merely a fashionable 'worldliness' which despises the ways of the generation just gone by, seeks change for the sake of change, and imagines that the new must always be better than the old. It should not be beyond the wit of man to disentangle what was good and permanent in Amaziah's way of life from what was bad and transient, and to value and imitate the former.

### b. The consecration of one's own heart

On the other hand, there is never any guarantee that the legacy of the last generation will keep this one solvent. Had Amaziah been ten times the man he was, his godliness would by no means have ensured of itself that his son would rule well. Uzziah personally must 'set himself to seek God' (26:5), for the tradition of the past is of no value without the convictions of the present.

This might seem a point so obvious as to be scarcely worth making, were it not for the way in which the effects of tradition (not just ill effects, but those also which seem good) do persist. Among God's people as in the world at large, the structures of the past have the property of 'inertia' – an 'inert' object being not simply one which remains still unless something moves it, but also one which keeps moving until something stops it. Uzziah must have known, as every leader knows, that the machinery he had inherited would keep going of its own accord if he let it. So the activity of the church will continue over the months whether or not its pastors set themselves to seek the Lord, and its organizations and services will seem to have a persistent life of their own which has very little to do with real spiritual life. We might well ask ourselves more often the salutary question, 'How many of my church's activities would carry on regardless even if the Holy Spirit were taken away from among us?'

It is essential therefore for an effective pastoring of the people of God that their leaders should constantly seek *for themselves* God's direction and blessing – that along with what is good in inherited tradition there should also be daily personal consecration.

### c. *The ministration of one's friends*

With a note of his own which he adds to the Samuel/Kings account, the Chronicler completes his picture of the threefold source from which Uzziah drew his strength. We are told little about Uzziah's friend Zechariah, 'who instructed him in the fear of God' (26:5); there are nearly thirty Zechariahs in the Bible, and the verse before us seems to be the only mention of this particular one. But what we do know about him is that Uzziah's spiritual welfare was closely linked with his influence. The relation between the two is very like that between Joash and Jehoiada in 24:2. The natural way to read 26:5 is to see Zechariah as being for the whole of his lifetime Uzziah's mentor and the architect of his prosperous rule. We may presume that had the friendship not come to an end before the fateful temptation of 26:16 waylaid Uzziah, he would never have yielded to it.

For the greater part of his reign, however, he was willing to be guided by his friend. He was a man of many parts, and a great pastor, but he was humble enough to recognize that he did not have within himself all the resources he needed, and wise enough to know that God's resources could come to him through a human channel. No pastor can afford to isolate himself from such help.

And it is of particular interest that Uzziah finds a confidant within his own community. We might have thought that if he were going to seek the friendship and guidance of a man of God, there would be one person who for a variety of reasons would be the obvious choice. Amos of Tekoa was prophesying in Israel 'in the days of Uzziah king of Judah'.[9] As a God-fearing southerner, he had the same background as Uzziah; they talked the same language, as it were. On the other hand, he was now living in the north, and what could have been a greater tonic for Uzziah than to escape the cares of office occasionally, to leave his 'parish', and to slip away incognito to share his problems with a man like Amos? So the traditional view is sometimes expressed that a pastor ought not to share himself intimately with anyone in his own community, and should find his close friends only outside it. Uzziah did not believe this. Whatever cries of 'Favouritism!' there may have been, he made a confidant of this man of Jerusalem, and did so quite openly, to judge by the historian's account. So respecting the tradition he had inherited, and renewing daily the consecration of his own heart to God, he cherished equally the ministration of his friend, and found in these the source of his strength as a pastor.

## 3. The mark of a strong pastorate (26:6–15)

We have seen how at the beginning of the chapter the name 'Eloth', with all its overtones, struck the keynote of Uzziah's strength as a leader. It indicated the range of his vision, the scope of his 'oversight' over the welfare of his people. This is now spelt out in the paragraph that follows. Of all the kings of Judah, Uzziah has perhaps the widest interests, and the list of them is the mark of his strength.

He is concerned equally with foreign affairs (26:6–8) and with home affairs (26:9–15). Abroad, he is at pains to curb the power of Judah's traditional enemy Philistia, and that of other nations around his southern frontiers. (To his north, Israel is currently a friendly neighbour, and her king Jeroboam II is likewise extending his authority (cf. 2 Ki. 14:25–28); both nations are benefiting from a temporary decline, in the early eighth century, of the super-power Assyria.) His influence and wealth increase among the kingdoms of the eastern Mediterranean, till the authority of the two Israelite kings together falls little short of that of David or Solomon.

[9] Am. 1:1.

At home, Uzziah strengthens his capital's fortifications, damaged during his father's reign (25:23), sets up a regular army, provides it with more sophisticated armour, and introduces new types of defence. [10] Furthermore, he is interested also in the arts of peace, and is much concerned with his country's life and economy, which are still basically agricultural: in the simple but telling words of 26:10, he loves the soil. He is, at more levels than one, a pastor, and the strength of his pastorate is marked in this whole paragraph. Both the source and the result of it are indicated at the outset: because 'God helped him', 'he became very strong', and because he was strong 'his fame spread' (26:7–8). The end of the paragraph repeats the same three terms – helped, therefore strong, therefore famous (26:15). The main lesson of Uzziah's reign may turn out in the end to be one of warning against presumption; but he is nonetheless presented by the Chronicler as a great shepherd-king in the mould of David, Solomon, and Jehoshaphat.

Even what he did *not* do is a pointer to his strength. It is clear that he knew how to delegate. When we are told that *he* 'built cities' or 'hewed out ... cisterns', we are to understand that he mobilized the abilities of others, as the Chronicler makes explicit with regard to the organizing of the army in 26:11. It is foolish to expect the pastor to be himself a jack of all trades; why else are his people equipped 'for the work of ministry'? [11] But Uzziah's was the responsibility of seeing that these things were done. He *saw to it* that his people were *looked after*; these are the verbs of vision, which mark the true *episkopē*, the oversight, of the strong pastor.

In all those ages (and they make up the greater part of history) in which God's people have been something other than a political monarchy, their leaders readily find the equivalents of the many areas of the holy nation's life in which Uzziah interested himself. They recognize the forces arrayed against them, as Uzziah had to face the Philistines and the Arabs; they know how to fortify the central citadel of their community's life, as Uzziah restored the walls of Jerusalem. They love the soil, the countryside where the flocks feed and the fruit grows, and they care for it. They know what is meant by the building of guard towers and the digging of wells. They are aware of the latest weaponry and are concerned to equip

[10] On the question of whether these were some kind of catapult (so most modern versions), and if so, whether this is an anachronism, see Williamson, pp. 337f.

[11] Eph. 4:12.

their people with it. And their fame will be that God has helped them to be strong in the building up of a people for his name.

## 4. The danger of a strong pastorate (26:16–23)

In spite of all this, the story of Uzziah is certainly not one of unbroken glory. Nearly half the chapter is devoted to a serious warning of the danger inherent in being a strong leader. In the latter part of his reign Uzziah's failure was as resounding as his earlier success had been. So the summary of 26:4 was accurate after all: 'he did what was right ... according to all that his father Amaziah had done'. Like Amaziah, and indeed like Amaziah's father Joash, Uzziah began well and ended badly. As 'Joash did what was right ... all the days of Jehoiada the priest' (24:2), so Uzziah sought God 'in the days of Zechariah, who instructed him in the fear of God; and as long as he sought the LORD, God made him prosper' (26:5). But for all three kings the day came when the help and guidance of God were rejected.

In this respect we see, as so often in Scripture, a pattern repeated.[12] We also see another pattern reversed. Uzziah's story here is the reverse of that of his great-great-great-grandfather Jehoshaphat. The earlier king was fundamentally a weak man who could not say no, and his weakness was blameworthy – until it came to the crunch. Then it was that in his real need he found that God came to his rescue; so his weakness was his salvation. Uzziah was a strong man, and his strength was praiseworthy – until it came to the crunch. Then his strength was his downfall.

The sequence of help leading to strength leading to fame is one noted twice already (26:7–8, 15). But strength can have, and in Uzziah's case did have, another result. 'When he was strong he grew proud, to his destruction' (26:16). The pride we have seen in other kings of Judah; the particular act of wickedness to which it led here has a precedent in the first king of Israel, Jeroboam I, more than 150 years before, when it had a similar result. Jeroboam's whole religious system was a counterfeit: 'he went up to the altar which he had made ... in the month which he had devised'; but it was when he, like Uzziah years later, 'was standing by the altar to burn incense', that God's messenger condemned him and he was physically stricken (1 Ki. 12:28 – 13:5). That was a ceremony which

[12] See my *The Message of Revelation: I Saw Heaven Opened*, pp. 37–39.

belonged to the priests alone. No-one else, not even the king, not even when the altar was a sham altar, should presume to offer incense.

That was the sin of Uzziah. He 'entered the temple of the LORD to burn incense ... But Azariah the priest went in after him, with eighty priests of the LORD who were men of valour; and they withstood King Uzziah ... "Go out of the sanctuary; for you have done wrong"' (26:16–18). Bold words to a great king! But then he had sinned a great sin. We should note two things about his wrongdoing.

### a. Not a sin of youth

It was 'when he was strong'. Perhaps he had always been strong in character, but now he was strong with age and experience also. The incident took place probably in the year 750 BC; he had already been king for seventeen years – indeed if we include the period when he had ruled also during his father's lifetime, he had been on the throne for forty-one years. He was a man in his mid-fifties, a highly experienced pastor, and a man of power and authority. His was not a sin of callow youth. If we call it presumption, we must know what we mean by that. Youth can be presumptuous in its ignorance; maturity is in danger of presumption of a different kind, and needs to beware of thinking itself exempt from the rules that apply to those who are less advanced. 'I am not an ordinary man', Napoleon once said, 'and the laws of morals and of custom were never made for me.'[13] But among the people of God no leader, however experienced, can risk such a cavalier attitude to the law of God. *Noblesse oblige* – nobility has its obligations, and the higher the greater. No-one is beyond the kind of temptation that came to Uzziah; it may lie ahead for any of us.

### b. Not a sin of wickedness

In one sense, of course, all sin is wickedness. But we could not call Uzziah a blatantly wicked man, and his sin has little to do with vice or villainy. On the contrary, it has to do with religion and worship. It takes place at the very heart of the life of the people of God, in the temple. It is a sin committed in the Holy Place. That is precisely what makes it the outrageous sin that it is.

[13] G. A. Chadwick, *The Book of Exodus* (Hodder and Stoughton, *Expositor's Bible* series, 1890), p. 86, quoting the *Memoirs* of Mme de Rémusat.

And yet it does not after all seem a very bad thing to do. Why should it have such a devastating effect? Why is Uzziah stricken there and then with leprosy, and from that day forward kept in isolation both from public worship and from affairs of state for the remaining ten years of his life (26:21)?

True, the offering of incense was not a bad thing, but a very good thing – provided it was done by the right people. It was a holy task, and it was not Uzziah's task. He took upon himself something which God had reserved for another of his chosen servants. Uzziah, of the house of David and the tribe of Judah, was the king; the priest was Azariah, of the line of Aaron and the tribe of Levi. We know now that the two functions, the priestly representing of man to God and the kingly representing of God to man, would one day merge in the person and work of our Lord Jesus Christ. We know too from history that in the days between Old Testament and New there would be a line of Jewish rulers who would themselves attempt to combine kingship and priesthood. But in the days of which the Chronicler writes the picture must be as God has drawn it. And though we no longer see his people living within the structure of the Old Testament monarchy, his composition of the picture is still of paramount importance. Each person in it has his own role in the mind of God, every calling is holy, it is wrong for any either to neglect his own function or to arrogate to himself someone else's. In terms of Paul's illustration of the people of God as a body, the foot must not say, 'Because I am not a hand, I do not belong to the body', and the ear must not say, 'Because I am not an eye, I do not belong to the body'.[14]

We have in fact come full circle back to Jehoshaphat. He could not say no to others; Uzziah could not say no to himself. He was a foot wanting to be a hand, an ear wanting to be an eye; and his sin was crowned by the fact that he resented Azariah's criticism of it. It was 'when he became angry with the priests' that 'leprosy broke out on his forehead' (26:19). To use another of Paul's illustrations, describing exactly such a situation, he was a man who for forty years had demonstrated to others the ways of God for his people, and now found himself disqualified.[15] He had as it were been preaching the

---

[14] 1 Cor. 12:15–16. *Cf.* McConville's comment on the death of the similarly-named Uzzah (1 Ch. 13), which, 'while seeming to come grimly to us from an alien thought-world, has a message for us in terms of careful attention to our own God-given role within the Church' (p. 38).

[15] 1 Cor. 9:27.

231

good news of the kingdom of God, but having then placed himself above that rule, he lost the privilege of proclaiming it. Perhaps even the note of his interment is a sad epitaph reminding all his successors of the possibility of the final setting aside of one formerly in the centre of God's will: 'they buried him with his fathers', in a sense, but only 'in the burial field which belonged to the kings' (26:23), and not in the royal tombs: in death, as in the last years of his life, a leper and an outcast, betrayed by his own strength.

# 2 Chronicles 27 – 28

# 20. Jotham and Ahaz: Israel re-emerges

Uzziah died in 740 BC. Of his successors on the throne of Judah, his son Jotham was a good king and his grandson Ahaz a bad one. This kind of black-and-white simplification is not as common in Chronicles as it is sometimes said to be. The very human mixture of good and evil which we have noted particularly in the cases of Joash and Amaziah is actually typical of several generations of the royal family. Jotham and Ahaz present a couple of uncomplicated portraits of virtue and villainy such as we have not seen for some while. In this respect, the last king comparable to Jotham was Abijah, Solomon's grandson, and though greater and better men sat on the throne in the intervening 170 years, of these two only did the Chronicler have nothing bad to say. Ahaz, on the other hand, did not have to look quite so far back to find a precedent for his wickedness, but even the thirteen years during which Jehoram, Ahaziah, and Athaliah in turn ruled the nation, a century before him, were not so disastrous a time as his reign would be.

The Chronicler's presentation of Jotham the Good and Ahaz the Bad suggests a new perspective on the history of the monarchy, and a way of interpreting and applying its lessons slightly different from those which we have used so far.

First, David and Solomon were depicted as ideal figures, so lofty that they are clearly not an example which we are to imitate, but the embodiment of principles to which we are to submit. For us, the principles have now been re-embodied in a Person, and teach us something of the kingly rule of Christ.

Nine kings followed, from Rehoboam to Uzziah, each called to govern the people of God according to those principles. Some did it well, some badly, but all were meant to be leaders and guides of Israel, as God's under-shepherds. To them, all who have equivalent responsibility today may look for examples to follow or warnings to heed.

But now comes an account of two reigns which have perhaps a different purpose. The very starkness of the picture indicates that in this case realistic lessons are to be learned not from the righteous King Jotham or the appalling King Ahaz, but from the experience of the people they ruled. Judah – or should we say Israel? – re-emerges here as a living, suffering, sinning and repenting community. The story is still, at one level, about the monarchs of the house of David. But what about the people? What is happening to them? What do we find to be the knots in the thread of *their* story, the story of the common man? Experiences more mixed, says the Chronicler, than the one-colour characters of these two kings.

## 1. Corruption (27:1–9)

Jotham was a good king, following the example of his father Uzziah in every respect but that of the older man's sin. Uzziah had become a powerful ruler, and it had led him into sin (26:16ff.). Jotham too became powerful, but recognized that power depended on obedience (27:6). This was why God blessed him. The Chronicler, with the Samuel/Kings account before him (2 Ki. 15:32ff.), adds and omits in such a way as to emphasize the signs of blessing: Jotham was a builder – yes, a great builder, as Solomon had been, and a winner of victories too, like David, exacting tribute from defeated foes; though to skirmishes on the northern border (2 Ki. 15:37) we have only the vaguest reference (27:7), leaving these over as more apt material for the story of Ahaz.

'But the people ...' Alas, a sour note among the praises of a good man. 'But the people', the Chronicler tells us, 'still followed corrupt practices' (27:2). Up to now he has generally been recounting the story of the kings, and we have tended to take for granted that on the whole the people will follow the lead of their rulers, whether for good or ill. But it has not been altogether so. When rulers have turned aside from the right way, it has not been prophets and men of God only who have spoken and acted against them. It was the people who at Jehoram's funeral pointedly withheld the normal honours (21:19–20); multitudes gladly joined the movement to oust Athaliah, and rejoiced when she died (23:1ff., 21); Joash's servants conspired against him because he had murdered Zechariah (24:25), and Amaziah too was the object of a conspiracy 'when he turned away from the LORD' (25:27). And as we are thus given hints of the revulsion felt by good subjects towards bad kings, so here we have the first indication that bad subjects may go their own way despite the efforts of good kings. There was in Jotham's time a corruption in the heart of Judah which was not shamed by the king's goodness, and which would reappear particularly in the reign of Josiah a hundred years later. It is worth noting what that corruption means: not what it consisted of at the time ('the people still sacrificed and burned incense on the high places', 2 Ki. 15:35), but what it shows of an inner attitude.

For the Chronicler discounts the beginnings of trouble on the northern frontier (2 Ki.15:37), and clearly wants us to see Jotham's reign as one of success and prosperity, which are related directly to the king's godliness. Those are the circumstances in which many in Judah are practising a religion that displeases God. What we see here is a special and familiar kind of corruption. The welfare of society is reckoned by many to be based on certain values – modern Western society might call them Christian values; but (people say) I seem to get by, and to get by quite comfortably, with a set of values of my own choice; I don't do anyone else any harm; Jotham has his beliefs, I have mine, where's the problem?

The problem becomes apparent when the spiritual capital runs out, and when Jotham, for whose sake I have been left in peace to practise my disobedient 'religion', is replaced by Ahaz.

## 2. Captivity (28:1–8)

Ahaz is as bad as Jotham was good. In the whole history of the southern kingdom up to this point, 'only the reign of Ahaz' (says

Williamson) 'is recorded without a single redeeming feature'.[1] Again, the Chronicler puts together his material, adding considerably to Samuel/Kings from a very interesting parallel account, in such a way as to stress the dominant features of Ahaz's character and reign. 'Faithless' will be the keyword (28:22). 'The ways of the kings of Israel' (28:2) were originally a mishmash of religion, paganism together with the true faith. By the end of his life Ahaz has 'shut up the doors of the house of the LORD' (28:24), and we have paganism instead of the true faith.

And his people are dragged down with him; or rather, their own inner corruption betrays them, now that the framework of their society is no longer upheld by a godly king. The responsibility for their downfall is his, but it is also theirs. They are exactly the generation that Moses foresaw, when he spoke of the man who 'blesses himself in his heart, saying, "I shall be safe, though I walk in the stubbornness of my heart"'. That was Judah in the days of Jotham. Sooner than they bargained for, Moses' prophecy came true, and 'the LORD uprooted them from their land in anger and fury and great wrath, and cast them into another land'.[2] That would be Judah in the days of Ahaz.

For deportation from the land was to be their punishment. Read the story of 28:1–8 through the Chronicler's eyes. First he looks back to the historic time when Israel was brought into Canaan. That is the ominous background to 28:3: Ahaz had adopted 'the abominable practices of the nations *whom the LORD drove out*'. There is no mistaking the implication. Because of such sins, the Canaanites had forfeited the land; if Ahaz too indulged in them, he should not have been surprised when 'the king of Syria ... took captive a great number of his people and brought them to Damascus', or when 'the men of Israel took captive' another multitude of prisoners 'and brought the spoil to Samaria' (28:5, 8). Here the Chronicler is also looking forward, for he knows that although the kingdom of Judah will last for more than a century after the death of Ahaz, when it does end it will end in another captivity. This he sees foreshadowed here. Notice how often the word 'captive' appears in this chapter. The people's experience under Ahaz will be a repeat of the original expulsion of the Canaanites, and a foretaste of the eventual captivity of Israel.

[1] Williamson, *Israel*, p. 117.
[2] Dt. 29:19, 28.

Thirdly, the Chronicler looks inward, deep into the heart of God's people – that is, the people of the southern kingdom. What is there about them that would ever have caused the favour of God to rest upon them? At the present time, indeed, they deserve nothing but punishment, but there is no denying that God has richly blessed them in the past. Why? Is it because they have Jerusalem? or the temple of Solomon, and the true priesthood? or the throne of David, and the true kingly line? They might have banked on any or all of these. We belong to the right organization, they might have said, we talk the right language, we bear the right label, the personal sins we are too genteel to talk about do not affect our certainty that God is on our side.

Does the Chronicler share the view that God's blessing is the special prerogative of the south? If anything in a superficial reading of his book may have suggested that, this chapter demolishes the idea. He surely intends it to recall chapter 13, and the remarkable eve-of-battle address by the otherwise undistinguished king Abijah. At that time the reign of Rehoboam, through whose stupidity the kingdom broke in two, had recently come to an end; and the new king wanted to reunite Israel. The division had been 'a turn of affairs brought about by God' (10:15), but with Rehoboam gone, it was no longer appropriate. Then, it had been right for the northern rebels to leave; now, it was right for them to return. And the reason was that the south, not the north, had the true worship of God – not its outward forms only, but its inward spirit.

Now see how across two hundred years the worlds of Abijah and Ahaz answer to each other. In the tenth century BC, the northerners have forsaken the Lord, the God of their fathers; they are therefore defeated by the southerners, are given into their hands, and suffer a great slaughter (13:11–12, 15–17). In the eighth century, the *south* is given into the hand of the *northern* king, and defeated with a great slaughter, because it has forsaken the Lord, the God of its fathers (28:5–6). In the plainest possible way, by using identical words and reversing their reference, the Chronicler shows that divine favour does not belong automatically to any place, community, or form of religion as such, but only to those whose hearts are right with God. So that, again repeating his wording (Hebrew *kānaʿ* in both places), he tells us 'the men of Israel were subdued' – brought low – 'at that time', the time of Abijah, while afterwards 'the LORD brought Judah low because of Ahaz' (13:18; 28:19).

## 3. Conviction (28:9–15)

We come now to one of the most fascinating paragraphs in the whole of Chronicles. It is unusual, in that it deals with events in Samaria, in the northern kingdom. It is important in developing the lessons the Chronicler wants to draw from the relation between north and south. And it is prophetic, setting the scene for an immensely influential passage in the New Testament.

Moving into the unfamiliar territory north of the border, the Chronicler begins by drawing out likenesses between north and south. He has just been saying, in effect, 'In the reign of Abijah, north was bad; in the reign of Ahaz, south is bad.' But he does not take the further step of saying 'Then, north was bad and south was good; now, south is bad *and north is good.*' The faithlessness of Ahaz does not automatically mean that his northern opponent is on the side of the angels. As on other occasions,[3] a punitive campaign ordained by God is taken too far. The northern king Pekah, given victory by God over the southerners, has slaughtered them 'in a rage which has reached up to heaven' (28:9). This is one more sin added to the 'guilt … already great' (28:13) which has accumulated in the north through the centuries of its rebellion.

So the wrath of God is now upon *both* the south (28:9, 25) *and* the north (28:11, 13). But being thus in the same case, each is equally in need of the mercy of God; and to the north now, as so often to the south already, a prophet is sent (28:9) with a message about the southerners killed or captured in the battle. What is more, his message is heeded. The conviction of sin, through which Judah has repeatedly been brought back to God, now for the first time comes down upon Israel too. Conviction leads to repentance, and repentance to action: the northerners 'took the captives, and with the spoil they clothed all that were naked among them; they clothed them, gave them sandals, provided them with food and drink, and anointed them; and carrying all the feeble among them on asses, they brought them to their kinsfolk at Jericho, the city of palm trees' (28:15). This astonishing verse, shining like a good deed in a naughty world,[4] is one to which we shall return.

When Israel as well as Judah knows at last what it is to be convicted by the Spirit of God, both are abased to the same level, and the Chronicler is in a position to take his story forward into its

[3] *Cf.* Is. 10:5–19; Zc. 1:15.
[4] Shakespeare, *Merchant of Venice*, V.i.91.

next stage. He has never approved of the northern kings; for him the descendants of David are the only royal line. The ordinary people of the north, on the other hand, he regards as 'brothers' to those of the south. Not only under the united monarchy (1 Ch. 12:39; 13:2), but also at the time of the division (11:4) and here again in this story (28:8, 11, 15),[5] the word is used to bind all the tribes together as a single family.

And now something else seems to have happened to bring one step nearer the reunion of the family, so that its political structure may correspond to the spiritual facts. Who in Samaria, the northern capital, gives orders for the southern captives to be returned? Not King Pekah, nor yet his successor Hoshea, but 'certain chiefs ... of the men of Ephraim' (28:12). It may well be that between the slaughter of 120 southern 'thousands'[6] in 28:6, and the capture of 200 more in 28:8, momentous events have taken place: the Assyrian invasion of the north, the fall of Samaria, and the abolition of the northern monarchy.[7] If so, the Ephraimite chiefs no doubt represent the only local authority left. It would be just like the Chronicler to treat the downfall of the northern kingdom with such casual indifference – 'Oh, by the way, affairs in the north are now run by chiefs, not kings.' And his occasional use of the title 'king of Israel' for a southern king is perhaps after all not careless but deliberate, especially here in 28:19. The removal of the last king in Samaria is the removal of one more barrier to the unification of the kingdom. It reminds us again of one of the Chronicler's main themes, that God promises his blessing to a people united around a Davidic king.

However that may be, no royal personages confuse the issue in the paragraph before us. It is not kings, but commoners, who occupy the stage, and we are dealing not with principles or patterns, but with flesh-and-blood people, 'of like nature with ourselves'.[8] As in 27:1–9 we saw people sinning in spite of a good king, and in 28:1–8 people suffering partly because of a bad king, here in 28:9–15 we see

---

[5] 'Kinsfolk' (RSV) is *ahîm*, 'brothers', as in the other instances.

[6] *Cf.* p. 38 above.

[7] 2 Ki. 18:10 says that Samaria fell in the sixth year of Hezekiah, Ahaz's son, and seems to contradict the view put forward here, that it fell during the reign of Ahaz. In fact both are true, because of Judah's co-regency system. When Pekah ruled Israel (28:6), Ahaz was ruling Judah jointly with his father Jotham. When Samaria fell in 722 BC and there were no more kings in the north, Jotham was dead, and Ahaz and his son Hezekiah were ruling jointly in the south.

[8] Jas. 5:17.

people convicted even where there is no king. The Spirit of God is at work among his people still, although the formal instrument of his rule is missing. Whatever significant events may be happening on the higher political levels, the daily life of ordinary people, and the dealings of God with their souls, continue.

## 4. Conscience (28:16–27)

Ahaz flounders deeper and deeper into the quagmire of faithlessness, and one can only assume that the spiritually-minded among his subjects become more and more unhappy with his leadership. Where sin and suffering have been understood, and the Spirit has brought conviction, conscience will be tender. The resultant opinion in the collective mind of Israel will emerge when she finally takes stock of the reign of this regrettable king.

Meanwhile he goes from bad to worse, panicking under the pressure of a series of assaults by enemy armies. Help, often in the Chronicler's story sought from God by his people in their time of need, has equally often been his gift to them, the simple but practical answer to their prayers. It is a measure of Ahaz's wickedness that in his need he looks for help to anyone except the Lord. His land is invaded, his forces defeated, and his subjects taken captive, again and again – by Syria (28:5a), by Israel (28:5b), by Edom (28:17), by Philistia (28:18). He cries out for help; but to whom? An appeal 'to the king of Assyria for help' (28:16) had thoroughly unsatisfactory results: 'Tiglath-Pileser ... came to him, but gave him trouble instead' (28:20 NIV); when all was said and done, the expensive appeal 'did not help him' (28:21). Then 'he sacrificed to the gods of Damascus which had defeated him, "... that they may help me." ' But there was no help there either; 'they were the ruin of him' (28:23).

Indeed, says the Chronicler, 'they were the ruin of him, and of all Israel'. But there were some left whose conscience must have rebelled long before that. They were people of influence, for it is in connection with the arrangements made for the royal funeral that we eventually hear their indignant protest. It is the voice of the true Israel which says 'This really will not do', and which declares, when at last Ahaz dies, that he shall not have the honour of burial among the tombs of the kings (28:27). Conscience knows that just as Saul was faithless (1 Ch. 10:13–14), so that the nation needed a David to put things right, so Ahaz has been faithless (28:19), and a Hezekiah will be needed to repair the damage.

So in the reign of 'the dreadful Ahaz', 'an all-time low' as McConville calls it,[9] there is a gleam of hope. Conscience is awake, the word of God is still 'living and active',[10] and a remarkable incident has reminded ordinary Israelites in both north and south of what it really means to be God's people.

This is the one described in the paragraph 28:9–15, to which we have already referred, the sending back to Judah of prisoners who had earlier been captured and taken to Samaria. The prophet Oded has rebuked the victorious northern soldiers, and supported by Ephraimite chiefs has told them that that is what they must do. Let us now take the story on from there, and ask ourselves, as we do so, what we are reminded of. Do we hear pre-echoes of another, much more familiar, passage of Scripture?

It is a story which will eventually take us down the road to Jericho. But much happens before we get there. The people concerned have been attacked by brigands, and we should picture them, when Samaria sets eyes on them, as being stripped, beaten, and half dead. It is this same Samaria, however, which then has compassion on the victims, anoints them, clothes and feeds them, mounts all the feeble among them on asses, and brings them on their homeward way.

Now where have we heard all this before?

One of the delights of reading Chronicles is the frequency with which one can say with the Psalmist, 'I rejoice at thy word like one who finds great spoil.'[11] Often in our study of these books we have found springing out from the page words which we remember well from hymns or sermons or liturgies, and we have said 'So *that's* where they come from!' In this passage, I for one find myself exclaiming, 'So *that's* where the story of the Good Samaritan comes from!' We do not have space here for a detailed study of the relation between Luke 10 and 2 Chronicles 28.[12] Suffice it to say that Jesus, his quick perceptive brain stored since childhood with the scriptures of the Old Testament, must have known this narrative of the Chronicler's, and could not but have had it in mind when telling the

[9] McConville, p. 224.
[10] Heb. 4:12.     [11] Ps. 119:162.
[12] *Cf.* F. Scott Spencer, '2 Chronicles 28:5–11 and the parable of the Good Samaritan', in the *Westminster Theological Journal*, 46, 1984, pp. 317–349.

parable of the man from Samaria who showed such practical loving care towards the man from Jericho.[13]

It is not perhaps unreasonable, therefore, to assume that Jesus would have understood the original story to be illustrating the kind of point that he wanted to make in his re-telling of it. In other words, both stories have to do with the question 'Who is my neighbour?'.[14] The answer in each case is that Samaria is my neighbour. It is true that the phrase 'man of Samaria' means something different in Ahaz's time from what it means in the Chronicler's time, or in Jesus's time. But it always means someone whose connection with the true faith (*my* faith) is suspect, but who to my surprise shows me the kind of love that one finds only among the people of God.

I have suggested that in these chapters the kings recede, and the common people come to the footlights. In Chronicles, kings and commoners alike are no doubt in one respect actors in a drama staged for our instruction. But in another respect the actors are human under the greasepaint, and teach us other lessons by their real-life relationships; not least when the train of asses from Samaria brings the repatriated prisoners home to the city of palm trees, to illustrate the sentence which sums up all the commandments, 'You shall love your neighbour as yourself.'[15]

# 2 Chronicles 29 – 32

## 21.  Hezekiah: the kingdom renewed

So we come to one of the greatest, perhaps *the* greatest, of all who succeeded David and Solomon on the throne in Jerusalem. From

---

[13] 'The man from Jericho', because if the Old Testament story is indeed the background to the New Testament one, the man Jesus describes as going *to* Jericho was presumably going home.

[14] Lk. 10:29.      [15] Rom. 13:9.

their time onwards there is no king quite like Hezekiah. He is the 'golden boy' of Chronicles. He is not faultless, and the Chronicler is not uncritical of him, but he is nevertheless greatly to be praised, and we shall find that reasons for both blame and praise are brought out as the Chronicler rewrites the Samuel/Kings story.

For here, as everywhere, a comparison between the earlier and later histories is of keen interest. Three chapters of 2 Kings (18–20) run parallel to four chapters of 2 Chronicles (29–32), but the two accounts are very different. As we have noticed often before, it is not at all the Chronicler's intention to contradict Samuel/Kings. He is neither falsifying something true, nor correcting something false. He wishes rather to show the importance of a particular kind of truth, and does so by enlarging on certain aspects of the reign in question and minimizing others. To put it another way, he shifts the hub of interest: regard *these* facts as the circle's centre, he says, and leave *those* out towards the circumference, and a new truth will emerge.

This is what happens to the earlier account of Hezekiah. The mere four verses at its beginning which deal with his religious reforms are expanded to three whole chapters, three-quarters of the Chronicler's narrative (2 Ki. 18:3–6; 2 Ch. 29–31). The Assyrian invasion of both Israelite kingdoms, in the course of which the northern one was destroyed, occupies sixty-six verses in 2 Kings; this is reduced to twenty-one in 2 Chronicles (2 Ki. 18:9–19:37; 2 Ch. 32:1–21). To the events of Hezekiah's later days the Chronicler gives only half the space which Samuel/Kings has devoted to them (2 Ki. 20:1–21; 2 Ch. 32:24–33). Chameleon-like, the story takes on a new colour as some cells expand and others contract against the background of the Chronicler's theology of history.

We shall spend most time on the matters which he treats at greatest length, since he obviously thinks them so important. On the other hand, there are things he touches on briefly, near the end of his account, which are also worth attention. Like the reference to Eloth in the 'headline' to the story of Uzziah (26:2),[1] they are presumably significant even though they are given so little space — as if the Chronicler were saying, 'Don't forget, will you, that Hezekiah was the king who ...'. There must be a reason why, when such things are mentioned so briefly, they are in such a carefully

---

[1] See above, pp. 222–224.

edited work mentioned at all. Thirdly, there are matters which are actually left out of the Chronicler's narrative altogether, not because he considers them unimportant, but because they will be taken for granted by his readers. They form the historical backdrop to the story. As we embark on it – the story of this remarkable shepherd-king pastoring his flock through one of the most critical periods of its history – it is with these unspoken assumptions that we begin.

## 1. The pastor facing crisis

It is no ordinary crisis that Hezekiah faces, none of your minor day-to-day upsets which will be forgotten this time next year, nor yet the kind of emergency which, though dire in itself, is nonetheless that of one person alone. What is hinted here and there in the story, nowhere spelt out but everywhere implied, is the black background to the whole of this period. We return to the chapter which deals with the reign of Hezekiah's father Ahaz, and in the simple words 'At that time king Ahaz sent to the king of Assyria for help' (28:16) we can already hear the growl of distant thunder. Ahaz was in trouble, harassed on every side by the other kings of the Mediterranean seaboard, and he eventually took the desperate step of appealing over the heads of his neighbours to a greater power, the king of Assyria. But the growing might of Assyria was itself one of the main reasons for the turmoil among the petty states of the region. It was because of this that Israel and Syria had formed an alliance, and were trying to unite the neighbouring nations with them in opposition to the threat from the east. Ahaz of Judah could not be allowed to step out of line (28:5). In this situation Ahaz was (as it no doubt seemed to him) more realistic than to imagine that all the states of the Levant put together could in the end withstand the Assyrian juggernaut. He chose the strategy 'If you can't beat it, join it'. And although he was sowing the wind, and would reap the whirlwind – Tiglath-Pileser, when he came, 'afflicted him instead of strengthening him' (28:20) – he did at any rate recognize that Assyria was the ultimate bogey.

We quite misunderstand the situation if our picture of this ancient empire is only that of Byron's lines: 'The Assyrian came down like the wolf on the fold, And his cohorts were gleaming in purple and gold; And the sheen of their spears was like stars on the sea, When the blue wave rolls nightly on deep Galilee.'[2] Colourful it may have been, but its contemporaries were a great deal more impressed by its reputation as the most brutal, barbarous, ruthless war-machine the world had ever known. Its atrocities were a byword, and its name was universally loathed and feared. This was the threat that loomed over the peoples of the Bible lands in the latter part of the eighth century BC.

Is it misleading to compare such a threat with those which dismay the nations of our own time? I think not; and for two reasons. It might be argued that what today's world fears is a destruction infinitely more terrible than any the ancient world could have imagined. But what difference does that make in actual experience? It is foolish to say that if Ahaz and Hezekiah had known something about the horrors of nuclear war, they would have found Assyria considerably less terrifying. The fact was that the whole fabric of their society, human life as they knew it, with all that made it worth living, was threatened. It might on the other hand be argued that the two situations are different not so much in degree as in kind, since the drama of Old Testament days, though played out on the stage of international politics, focuses on the people of God, and they do not now form a political entity as they did then. This is true, and is indeed my contention throughout these studies. For example, a lesson on 'How to be a king in Judah' is to be understood by us as a lesson, not on 'How to run a secular twentieth-century state', but on 'How to be a pastor in the Christian church'; because the subject of such a lesson is fundamentally leadership among the people of God. But having said that, we should remember that Assyria does have its modern equivalents on the political scene as well as in the spiritual world, and we have to know how to face both kinds. The world in which today's church lives is surely more aware than it has been for two centuries past of the many types of 'Assyrian' menace that threaten to engulf it. How well equipped are God's people to face crises of such magnitude?

When on the death of Ahaz Hezekiah assumed sole control of the kingdom, he knew exactly how he was going to approach the problem. This was partly no doubt in reaction against the follies of his father. Even if it were excusable fear and panic which had driven Ahaz from one godless expedient to another, his refusal to look for help in the one place where it was to be found must have been an

---

[2] Lord Byron, *The Destruction of Sennacherib*.

object lesson to his son. More than that, Hezekiah accepted the crisis as a positive challenge. Samuel Johnson once wrote to his friend Boswell, 'Depend upon it, Sir, when a man knows he is to be hanged in a fortnight, it concentrates his mind wonderfully'.[3] By this time the Assyrian is at the very frontier of Judah. The northern kingdom, its capital Samaria, and its last hopeless kings, have been destroyed. An outlook so obviously dreadful that the Chronicler thinks it scarcely worth mentioning again certainly concentrates the mind of this leader of God's people. Hezekiah faces the grim prospect with a clear eye, and rises to the occasion.

## 2. The pastor coping with crisis

We move from an aspect of the story which for the Chronicler almost goes without saying, to one on which he has a great deal to say – almost four full chapters. He takes it for granted that his readers know about the world crisis which Hezekiah had to face on his accession to the throne. But he wishes to describe at length how the young king coped with it.

He did so, this 'golden boy', by returning quite deliberately, in mind and spirit, to the Golden Age of his nation. Read chapters 29 to 32 alongside chapters 7 to 9, and you will find a remarkable number of parallels between the achievements, both religious and secular, of Hezekiah's reign, and those of the reign of his ancestor Solomon.[4] Note also that he is the first of the twelve kings since the kingdom split in two of whom it is said that he did 'according to all that David his father had done' (29:2). Jotham had followed 'all that his father Uzziah had done' (27:2); Uzziah, 'all that his father Amaziah had done' (26:4); but Hezekiah went right back to David and Solomon, to the roots of his kingdom's life and worship, seeing clearly that the crisis which threatened him with being 'hanged in a fortnight' at the same time provided him with the opportunity to give his people a new lease of life.

But everything in its order. A clear view of how to cope with the crisis meant that he must look first, not to the threat, nor to the threatened, but to the God who was over both.

---

[3] James Boswell, *Life of Johnson*, iii.167.

[4] 'The Chronicler has gone out of his way to present Hezekiah as a second Solomon' (Williamson, pp. 350f.). Williamson elsewhere (*Israel*, pp. 119–125) draws out the parallels in detail.

### a. Looking up to God (29:1–36)

Before anything else, the concern of the pastor of God's people is God himself. 'In the first year of his reign, in the first month' – indeed on the very 'first day' – 'he opened the doors of the house of the LORD', long neglected, even desecrated (29:3, 17).[5] God, and the worship and obedience of God, must come first.

Within this first enterprise also the order of events is significant. The king takes the initiative, and does so by a formal address to Judah's religious leaders (29:4–11). He speaks as a prophet.[6] Through him God is directing his people to recognize that their troubles are the result of sin, and to be diligent in setting right their religious life and re-consecrating themselves to the Lord's service. Then, because this is a prophetic word from God and therefore effective, the Levites respond; practical and thorough repentance means in their terms a literal cleaning out of the temple (29:12–19). Next the rituals of sacrifice (29:20–24) and praise (29:25–30) are recommenced. Here Hezekiah is reaching even further back into the past; 'with rejoicing and with singing, according to the order of David', are linked 'burnt offerings to the LORD, as it is written in the law of Moses'.[7] The burnt offering represents the total consecration of oneself to God. How many of his servants can testify that that handing over was for them not a deprivation, but a joyous fulfilment! 'When the burnt offering began, the song to the LORD began also' (29:27).[8] Lastly the whole assembly joins in 'the service of the house of the LORD' (29:31–36). It is important to note that the entire festival, a splendid beginning to Hezekiah's reign, was on the one hand a matter of grace – it was 'what God had done for the people' (29:36); yet it was on the other hand a matter of obedience to the preached word, for we are reminded frequently that all was done at the king's command, which was at the same time the

[5] The mention in the next chapter of 'the passover in the second month' (30:2) seems to indicate that the Chronicler is talking about the first/second months of the calendar year, *i.e.* Nisan and Iyyar in Hezekiah's first full regnal year, rather than the first/second months after his father's death. But his interest is clearly not so much in dates as in what came 'first' on Hezekiah's agenda.

[6] On the relation in Chronicles between the roles of prophet, priest, and king, see above, pp. 218–220.

[7] A connection noted at the time of an earlier temple restoration, that of the days of Joash and Jehoiada (23:18).

[8] If I may add my own testimony, I have never forgotten this text, or its personal significance for me, since I heard Fred Mitchell preach on it at the Keswick Convention over thirty years ago (July 16, 1952).

commandment given through kings and prophets from the Lord himself (29:25).

Such is the revival of true religion which is, for Hezekiah, of prime importance as he faces the Assyrian threat. It is the beginning of a process which will result in tiny Judah surviving when her mighty enemy has crumbled to dust.

The irony is that Assyria, for all her power and sophistication, simply cannot see the relevance of it. As John Hercus suggests, it will rate an inch or two in the *Nineveh Morning Advertiser*, and be good for a passing laugh in 'a culture where Aggressiveness, Pride and Greed are the Holy Trinity'.[9] The world expects everyone to react to a crisis in terms of that crisis. And the church, if it is sufficiently infected with worldliness, will readily oblige. When there is a financial crisis, the first thing we think about is money. When there is a communications crisis, our prime concern is to learn how to talk the language of the modern generation. When there is a church attendance crisis, we make it our chief aim to get numbers up. If Hezekiah had responded to a military threat in a military way, the Assyrians would have understood that. Army would have been matched against army, with dire consequences for Judah. But instead he first looked up to God. Were he and his people right with God? Was God's temple open, clean, glorious with offerings and praise? The result was that when the invaders did reach Jerusalem the presence of God filled it, and it was impregnable.

### b. Looking round at the church (30:1 – 31:1)

Hezekiah's looking to God meant in practical terms the reopening of the temple with great celebrations. An event more formal and official, though no less celebratory, is in order as he extends the scope of his reforms to include God's people as a whole. The passover, the festival of the first month, is imminent, and nothing could be more appropriate than that reminder of the great acts by which God at the time of the exodus rescued Israel from slavery and constituted them his own people.

Few of the continuities between Old Testament and New are as well-established as that between the death of the lamb in Egypt and the death of the Lamb on Calvary. It is in no way a fanciful notion to see in Hezekiah's invitation to all Israel to 'come to the house of the

[9] John Hercus's racy retelling of various episodes in Old Testament history, *More Pages from God's Casebook* (IVP, 1965).

LORD at Jerusalem, to keep the passover' (30:1), a precedent for the Christian leader to recall the church to its true unity around the cross of Christ.

There is a significance which the Chronicler does not fail to note in the delay of the passover's date (30:2–4). It should have taken place on the fourteenth of Nisan, the first month of the year. But 'the plan' to hold it a month later 'seemed right to the king and all the assembly'. Though this looks at first glance like the very attitude for which Jeroboam, first king of Israel, had been condemned (he 'appointed a feast on the fifteenth day of the eighth month ... in the month which he had devised of his own heart', 1 Ki. 12:32–33), it is in fact the opposite. Hezekiah is going back to the original rules, where the law lays down that in certain circumstances the passover may be delayed by one month: 'If any man ... is unclean ... or is afar off ... he shall still keep the passover to the LORD' by observing it on the fourteenth of Iyyar instead.[10] As the Chronicler points out, this is in effect the situation here: 'they could not keep it in its time because the priests had not sanctified themselves ... nor had the people assembled in Jerusalem' (30:3). Defilement and distance are the permitted grounds for postponing the festival.

With regard to the first, it is interesting to notice that Hezekiah is concerned both with outward, ritual, cleansing, and with inward cleansing. The passover cannot be held till the priests, like the temple itself, are ritually clean (29:17; 30:3). On the other hand, he does not think it wrong to waive the rules on behalf of many visitors from the northern tribes, provided their hearts are right with God (30:17–20).

The Chronicler may want his readers to hear other overtones, in that the particular kind of defilement which the law instances as a reason for postponing passover is contact with a corpse; for the pagan influence of the surrounding nations has been the touch of death infecting Judah, and still more Israel, down the years. The other clause in Numbers 9:10 is even more symbolic, for the whole nation has been 'afar off on a journey', wandering away from God. Indeed the reference is extraordinarily apt in the context of Hezekiah's reign, for his invitation does literally draw men back from great distances. He is able to send messengers through the ravaged lands of the north, where Assyrian governors now rule instead of Israelite

10 Nu. 9:10–11.

248

kings. Much of the population of Israel has been deported, and of those who remain, few respond to his call (30:10–11). But the important thing is the breadth of Hezekiah's vision. It is universal, embracing the breakaway tribes, and reaching the limits of the land: 'all Israel ... Ephraim and Manasseh', 'all Israel, from Beersheba to Dan' (30:1, 5). This is why the Chronicler can say of the festival which followed that 'since the time of Solomon the son of David king of Israel there had been nothing like this in Jerusalem' (30:26). He is speaking of something more than the magnificence of the occasion. Only David and Solomon had ruled the united monarchy; since the days of Rehoboam, Solomon's son, it had been divided. At Rehoboam's death his son, Abijah, had tried unsuccessfully to reunite it, but now, ten generations later, with the northern throne destroyed, it was at last possible at any rate in theory for representatives of all the tribes to draw together again in fellowship. Their true centre was, as it always is, the kingship and priesthood appointed by God, and the theme of their worship the redemption which makes them his people. As with the earlier assembly, all is due to the grace of God (30:12), yet at the same time springs from a full-hearted response, which in this case says 'That was good – let's do the whole thing again!' (30:21–23).

### c. Looking into the heart (31:2–31)

The new king has shown himself a man of spirituality, as with the restoration of proper temple worship he has looked first to God; then a man of broad vision, as in inviting his people to his first passover his gaze has ranged far and wide round all the tribes of Israel. Now the newly-restored religious life of the nation needs to be established as an ongoing thing. The chapter which describes this process looks into the hearts of God's people, and sees behind the outward organization of Israelite religion a remarkable inward devotion in both king and subjects.

We have commented already on the way Hezekiah's reign mirrors those of David and Solomon. Like Solomon, Hezekiah now appoints the divisions of priests and Levites, and makes offerings for the sacrifices; Solomon himself was simply following out the directions of his father, and Hezekiah like David also contributes lavishly 'from his own possessions' (31:2–3; cf. 8:12–14; 1 Ch. 29:3). This is not however a mere repeat of that golden age 250 years earlier. The founders of the dynasty were, as the Chronicler depicted them, providing a blueprint; Hezekiah is at work on the actual building. In a sense Hezekiah's situation is more 'real' than Solomon's. It is as though his great ancestors (in the halcyon days of yore, so to speak – it was all very well for *them*!) conjured up a vision of how things ought to be, while Hezekiah has to try to make it come true in his modern world of hard facts, hard cash, and perhaps hard people.

If he did have fears about the hardness of his people, they were blow 1 away in the astonishing sequel. The practical question, which has been asked before in Chronicles,[11] is how one may know that a real spiritual work is going on in the hearts of God's people; and as before, the practical answer is the thoroughly earthy one of the pocket, the purse, and the cheque-book. The need of the moment is the ongoing support of the ministry, the providing of a livelihood for those whose calling is to 'give themselves to the law of the LORD' (31:4). The challenge comes initially to the residents of Jerusalem, but the news gets out, and people all over the country begin to contribute. Hezekiah himself is taken aback by the way his proclamation is heard not as an irksome demand but as a welcome opportunity to be generous (31:4–10). Those who live near enough to drive cattle and sheep to the city as offerings do so, contributions of all kinds come in abundance, and from the Feast of Weeks at the beginning of harvest to the Feast of Tabernacles at the end of it ('third month ... seventh month') the gifts flow in till there is far more than enough. It is the days of David come again, and as then, what it shows is the inward state of the giver: 'I know, my God, that thou triest the *heart* ... in the uprightness of my heart I have freely offered all these things, and now I have seen thy people ... offering freely and joyously to thee' (1 Ch. 29:17).

Are we to imagine that the detailed organizing which followed – storage arrangements, a hierarchy of officials, registration lists, all the paraphernalia beloved of bureaucrats (31:11–19) – is out of keeping with the heart-devotion expressed in the first part of the chapter? Not at all. The response of the heart may sometimes ignore rules and regulations, but there is a difference between structures which hinder the flow and those which channel it. What we see operating here is a principle to be found throughout Scripture, that of the proper relation between organism and organization, spontaneity and preparedness, content and form, spirit and word. In each case, not only is the latter as important as the former, it is actually

---

[11] See above, pp. 93, 113–114.

an appropriate expression of it. Three times in this part of the chapter we find the word 'faithful' or 'faithfully', which speaks of the diligence and perseverance of people who know how easily the first impulse can be lost. But the fact remains that the structures of 31:11-19 would have been a lifeless skeleton if Hezekiah had not seen, when he looked into the hearts of his people in 31:4-10, a true love for God, which God himself had put there.

And all this, we remind ourselves, with the Assyrian menace at the gates, its sword only temporarily sheathed! But it is now, after three chapters of preparation, that Hezekiah is at last ready to face the drawing of that sword.

### d. Looking out to the enemy (32:1-23)

The last three chapters have been an enormous expansion of a few short verses at the beginning of 2 Kings 18. Now the Chronicler is ready to take up the subject of the eventual arrival of the Assyrians at Jerusalem, and in this case he condenses the account in his main source-book – sixty-two verses there (2 Ki. 18:13 – 19:37) become twenty-three here. The Samuel/Kings narrative is complicated, and the Chronicler simplifies it considerably.[12] His attitude to history is well shown by the first verse of this chapter. He is, as we have often seen, passionately interested in facts, but that is not to say that he is interested in dates. His readers can learn elsewhere that the invasion finally took place 'in the fourteenth year of King Hezekiah' (2 Ki. 18:13); he is more concerned with the order of events and the theological relation between them – 'after these things and these acts of faithfulness', after, that is, Hezekiah's religious reforms and spiritual preparation, 'Sennacherib king of Assyria came and invaded Judah' (32:1). Having first looked up to the God who appointed him a shepherd of his flock, then around him with a gaze which embraces all the scattered sheep of Israel, then into the hearts of his people to find there a true practical response to his call, Hezekiah is now at last in a position to look out to the enemy, whom the providence of God has kept at bay for these fourteen years of preparation.

His spirit of confident *resistance* comes across clearly in 32:1-8. It would be easy to contrast this with an apparent spirit of craven fear in the older account, where his message to the Assyrian king is 'I have done wrong; withdraw from me; whatever you impose on me I

[12] See the discussion in Williamson, pp. 378ff.

will bear' (2 Ki. 18:14), and the invaders are bought off at great cost. But there is no reason why Hezekiah should not have been deliberately buying himself a brief respite in which he might 'set to work resolutely' (32:5) on a defiant strengthening of his capital against the renewed attack he knew would come.

His resistance is a matter of both action (32:2–6) and trust (32:7–8). The two can of course be mutually exclusive, and the harsh words of Isaiah, addressed to just this situation,[13] were for those in Jerusalem at the time who were active precisely because they were faithless: 'In that day you looked to the weapons of the House of the Forest, and you saw that the breaches of the city of David were many, and you collected the waters of the lower pool, and you counted the houses of Jerusalem, and you broke down the houses to fortify the wall. You made a reservoir between the two walls for the water of the old pool. But you did not look to him who did it, or have regard for him who planned it long ago.' Hezekiah, however, did have regard for that mighty God, and knew that he expected both faith and action. In another age he would have told his armies to trust in God and keep their powder dry.

As he and his people look out at their enemies, listening to the 'voice of the dragon',[14] they are given a spirit of *perception*. As Paul will say concerning the ultimate enemy of God's people, 'We are not ignorant of his designs.'[15] In the very taunt that Hezekiah is misleading Judah, the Assyrian spokesman betrays the fact that he does not understand the situation. No other nation's god has been able to rescue it from Assyria; 'how much less' can Judah expect to be rescued by a God whose altars Hezekiah has himself torn down (32:10–15)! There was surely at that point, to the enemy's puzzlement, derisive laughter from the walls of Jerusalem. So the Assyrians assumed that the destruction of the 'high places' was an *insult* to Yahweh! To think that behind the fearsome assault mounted against God's people there should be so total a misunderstanding of the principles on which they built their resistance! Powerful and subtle though their enemy may be, he cannot see through them as they can see through him.[16]

[13] Note the close parallels between this passage (Is. 22:8b–11) and 2 Ch. 32:3–5.
[14] *Cf.* Rev. 13:11.    [15] 2 Cor. 2:11.
[16] It is again with reference to the great Enemy, and the ridicule to which perception leads, that C. S. Lewis adduces two telling quotations on the flyleaf of *The Screwtape Letters* (Geoffrey Bles, 1942): from Martin Luther, 'The best way to drive out the devil, if he will not yield to texts of Scripture, is to jeer and flout him, for he cannot bear scorn'; from Thomas More, 'The devill ... the prowde spirite ... cannot endure to be mocked'.

However, perception leads not only to presumed derision, but to an expressed *revulsion*. The Chronicler, at any rate, expresses such a feeling, and without doubt intends us to believe that Hezekiah and his people felt it too (32:16–19). In speeches the Assyrians speak 'against the LORD and his anointed' (32:16 is a clear echo of Psalm 2:2), in letters they 'cast contempt on the LORD the God of Israel' (32:17), and in the howl of the mob the God of Jerusalem is degraded to the level of 'the gods of the peoples of the earth, which are the work of men's hands' (32:19). Those whose perception has been sharpened through spiritual exercise are quite properly revolted by such insults to their God and Saviour. The Chronicler reveals finally the spirit of *prayer* through which the outcome is to be decided. Where there is, as here, 'a direct challenge to God's sovereignty ... Hezekiah acts in the only appropriate manner',[17] and with Isaiah cries to heaven. It is an appeal to the One whose authority is being called in question, and he is vindicating himself when he destroys the Assyrian menace (32:20–23). Maybe it was originally the threat of being 'hanged in a fortnight' that had concentrated Hezekiah's mind. But the key to the final victory was that he looked beyond the threat to the power and glory of the Lord, and saw to it that he and his people were in a right relation to their God.

## 3. The pastor finding resources (32:24–33)

Why now, after dealing with what are clearly to his mind the major events of Hezekiah's reign, does the Chronicler add these final paragraphs? His notes are brief, not to say cryptic, but we are surely intended to see meaning in them. And they do, on reflection, tell us something of where Hezekiah found the resources to cope with the crises of his time.

He is not perfect. To depict him as a superman would be the exact opposite of the Chronicler's intention. He is a fallible human being, trying, as every other leader and pastor must try, to care for God's people according to the David/Solomon ideal, and his very failures should encourage us. For failures there were. The reference to Hezekiah's illness could scarcely be briefer, but readers of the older history know the details, the king's prayer which was encouraged by his friend Isaiah, and the sign which God gave to confirm his

[17] Williamson, pp. 384f.

promise of healing, namely the miraculous going backwards of the
shadow on the sundial (2 Ki. 20:1–11). In this matter Hezekiah's
heart was right. But 'in the matter of the envoys of the princes of
Babylon, who had been sent to him to enquire about the sign', God
was testing him (32:31), and found that his heart was not right.
Again, the details are in 2 Kings 20 (verses 12–19). The pride with
which Hezekiah showed his wealth to his visitors – there was no
doubt a political motive in the visit, as Babylon and Judah each
sized up the other, and the possibility of an anti-Assyrian coalition –
was a pride which God did not approve (32:25). In this case also
Isaiah stood at the king's elbow, though now the quiet counsel was a
word not of encouragement but of rebuke.

The two incidents together take us to the heart of the matter, and
to one of the most unforgettable images of those historic times. Let
me remind you, says the Chronicler, that Hezekiah was the man
who 'closed the upper outlet of the waters of Gihon and directed
them down to the west side of the city of David' (32:30). Like many
other visitors to Jerusalem, I have myself walked, or rather waded,
the length of the underground conduit through which he 'directed'
the city's all-important water supply. Although in general old
Jerusalem crowned a hilltop, and its walls enclosed the higher
ground, the lie of the land is such that this southern point of the city
was slightly lower than the spring of Gihon, even though the latter
was outside the walls. Down a gentle gradient, therefore, through a
tunnel cut in the solid rock of the hillside, the precious water flowed
to its reservoir.

Did this feat of engineering in fact show a lack of faith, as Isaiah
says it did?[18] As we have noted,[19] that depends on the person
concerned; and the Chronicler seems to imply clearly that for
Hezekiah at any rate it was one of the works by which he actually
showed faith, not the lack of it.[20] For these are the waters of Siloam,
or Shiloah; and although a New Testament reference may come at

---

[18] Is. 22:11.

[19] See above, p. 252.

[20] Cf. Jas. 2:18. On the other hand, Alec Motyer suggests in a private communication that
in the light of Is. 22 the Chronicler may intend a contrast between faithless labour, i.e.
Hezekiah's military preparations (including the tunnel), and the proper response to the
Assyrian threat, namely trust and prayer (including leaving the waters of Shiloah as God had
made them). McConville (p. 247) takes the view expressed in my own comments: the tunnel
project 'is one of the tokens that Hezekiah "prospered in all his works" (v. 30). Had the
Chronicler taken a dim view of the matter he could easily have referred to it as a part of
Hezekiah's failure (v. 25).'

once to our mind,[21] perhaps the Chronicler is pointing us to another Old Testament one, again in the writings of Isaiah. In the reign of Hezekiah's father Ahaz, before the tunnel was built, the spring had fed another Shiloah pool, through an open channel outside the city wall. But even then the water was symbolic. Ahaz and his people, turning from one hopeless political expedient to another, but unwilling even in the terror of those days to turn back to God, 'refused the waters of Shiloah that flow gently'.[22] His son knew better. He could rely on God, and he could rely on Isaiah, the mouthpiece of God's word, just as he could rely on the waters of Shiloah that flow gently. He saw to it that that quiet, unspectacular, but never-failing source of renewal could always be looked to within the walls of the city of God.

> See, the streams of living waters,
>   Springing from eternal love,
> Well supply thy sons and daughters,
>   And all fear of want remove;
> Who can faint while such a river
>   Ever flows their thirst to assuage –
> Grace, which like the Lord, the Giver,
>   Never fails from age to age?[23]

# 2 Chronicles 33

## 22.  Manasseh and Amon: God's dealings with the worst of men

The difference between Hezekiah and his son Manasseh is so striking that one might almost wonder whether the Chronicler is deliberately setting one against the other, repeating on the grand scale the

[21] Jn. 9:7.
[22] Is. 8:6.
[23] John Newton, *Glorious things of thee are spoken*.

contrast between the two previous generations, Jotham the Good and Ahaz the Bad. In the longer perspective, however, we shall find that chapters 29 to 33 are not meant to be larger-than-life portraits of Hezekiah the Very Good and Manasseh the Very Bad, contrasting with each other. The Chronicler sees in this period a more complex and instructive pattern than that; and it is not he, but the earlier historian, the author of Samuel/Kings, who 'can say no good word of Manasseh, but instead brands him as the worst king ever to sit on David's throne, whose sin was such that it could never be forgiven'.[1] Before we consider how the Chronicler depicts Hezekiah's son and successor, let us see the picture which would have been familiar already to him and his readers.

## 1.   Manasseh in Samuel/Kings

The fifty-five-year reign of Manasseh was longer, and worse, than that of any other king of Judah. He was more provocatively wicked even than his grandfather, the deplorable Ahaz. The Chronicler will reproduce practically everything which Samuel/Kings includes in the catalogue of Manasseh's sins (2 Ki. 21:1–9). No doubt they are evils which in themselves are hardly likely to tempt the modern reader; but seeing them against their biblical background, we can deduce the attitudes of moral perversity which lay behind them.

For whatever reason (and he should at least be given the credit for sinning for a reason: he was an able politician!), he broke down the dikes which had been built against the old pagan religion of the surrounding nations, and it came flooding back in. The outward forms of the worship of Yahweh, the God of Israel, would have continued, but the ranging of Canaanite practices alongside them emptied them of meaning. Monotheism (one God over all the nations) could so easily become henotheism (one god for each of the nations). Manasseh was in fact distrusting God's providence. The attitude is modern enough: we say we believe in God, but in practice we hedge our bets by trusting several other sources of help besides, just in case he lets us down.

Further, Manasseh was desecrating God's sanctuary. There in his capital city stood the temple, 'of which the LORD said ... "In this house ... I will put my name"' (2 Ki. 21:7). Manasseh, if he was to be consistent, could not leave that one place as a testimony to the

[1] J. Bright, *A History of Israel*, (SCM, 1960), p. 291.

exclusive claims of Yahweh. There also he must set up his belt-and-braces religion. Of this sin too every generation stands in danger: in the very sanctuary – wherever, that is, we are face to face with God in prayer and worship – to allow other things to dominate our minds, so that he is not at that crucial point the only true God.

Then, Manasseh degraded God's creatures. He had not been blessed with sons in order to burn them alive. He would have pleaded that his motive was not sadism, but (given the religious opinions of the time) a patriotic desire to enlist the help of some further god. The fact would have remained that in God's order of creation that was not what children were for. Manasseh's sin is repeated, in essence, whenever man uses or manipulates his fellow-men for some supposedly higher good than their own welfare – or, indeed, uses any part of God's creation for purposes other than those which God intends.

The list of sins headed by the burning of his own sons is all to do with magic and the occult. In these Manasseh was despising God's word – not simply in the sense that the law explicitly forbade such practices,[2] but in the sense that magic is the attempt to make the forces of nature and supernature do what *I* say, when in truth I ought to be happy to submit to what *God* says.

The long and the short of it was that Manasseh was determinedly cutting himself off from the everlasting covenant name of God, as the record states twice over (2 Ki. 21:4, 7). The irony was that Manasseh's object in all this was without doubt to strengthen his position, when all the time the covenant had said plainly that a nation following those ways would lose the land (verse 2) while a nation following the Lord's ways would keep it (verse 8). Since the doings of Manasseh were the kind of thing which had caused the Canaanite nations to forfeit their place in it, they would now cause Israel likewise to forfeit it. Such was the irreversible damage he was doing to his own nation's destiny, and the bloodshed with which he filled Jerusalem was a foretaste of how Judah's enemies would later treat her because of him. Six more reigns were to elapse before the kingdom of Judah finally fell, but already the die was cast.

This is the conclusion which the author of Kings emphasizes three times over (2 Ki. 21:10–15; 23:26–27; 24:3–4). He takes a long-term view of the historical consequences of Manasseh's reign which moves him to sum it up as 'the acts of Manasseh, and all that

[2] Dt. 18:10–12.

he did, and the sin that he committed' (2 Ki. 21:17). The Chronicler, however, reflecting on the same events, sees that they will bear a further interpretation.

## 2. Manasseh in Chronicles

The Chronicler is as concerned as his predecessor was to point out the effects of sin. Both historians note the moral consequences of the actions of men. But the Chronicler regularly deals in immediate consequences: 'the soul that sins shall die'.[3] Though it is true that one man's sin can cause others to suffer sixty years after he is dead and gone, this is not the kind of lesson which Chronicles as a whole aims to teach. It would be easy therefore to say that a new second half of the story of Manasseh has been more or less invented (with or without some foundation in fact, that is) by the Chronicler. What Manasseh's sin leads to is not the fall of Jerusalem long after his death, as Samuel/Kings says, but 'distress' for him himself, as he is taken by Assyrian forces 'with hooks and ... fetters of bronze' to Babylon (33:11–12). This in turn leads to a personal repentance, through which he comes at last to a true knowledge of God, and a restoration not only of the man but of the religious life, public works, and military strength of his nation. Thus the summary in Chronicles, unlike that in Samuel/Kings, refers to 'his prayer' as well as 'his sin' (33:13–20).

If this sequel is a fabrication, it is simple enough to see why the Chronicler has made it up. But we must ask yet again the prior question: does the Chronicler, in his whole approach to the story of Israel, believe that God is more likely to convey his truth through fact or through semi-fiction? If by this time the premiss is well-established (as I believe it to be) that the Chronicler's interest is facts, then it has to be said that there is actually no reason why the events of 33:11–13 should not be historically true as he has recounted them. The omission of them in Samuel/Kings is neither here nor there, since there is by the same token no reason why the author of Kings should not have as good a motive for leaving them out as the Chronicler had for putting them in. All writing of history is selective, and we have to allow that, having an unknowably great array of material before them (for who are we to say what resources were or were not available in Bible times?), these historians might

[3] Ezk. 18:4, 20.

deliberately exclude much that we would think important, and include and amplify much that we would belittle. And if we were to say to them that in doing so they were misleading their readers as to the true import of history, they would have every right to reply that they were doing just the opposite. After all, is it we or they who can claim without arrogance to be closer to the mind of the God of Israel?

The import of the Samuel/Kings account is that Manasseh's sin will *in the long term* destroy his nation. No subsequent repentance on his part will undo that dreadful achievement, so there is no point in describing such a repentance. The Chronicler does not deny the wickedness of Manasseh. But he is concerned to show its *short-term* effects, because paradoxically they convey the deeper truth. 'There are two or three occasions', says Williamson, 'when either as a loyal vassal or as a discomfited rebel Manasseh may have found himself taken to the Assyrian court',[4] and since the experience was one of such distress that it led to a radical change in his attitude to God, the latter seems more likely. In other words, the Chronicler highlights an incident which for Samuel/Kings, as for other contemporary historians, may not have seemed particularly important, but which illustrates the simple principle that sin leads to punishment. Specifically, *Manasseh's* sin leads to *Manasseh's* punishment. Which is in the last analysis, and in the perspective of eternity, *the* truth about sin; and it leads directly to the necessity for the substitutionary atonement of Christ at Calvary, where 'he himself bore our sins in his body on the tree'.[5]

We ought not on this account to imagine that the Manasseh depicted in Chronicles is meant to be simply another 'awful warning' about the consequences of sin. We may certainly take him in that way, and try to think through what would be the equivalents in our time of those ancient wickednesses. But Manasseh is not a private individual. He is a public figure. If secular history can speak as highly as it does about King Omri of Israel, though the Bible dismisses him in a few verses as a bad man (1 Ki. 16:23–28), Manasseh might be equally admirable in the eyes of the world. There must have been no mean ability in a king who was able to keep his throne longer than any other monarch of his line, and that in such a difficult time as his. It is not simply as a man, but as a

[4] Williamson, p. 393.
[5] 1 Pet. 2:24.

king of Judah, a ruler of Israel, and a son of David, that Scripture judges him.

On the other hand, there are kings and kings, and we have to classify him properly among them. It goes without saying that he is not to be put in the same category as David and Solomon themselves. There is a difference in kind, not simply in degree, between him and them, since, as we have seen, they represent for the Chronicler the twin ideal of pastoral kingship; in this sense they stand apart from even the best of their successors, let alone the worst. Then again, among their descendants Manasseh is obviously not to be ranged with Asa, Jehoshaphat, and the others who tried to live up to the ideal, but with Rehoboam, Ahaz, and the rest of those who rejected it.

But even then there is something unique about Manasseh. Not only is he more than just a bad man, he is more than just a bad king. His particular place in the Chronicler's gallery of instructive portraits is related to the situation in which the Israelite readers of Chronicles lived. Of that we must now remind ourselves. Having hindsight, they knew the calamity with which the reigns of Manasseh and his half-dozen successors would end. The capture and destruction of Jerusalem and the exile of the nation, together with the restoration which was to follow, were the outstanding events of their own recent history. The Chronicler has been at pains to show that the exile was not unprecedented, and should not have been unexpected. He has depicted the reign of Saul, at the very beginning of the story of the monarchy, as an 'exile' experience for the people of God. At that time also, in the eleventh century BC, the Lord and his covenant were rejected, and as a result the fabric of Israelite society began to disintegrate under the onslaught of foreign enemies. Peace and stability were in due course restored through the establishing of God's chosen government, that of David. The whole pattern of events can be seen by the Chronicler's first readers as an analogy of the exile of the sixth century, and of the restoration which has followed, things which are fresh in their minds. But Saul is not the only foreshadowing of the exile, nor David of the restoration. As the end looms in sight, the nation of Ahaz's time also suffers many of the pains of exile – even, for some, actual deportation; while under Hezekiah it is restored and enjoys renewed prosperity. And now the pattern is repeated yet again, in still sharper focus, as Hezekiah is succeeded by Manasseh, and the Chronicler sees within a single reign a picture of both 'the fall and rising of many in Israel'.[6] Manasseh is in this respect both Saul and David; he is both Ahaz and Hezekiah; he represents his whole nation, and what happens to him is a preview of what is to happen to it, both in its exile and in its restoration.

So the two halves of this account, the story of Manasseh's sin, drawn from Samuel/Kings, and the story of his repentance, which for the older historian was irrelevant, are seen to be equally important for the Chronicler. Just as it is not a case of his inventing tales in order to illustrate his point, so neither is it a case of his falsifying history for the same purpose. It is not even a case of his noticing that by a happy accident the actual events of history will serve that purpose. Rather, he is bringing out lessons which these events necessarily teach.

And that is what makes his narrative relevant to readers in every age. The first half of this particular story is a caution. *Whenever* the people of God, and especially their leaders, reject the ways of God as Manasseh did (33:1–9), and most of all when they set the seal on their wickedness by rejecting also his warnings (33:10),[7] they will find themselves in some sense or other taken with hooks, bound with fetters, and brought to Babylon (33:11). That city belonged in the time of Hezekiah and Manasseh to the Assyrian empire,[8] and Manasseh's stay there was no doubt very unlike what his people were to suffer in the following century, when Babylon had superseded Assyria as a world power, and the words 'Babylonian captivity' meant something on a national scale, real, lasting, and catastrophic. But 33:11 has all the right overtones of menace, to make the Chronicler's readers shudder and vow that if they can help it no such disaster shall befall *them*.

The second half of the story is an encouragement. *Whenever* the people of God, and especially their leaders, are moved in a time of distress to humble themselves and turn back to God, as Manasseh did (33:12), they will find that the Lord forgives, restores, and blesses (33:13). For a king of Judah, the signs of that blessing are typically a successful building programme, a sound military organization, and a cleaned-up national religion (33:14–17). Of this kind of restoration – not its details, but its equivalents in their own

[6] Lk. 2:34.

[7] The ultimate in provocation, as we have already seen in the cases of Asa (16:7–10) and Joash (24:19–22), and will see again in the summary of 36:15–16.

[8] As in 32:31, and 2 Ki. 20:12ff.

rather different circumstances – the Chronicler's first readers have had happy experience. They are encouraged to know that the Lord does indeed restore the years that the locust has eaten.[9] The same will be true for every subsequent reader, each in his own situation. He may not be a builder of walls, a commander of armies, a destroyer of idols; but as a humble and obedient servant of God, his witness and work may very well be described as edifying, strong, and holy.

## 3. Amon

In spite of the change in Manasseh's fortunes of which Chronicles tells, the ills of Judah were by this time incurable. The passage we have just been considering represents one remission in the disease, and another would shortly follow, with the reign of Manasseh's grandson Josiah. But the spiritual decline could not now be reversed.

The reforms carried through by Josiah were on any reckoning a notable personal achievement. Neither the Chronicler nor the author of Samuel/Kings will want to deny it. But they have painted two different portraits of Manasseh; and that means that their depictions of his son Amon serve two different purposes. Samuel/Kings simply says that Manasseh was the worst of all the kings of Judah, that his sins sealed the nation's fate, and that his successor repeated those sins. In the older history, therefore, the famous reforming zeal of Josiah is an attempt to put right the evil which has been the chief characteristic of both the preceding reigns. That is, Amon has continued in his father's wicked ways. In Chronicles, however, Manasseh's reign is a mixture of bad and good. We have seen highlighted the reforms which he himself set in train. To present Josiah too as the reformer he undoubtedly was, the Chronicler needs to draw attention to the intervening two years, the reign of Amon, as the time when everything went wrong once more, and when such good as Manasseh might have done was again undone. Here Amon's guilt is contrasted with his father's repentance.

But for both historians the sins of Amon are a pointer towards the ultimate fate of Judah. The sins of Manasseh warned of the flowing of a tide of national retribution, and those of Amon are a confirmation that this is indeed the way the tide is moving. Josiah,

[9] *Cf.* Joel 2:25.

for all his valiant efforts to stem it, will in some respects turn out to be as impotent as King Canute on the sea-shore telling the waves to retreat. His father, and with him the nation, has 'incurred guilt more and more' (33:23), and there can be only one end.

Yet it is as though the Chronicler is using the very wickedness of one generation as a foil to emphasize the penitence of the previous one. Amon 'did not humble himself before the LORD, *as Manasseh his father had humbled himself* (33:23). There is in the experience of the earlier king a pattern of mercy which even the follies of his wretched son cannot obliterate – which indeed they actually stress by contrast, so that the lesson of Amon is that we should learn the lesson of Manasseh. The darkest cloud has a silver lining. Concerning the father, we should say to ourselves, 'This man was of all the sons of David the most resounding failure; but if *even Manasseh* could find a place of repentance, then however I may have failed there is hope for me.'

Two things need to be added to drive the lesson home. First, the Chronicler is speaking to a people, a community. Manasseh is not just the sinning but repentant individual, nor even just the sinning but repentant leader; he represents his nation. While the point of the Samuel/Kings account remains true, that what happened to Manasseh *led to* what later happened to Judah, the Chronicler makes the point that what happened to Manasseh *is* what later happened to Judah. That is why he wants to impress upon us that the story of Amon's father is not about sin alone, but about sin and restoration. It is not only a warning but also a promise. The man, or the leader, *or the community*, which repents will be restored. If the Chronicler's own generation will appreciate what their resettlement of the land means, they will see it as a vastly encouraging sign that their God is one who forgives and renews his penitent people. Behind the justice which sent them into exile is an even greater thing, covenant grace, which brings them back. What Amon would not recognize (33:23), his father in the end had come to know: 'that the LORD was God' (33:13), and that that meant a God whose name of covenant mercy would be a real and living thing 'for ever' (33:4, 7).

This leads to the second and last consideration. For if the God who put Manasseh right is everlastingly that kind of God, this will be his name also in our own Christian times. So indeed we find it to be. Is not this the grand good news which is trumpeted across the divide from Old Testament into New, that '*whoever* calls on the

name of the LORD shall be saved'?[10] And is not this the background
to the first of Paul's 'faithful sayings' in the Pastoral Letters, that
'Christ Jesus came into the world to save sinners'? For, as the apostle
goes on to explain, he was himself 'the worst' of sinners; but, he
says, 'for that very reason I was shown mercy so that in me, the
worst of sinners, Christ Jesus might display his unlimited patience
as an example for those who' in time to come 'would believe on
him'.[11] In other words, if God can save Paul, he can save anyone. If
God can restore Manasseh, he can restore even me.

# 2 Chronicles 34 – 35

## 23.   Josiah: the pastor alone

With the violent death of Amon while still in his twenties, the
crown passed to his son Josiah, at that time a child of eight. As a
shepherd of the people of God this remarkable man will take his
place alongside the other good kings of Judah, and will in the event
turn out to be the last of them.

On the face of it he might seem to be simply one more reformer,
who 'did what was right in the eyes of the LORD' (34:2). In his early
years his love for 'the God of David' resulted in a desire to put things
straight in the faith and practice of his people's religious life
(34:1–7). This led to a thoroughgoing restoration of the temple in
Jerusalem (34:8–13), in the course of which a copy of 'the book of
the law of the LORD' was found. The reading of this moved Josiah to
a fresh zeal to hear and obey what God was saying (34:14–28). He
gathered his people together and with them renewed the covenant
between Israel and the Lord (34:29–33), and celebrated such a
passover as had not been seen 'since the days of Samuel the prophet'

[10] Acts 2:21; cf. Joel 2:32.
[11] 1 Tim. 1:15–16 NIV.

(35:1–19). He died, tragically because unnecessarily, in battle with an Egyptian army on its way to fight a different enemy (35:20–27).

So he does in general follow in the steps of the other good men who have been shepherd-kings before him, though even in this brief outline we notice points which set him apart. A closer consideration of his story, especially when we set the Chronicler's version alongside that of Samuel/Kings, will enable us to see his individual greatness more clearly.

It is true that in the older book his reign is the climax of Judah's history, and he is regarded as the finest of all the kings ('Before him there was no king like him, who turned to the LORD with all his heart and with all his soul and with all his might, according to all the law of Moses; nor did any like him arise after him', 2 Ki. 23:25), whereas in Chronicles a greater importance seems in many ways to be attached to Hezekiah. Yet it is the Chronicler who tells us that Josiah's reforms were even more thorough (34:3–5) and far-reaching (34:6–7) than Hezekiah's (31:1), and who dwells at length on Josiah's grand celebration of the passover, which in this book as in the older one is an even greater occasion than the one in Hezekiah's reign (35:18; *cf.* 2 Ki. 23:22). For the Chronicler, Josiah is a devout spirit who is seeking his God already as a boy of sixteen, and not simply after he rediscovers the 'book of the law' ten years later (34:3, 21); he is a zealous pastor whose religious reforms are first set in motion not by the reading of the book, but by his own wishes six years before that (34:3b, 8ff.).[1]

And in one respect more than any other the Chronicler seems to want us to recognize in Josiah an outstanding shepherd-king of the people of God. As we stand back from the total picture of his reign, we see that of all the figures grouped round him none is really close to him. What we must find increasingly impressive is the isolation of this heroic man. It is this loneliness which becomes a dominant feature of the Chronicler's portrait of him.

---

[1] The commentaries deal with the two histories' different treatments of the chronology of these days. 'There are reasons to think that Chronicles has preserved an account of the matter that conveys more precisely what actually happened. The author of Kings has evidently telescoped and schematized his material because he wants to stress the penitence of Josiah following the reading of the book, and the consequences for his reign. Chr. has wanted to insist that the circumstances of the discovery – or loss – of the book did not materially affect the opportunity for Josiah to act righteously, and has therefore made known the actual chronology of events' (McConville, p. 256). See also D. W. B. Robinson, *Josiah's Reform and the Book of the Law* (Theological Student Fellowship monograph, Tyndale Press, 1951).

## 1. The causes of Josiah's loneliness

The young king carries through the sweeping reforms of chapter 34 in a strangely solitary way. His foes are many, his allies are few. In his endeavours to lead his nation forward in the ways of God, the times are not with him, as we shall see, and the people are not with him either. Even more striking, it seems the prophet is not with him; and that must have been the most painful isolation of all.

### a. The prophet is not with him

But she is, surely? – not a prophet, indeed, but for the first time in the tale of the monarchy a prophetess, Huldah the wife of Shallum (34:22)? God had guided each of the great reforming kings by words of prophecy. In the ninth century, Asa had had the counsel of Azariah (15:1–8), and Jehoshaphat that of no fewer than four other men of God (18:7; 19:2; 20:14, 37). In the eighth century, Uzziah had benefited from the instruction and friendship of Zechariah (26:5), and his great-grandson Hezekiah from those of Isaiah (32:20). Now here, where there is for once a king who actually, unlike most of his predecessors, seeks a word from the Lord without waiting for the word to come and find him, God has his servant ready: Huldah the prophetess.

Still, it remains true that *the prophet* is not with Josiah. For in addition to the fact that Huldah's message speaks only of the rebellious heart of Judah and the humble heart of its king, and ignores the whole subject of Josiah's reforms, the persistent question at the back of our minds must be 'What does *Jeremiah* think?' He, after all, is *the* prophet of the day. The book that bears his name tells us that it was in Josiah's reign that he began his ministry as a prophet (Je. 1:2). To that book we might well turn if we wanted to build up a rounded picture of this king. And the startling fact is that while both Kings and Chronicles present his religious reforms as the outstanding work of his reign, Jeremiah has scarcely more to say about them than Huldah does. He simply describes Josiah, after his death, as having been a just and righteous ruler, whom God blessed, and for whom no tears of regret need be shed.[2]

If Jeremiah hardly mentions the Josiah of Chronicles, the Chronicler returns the compliment, and has practically nothing to say about Jeremiah. He refers to the prophet's words concerning the

---

[2] Je. 22:10a, 15–16.

generations that followed (36:12, 21–22), but with regard to Josiah we are told merely that 'Jeremiah also uttered a lament' after the king's untimely death (35:25).

As the determined young man pressed ahead with his intention 'to purge Judah and Jerusalem' of false religion and to reinstate the historic faith of Israel, it must have been a puzzle and a pain to him that the prophet should be speaking only in condemnation of the people's sins, and not in approval of the king's piety. The reforms were Josiah's way of expressing his undeviating faithfulness to the ways of David, and of doing 'what was right in the eyes of the LORD' (34:2–3); and Jeremiah stood silent, uttering not a word of encouragement. Yet Josiah would not for that reason slacken his efforts. How his stature increases before our eyes! Though unsupported by the one whom later ages will recognize as the greatest prophet of his time, though in that respect he stands alone, he is determined to go ahead with what he knows must be done.

### b.   *The times are not with him*

They were stirring times in which Josiah lived. The Chronicler says little about them, just as he says little about the famous prophet who began his ministry in them. But he does provide at either end of the reign of Josiah unobtrusive pointers to what was happening on the political scene in those days.

Secular history tells us that the Assyrian empire, though larger than ever, was in fact nearing its end. Its very size was its downfall. In trying to quell the increasing number of revolts which began to spring up against its oppressive rule, in the end it would over-extend itself, and collapse before the onslaught of the rebel Babylonians.

We have seen in the Chronicler's account of Manasseh, Josiah's grandfather, an early stage in this process. Both Judah and Babylon are still firmly in the grip of their cruel overlord when the king of Assyria takes Manasseh 'bound ... with fetters of bronze' from one to the other (33:11). But some time after his return Manasseh sets about the rebuilding of the fortifications of Jerusalem (33:14). Is this by permission of the Assyrians, or in defiance of them? Even if it is the former, it points nevertheless to a weakening of their power. So does the mention in the next verse of Manasseh's repudiating of the pagan religion he had previously fostered. Here also there is a question as to what lay behind his earlier turning away from the God of Israel: did he hope to ingratiate himself *with* the enemy, or to find new helps *against* him? But again, in either case Manasseh's subsequent abandonment of the foreign gods shows that Assyria's hold over its subjects is slackening.

That is the picture of Middle Eastern politics before Josiah's accession. After his death, we are in a different world. Of the two sons who succeed him, Jehoahaz is deposed by the king of Egypt, and Jehoiakim by the king of Babylon (36:3, 6). These are now the great powers, and the very name of Assyria has disappeared from the pages of Scripture. Already in the last incident which the Chronicler records of Josiah's life he has touched on this change. An Egyptian army passes by on its way to Carchemish on the Euphrates; it is only because Josiah is determined to intervene that he dies at the hands of the Egyptians in the battle he has himself provoked at Megiddo (35:20ff.). The fact is that at this time Egypt is involved in a power struggle with nations and forces compared with which Judah is insignificant. The Egyptians have long been enemies of Assyria; but now that the latter empire is in decline, and Babylon is threatening to overthrow it and take its place, they change sides and opt for an Assyrian-Egyptian alliance to try to keep Babylonian pretensions within bounds.

In other words the three great powers of the late seventh century are fully occupied with one another's doings, and have little time to spare for the smaller nations of the Middle East. Although Josiah may think it worth while attempting to hinder Egyptian aid from shoring up the crumbling might of Assyria, he has equally been able to concentrate on home affairs without troubling himself too much about what the super-powers may think.

In this lies the difference between his reforms and those of his illustrious great-grandfather. Hezekiah's were carried through under the shadow of the Assyrian menace, Josiah's when the peril had wellnigh disappeared. The earlier king acted in spite of great pressure; by the time of the later one the pressure was off. Josiah was making hay while the sun shone, whereas Hezekiah had had to get in his harvest under a lowering sky. The fair-weather crop was actually, in the event, a less valuable one. The mere fact of being hard pressed does not in itself, of course, guarantee good results. It had the opposite effect with Manasseh. But critical times plus godly leadership produced the great reforms of Hezekiah's reign. It was in that sense that the times were not with Josiah. The godliness was there, but not the crisis. The atmosphere was becoming more relaxed, more optimistic. Perhaps there was even a passive approval of Josiah's aims. But it was shallow; it was too easy. All the more credit then to the godly king who in such times forged ahead with his programme of renewal among a people whose hearts, as Jeremiah clearly saw, had little real love for Josiah's God. For in that respect also (and this we must now consider) Josiah found himself alone.

### c. The people are not with him

We have read, in the Chronicler's account of Josiah's early days, of the uprooting of non-Israelite religion from Judah. It may be that the reforms of 34:3–7 included the abolition of idols and practices imported from Assyria in days when enemy influence was strong – the burning of incense 'to the sun, and the moon, and the constellations, and all the host of the heavens' (2 Ki. 23:5) no doubt comes into that category. Such a policy would have been popular because it would have been seen as a patriotic act. But these words from the Samuel/Kings account are omitted by the Chronicler. He focuses on a much less popular aspect of the king's work, the destruction of the Baal-worship which had been part of the religious scenery of the country for as long as anyone could remember. When so many people hankered after the ancient Canaanite religion, and had in any case often found it hard to see that the faith of the God of Israel was very different from it, it would have been too much to expect the nation as a whole to be enthusiastic about Josiah's doings.

In this we may notice a subtle change in the narrative, when we set him alongside the great reforming leaders of earlier times. The concept of 'all Israel' is, we have often seen, dear to the Chronicler, and it is very evident in those earlier chapters. Jehoshaphat's efforts to bring his people 'back to the LORD, the God of their fathers' are followed by an amazing demonstration, in a time of crisis, of their closing ranks around him in a heartfelt solidarity: 'from all the cities of Judah they came to seek the LORD', 'all ... Judah stood before the LORD', 'all Judah ... fell down ... worshipping the LORD' (19:4; 20:4, 13, 18). When Hezekiah issues a nationwide call to his people to return to the Lord, they are given 'one heart' to obey it, and phrases like 'many people', 'whole assembly', 'great numbers', 'all Israel', colour the entire passage that follows (30:6–31:1).

But when we come to the story of Josiah, the references to God's people are strangely different. 'They broke down the altars of the

Baals in his presence' (34:4); and one wonders whether they would have done it had he not been there to see that it was done, because as the tale proceeds one begins to realize how little they wanted to be involved. Any sense of a corporate unity of purpose is conspicuously missing. What had begun as a personal desire for God – 'while he was yet a boy, he began to seek the God of David his father' (34:3) – never really infected the rest of his people. *He* hewed down the altars, broke up the idols, burned their priests' bones; *he* purged the land and the house; when the book of the law had been found in the temple, it was he who sought help from the prophetess, and he who decided that the covenant must be renewed. *He* convened the great meeting, *he* read the book to the assembled company, and (in a revealing phrase) '*he made* all who were present ... stand to it' (34:4–5, 8, 19ff., 29–30, 32). The Chronicler's wording at the beginning of the chapter ('they broke down the altars ... *in his presence*', 34:4), is paralleled by a similar note at the end: '*All his days* they did not turn away from following the LORD' (34:33).

Through all this I feel an increasing sympathy, and then a growing admiration, for the shepherd-king. He knew the way his flock must go, but the flock had other ideas. It is this that accounts for Jeremiah's coolness towards the religious movement of Josiah's day. The king himself he respects, as we have seen.[3] But his reforms might as well never have happened, for all the notice they receive from the prophet. Is the godless Judah we read about in the early chapters of Jeremiah the same nation that is supposed to have been brought back to God here in 2 Chronicles 34 and 35? I look with new eyes at 34:2: 'He did what was right in the eyes of the LORD, and walked in the ways of David his father; and he did not turn aside to the right or to the left', though he trod that path practically alone. He was a shepherd whose flock never really accepted or understood him, though his concern was for its own welfare, and though that concern was not only sincere and active but also instructed and right. He foreshadows the greatest Shepherd-King of all, who came to his own, and his own received him not, but who nevertheless loved them to the end and completed the work he had come to do for them. And beyond that, he foreshadows also every pastor of the flock of God who, humbly sure of the way he must guide those in his care, finds himself practically alone in wanting to

[3] Je. 22:15f.

go that way, and can therefore look to this last great king of Judah for encouragement.

For there is, after all, encouragement in the story. Josiah's lonely labours did bear fruit.

## 2. The fruits of Josiah's loneliness

Although neither the prophet, nor the times, nor the people, were with him, yet he followed his own vision, and the Chronicler leaves us in no doubt as to where it took him. By it he was led to 'a *book*'; in the book were 'the words of the *law*'; it was 'the words of the *covenant* that were written in this book' (34:18, 19, 31). We have already noted that Samuel/Kings seems to make the discovery of the book of the law the springboard for Josiah's main reforming work, whereas the Chronicler has its finding, and the events that followed, as the climax of a process of reform which had been going on for some time.[4] It is worth noting also, however, that even in the earlier history repairs to the temple are already in progress, actively promoted by Josiah, at the time when the book is found (2 Ki. 22:3ff.). It was a fact, and not a fancy of the Chronicler's, that Josiah's heart was set to seek the Lord well before that memorable day, and the great discovery was the fruit of his devotion as well as the encouragement to further effort.

### a. *The rediscovery of the book*

His desire to do 'what was right in the eyes of the LORD' (34:1), however lonely the quest, led him first to a book. We find chronicled with unusual precision the stages of his spiritual journey. At his accession he was eight years old. In the eighth year of his reign, at the age of sixteen, he began to seek God – a teenage boy, with the cares of a kingdom on his shoulders, newly aware of the responsibilities and possibilities which that brought with it. Might we not in Christian terms call this a conversion experience, an awakening to the real meaning of faith? Then at the age of twenty, in his twelfth year as king, he set in hand the reforming of his country's religion. Perhaps twenty was 'the age of majority ... the earliest practical date'.[5] At twenty-six, in the eighteenth year, he embarked on the temple repairs which were to lead to the finding of the book.

---

[4] See above, p. 265 n. 1.    [5] Williamson, p. 398.

Unlike any of his predecessors, he has left us a kind of personal spiritual diary. His own inner drive to seek and then to follow the God of his fathers, and behind that the grace of God which created that drive in him, brought him to the day of the finding. The book was, in a sense, a reward. As God's blessing on other good kings before him is indicated by successful building projects or by victories in battle, so this is a blessing given to him for his faithfulness.

It is not a reward which is simply to be enjoyed at leisure; rather it calls for yet greater devotion and service. 'You have been faithful with a few things; I will put you in charge of many things.'[6] God's servants do not need to wait for their Master's return to learn that the reward of service is more service. Yet whatever the book actually was (we return to the question in a moment) there would have been more in it for Josiah than rebuke and warning. It did in due course bring joy; the celebrations of chapter 35 sprang from it. The one who when he 'heard the words of the law ... rent his clothes' (34:19) would certainly afterwards have been able to say with the Psalmist, 'I rejoice at thy word like one who finds great spoil'.[7]

And the finding of the book by those who seek the Lord is a repeated experience of God's people in all ages. It may sound naïve to say that what happened to Josiah is paralleled for us by the rediscovery of our own Bibles. Yet the Chronicler, who is forever challenging his readers to look for permanent principles in changing circumstances, would want us to see that what does not change in this case is the principle of an authoritative message from God made available in written form. Kingdom and priesthood, harvests, wars, and buildings, are in our day to be understood in new senses; but the book is still the book, though now much enlarged. Every devoutly-seeking Josiah is still met and rewarded by God in the pages of Scripture.

The double mention of David – 'the ways of David' and 'the God of David' (34:2, 3) – is not accidental. We cannot miss the fact that, in desiring to return to the values upon which the monarchy was founded in the days of David and Solomon, Josiah is led through a series of 'cleansings' to complete them by a restoration of the temple which dated from those times. The book, however, will take him back further than that in the history of his people. He had begun by seeking the God of David his father, but the search led him to 'the

6 Mt. 25:21 NIV.     7 Ps. 119:162.

*book of the law of the* LORD *given through Moses'* (34:14). Behind the king stands the legislator. We come to Jerusalem by way of Sinai. The temple of the Davidic monarchy is built upon the foundation of the Mosaic law.

### b.  The rediscovery of the law

Josiah's quest, then, had led him back to a book, and beyond that to what the book enshrined. It led him back to the law.

It would not be unfair to say that most of the kings of Judah faced their royal responsibilities in a pragmatic frame of mind. If they had any sense of duty at all, they confronted the duties of the day as best they could, and did what seemed right in each particular situation. The better among them were guided by the values they had inherited: Jotham by the principles of his father Uzziah, Uzziah by his father Amaziah's, and so on. Where there were sincerity and a love of God, and where the traditional values had been properly understood, and where the traditions were good ones in the first place, this rule-of-thumb piety would not go far wrong. But as the christianized nations of today's Western world are finding, you cannot go on indefinitely living off the spiritual capital of the past. A legacy is not the same *kind* of money as a salary. Unearned income is somehow a more perilous coinage than that which a man gains by sweat of his brow. Unless each of these rulers of Israel won through to a personal grasp of God's original strategy for his people, he was in danger of reflecting an increasingly distorted vision of that plan as he set about the everyday tactics of government.

The fact that this is a commonplace of Christian history, that again and again God's people (and especially their leaders) have found themselves drawn away from the high road into 'a way … which by degrees turned, and turned them so from the city that they desired to go to, that in little time their faces were turned away from it',[8] should not make us imagine that only past generations in their foolishness might do such things, whereas our own is enlightened and secure. We too tend to live by what we have inherited from yesterday, instead of bringing together the situation of our day and the truth of the Bible's day, the day of the original revelation.

The great kings of Judah's last century were aware of this danger. The kingdom was in such a sorry state when Hezekiah came to the

---

[8] John Bunyan, *The Pilgrim's Progress* (Christian and Hopeful deceived by Flatterer).

throne that he took his people right back to the beginnings of it, to show them what it ought to be. He and they dug down into the past, to the days of David and Solomon, to unearth the roots of the monarchy. There lay the ideal, the original. To the principles there rediscovered Judah must once more be made to conform. Hezekiah went back to the golden age of the monarchy; it was the kingdom that he wanted to renew.

What was for Hezekiah the goal, was for Josiah the starting-point. From the outset he 'walked in the ways of David his father' (34:2). God's design for his people was that Josiah should take them further forward than Hezekiah had, by taking them even further back. The book which was found in the temple of Solomon in the city of David was 'the book of the law of the LORD given through Moses', truth even more fundamental. The Chronicler makes this quite explicit. The crowning event in his account of Josiah is the passover which the king organized, and for it the people were instructed not only to prepare the temple worship 'following the directions of David king of Israel and the directions of Solomon his son' but also to celebrate the passover 'according to the word of the LORD by Moses' (35:4, 6). The great festival of Hezekiah's day, we are told, was a celebration unexampled 'since the time of Solomon the son of David' (30:26); but the entire period of the monarchy had seen nothing like Josiah's – there had been no comparable event 'since the days of Samuel the prophet; none of the kings of Israel had kept such a passover' (35:18).

And there was yet another result of the young king's lonely, determined quest as to how he should rule his people according to the will of God whether they would or no. In the book which gave him God's instructions Josiah had penetrated to something even deeper than the law.

### c. The rediscovery of the covenant

This was what it ultimately meant for Josiah to have gone back beyond David to Moses. What did the revelation of God through Moses show him? That behind the book was the law, and that behind the law was the covenant. Josiah returned to the very wellsprings of his people's existence.

We can see why it was necessary in the end to go further than Hezekiah had gone. It was of the essence of the monarchy established by David and Solomon that it should be geographical

274

and political, that it should have an actual city for its kings and a physical temple for its priests. Not only in New Testament days, but already among the Old Testament prophets and indeed by Solomon himself, was it recognized that God was not tied to particular buildings, and that he neither needed them nor could be confined within them.[9] But thoughtless people might easily 'trust in these deceptive words' (Jeremiah says they were doing just that, at this very time in Judah's history): 'This is the temple of the LORD, the temple of the LORD, the temple of the LORD.'[10] God told David and Solomon, such people might say, that this would be his city and his house for ever, it can never be destroyed, and as long as we are here we shall be safe; we need not trouble ourselves with disturbing thoughts about personal faith and obedience, since we belong to the indestructible church.

That was the danger of going back only to the beginning of the monarchy. The promise made to David and Solomon might well become the grounds for false hope. So Josiah was moved to go back to the days of Moses, and to the law, which is a ground for hope only so long as a man thinks he can keep it, but which becomes a quagmire of despair when he realizes how total and therefore how impossible are its demands. In theory, the keeping of the law is, as Moses says and as Paul agrees, the way to life; in practice, 'when the commandment came, sin revived and I died; the very commandment which promised life proved to be death to me'.[11]

But behind the law is the covenant. God sets these commandments before his people precisely because they *are* his people. He has already made them so. His gracious act in calling them out of Egypt precedes the revelation of his law for them at Sinai. Bible history presents a series of such covenants, in which he sets forth the basis of his dealings with mankind. He makes one with Abraham, he makes one with Moses, he makes one with David, and so on. Each represents a new stage in history, and each has its own distinctive terms; but all are manifestations of the basic covenant, which at bottom is not conditional on man's obedience or disobedience but rests on the unconditional grace of God. It is true that it often says, in effect, If you disobey me I will *punish* you; but God will never *reject* 'his people whom he foreknew', for 'the gifts and the call of

<hr />

[9] Acts 7:47–50; Is. 66:1f.; 2 Ch. 6:18.
[10] Je. 7:4.
[11] Rom. 7:9–10. *Cf.* Lv. 18:5; Rom. 10:5.

God are irrevocable'.[12] So Josiah demands, in 34:29–33, that Israel respond in obedience to the rediscovered covenant. That is what they are to do for God, what they owe to him. But they do *owe* it, as is made clear by the events that follow, in 35:1–19; for the passover is the great reminder of what God first did for them.

The Chronicler, as I have tried to show throughout this book, has been using the whole of Old Testament history as a text for a sermon, but has been very selective in his use of it. We may presume that the points he wants to make are sufficiently made by the material he has included, and we do not actually need to look elsewhere in the Old Testament in order to hear what he has to say. All the same, it is worth pondering the fact that the greatest prophet of these closing years of the monarchy, whom as we have seen the Chronicler scarcely mentions, is the one who speaks most of the covenant, and looks forward to the renewal of it. It will still be a matter of man believing and obeying, Jeremiah tells us; it will still be a matter, before that, of God calling and saving; but the new thing will be the radical change of heart which makes man truly able to respond.[13]

There is another characteristic of the way the Chronicler uses history in his preaching. Though he attaches great importance to facts, he (like the Bible writers in general) is much less concerned about chronologies and dates. For that reason one final observation on Josiah and the covenant would doubtless seem to him nothing more than a curiosity. Indeed the debate as to whether the exodus took place in the fifteenth or thirteenth centuries BC ('Whatever does *that* have to do with it?' I hear you ask!) may make the suggestion invalid in any case. If however the generally accepted view is correct, that Israel came out of Egypt in the later of those two periods (say, round about 1280 BC), it gives us a perspective on history which with regard to Josiah may capture the modern imagination. For the last great king of Judah, coming to the throne in 641 BC, stands at the midpoint in time between the covenant of Sinai and that of Calvary. From the last mountain-top of the monarchy he looks back across six centuries to Moses, determined to revive in his own day the old covenant which had failed so often before, and would fail again. For that law had 'but a shadow of the good things to come', and could never 'make perfect those who draw near'.[14] But from the

[12] Rom. 11:2, 29.    [13] Je. 31:31–34.
[14] Heb. 10:1.

276

same point the prophet Jeremiah looks forward, also across six centuries, to Christ the 'mediator of a new covenant' who 'by a single offering ... has perfected for all time those who are sanctified'.[15]

Seen in this light, it is poignant but appropriate that Josiah should be such a lonely figure, trying to lead back to God a people who did not want to be led. For the very weakness of the old covenant was that it could not *make* people good, whereas that was the very strength of the new one foreseen by Jeremiah.

'After all this' came the ill-advised decision to interfere in the power-struggle which was taking an Egyptian army past Judah to Carchemish on the Euphrates (35:20ff.). 'Cease opposing God, who is with me,' said the Egyptian king. Josiah might have been forgiven for discounting such words from the mouth of a pagan; but the Chronicler tells us that 'the words of Neco' really were 'from the mouth of God', and Josiah, going out to battle regardless, met an untimely end at Megiddo. Three sons and a grandson followed him on the throne of Judah, every one of them an unworthy pastor of the flock of God. With this determined, solitary man there perished the last of the true shepherd-kings of Israel, until the day when the great Shepherd should come, whose voice, though despised and rejected by many, his own sheep would heed and follow.

There is of course always a remnant, always a 'little flock'.[16] The role of the shepherd-king is meaningless without it. Josiah was never really alone; nor is any pastor; and all that has been taught in these chapters concerning leadership takes for granted a believing, obedient community, however small, and assumes the corporate nature of the church. But having said that, as I read for myself the story of Josiah I see that what matters in the last analysis for *me*, the shepherd of a flock, is to be what the chief Shepherd wants me to be. Whether or not anyone else is with me, I must base my service for him squarely on the covenant mercies of a loving and righteous God. My responsibility is to the flock. But first it is to him.

[15] Heb. 9:15; 10:14.
[16] Lk. 12:32.

# 2 Chronicles 36

## 24.   The last kings: war and peace

The story of Old Testament Israel, as the Chronicler casts it in
sermon form, ends with warfare and ruin. On the international
scene, the collapse of Assyria left first Egypt and then Babylon in
control of the lesser nations of the Middle East. The armies of the
one swept through Judah after the death of Josiah, those of the other
came in their wake only a few years later. In 609 BC Josiah's third
son, Jehoahaz, had been chosen as his successor, but had reigned
only three months before Neco of Egypt deposed him and set his
elder brother Jehoiakim on the throne instead. The latter had to
accept a new overlord when Nebuchadnezzar of Babylon defeated
Neco in 605, and when he finally rebelled he too was crushed, in
598, by a foreign war-machine. The hundred days for which his son
Jehoiachin ruled in Jerusalem were the hundred days for which it
was besieged by the Babylonians. The young king went into exile,
and Nebuchadnezzar set on the throne in his place his uncle, another
of Josiah's sons, with the official name of Zedekiah.[1] 'He also
rebelled against King Nebuchadnezzar' (36:13), and for the last
time the tide of war rolled across the land of Judah, burst against the
walls of Jerusalem, and in 587, after that final siege, overwhelmed
the city. Temple and palace, altar and throne, priesthood and
monarchy alike went down with it.

The twenty-three years covered by these four reigns, from the
death of Josiah to the sacking of Jerusalem, form one of the most
significant periods of warfare in Bible history. It was *total* war: the
attackers 'had no compassion on young man or virgin, old man or
aged', and all who were not slaughtered were exiled (36:17, 20).
Samuel/Kings tells us that 'some of the poorest of the land' were left,
but in practical terms the country was depopulated, and that is the

---

[1] All four kings have other names besides those chronicled here. Josiah's sons in order of age
(though the records are confusing) appear to have been Johanan, Eliakim, Shallum, and
Mattaniah; the third became king as Jehoahaz, then the second as Jehoiakim, then (after the
brief reign of Jehoiakim's son Jehoiachin, also called Jeconiah or Coniah) the fourth, as
Zedekiah. See 1 Ch. 3:15–16 and 2 Ki. 24:17, as well as the present passage.

picture the Chronicler wants to give us. This was the kind of warfare which we might call indiscriminate, except that the God who brought it about has long since been established as the God who will not destroy even the wickedest of cities while ten righteous men remain in it, who indeed *cannot* destroy it so long as it contains even one man whom he wishes to save; for he is the Judge of all the earth, and cannot do what is unjust.[2] Not indiscriminate warfare, then; but certainly total.

I have said that God brought it about, for that also is part of the Chronicler's picture. This is *holy* war. It is the Lord's messengers who have been mocked by his people, it is the Lord's anger which therefore rises against them, and it is at the Lord's instigation that the enemy comes to punish them (36:15–17). 'The LORD is a man of war',[3] not in the sense in which many in the history of Christendom have misused his name, claiming that he was for them in their bloody enterprises, but in the sense that those who think themselves to be his people find that he is actually fighting against them when they despise his way of righteousness.

Thirdly, it is the *last* war. When in our own century World War II began, to call the conflict of 1914–1918 'the Last War' could mean that it was the latest, the most recent previous one. But before 1939 there had been a more optimistic meaning to the phrase. People had called it 'the Last War' because they hoped it would be the final one, the war to end wars. That is the Chronicler's intention here. Beyond the horror there is hope. This, though the worst, is also to be the last war of the whole period of the monarchy; after it God's people enter a new age.

This is how we are to read the story of the closing quarter-century of Israel's existence as a kingdom. In particular, its character at a time of holy warfare reminds us to ask at every point what the intentions of God are. If we find moral difficulties in the picture of the Lord as a warrior, that is a separate issue, and so far as this study is concerned we must set it aside. It does after all recur in many other parts of Scripture. We are concerned here not with the morality of the method but with the purpose of the action. What is he intending to do through the events of these final war-torn years of the history of the monarchy?

---

[2] So the story of Lot in Sodom; Gn. 18:25, 32; 19:22.
[3] Ex. 15:3.

## 1. The dismantling of the system

In very many chapters we have noticed the Chronicler's fascination with the temple and its worship. It is not surprising that although for every reign of this period he shortens the Samuel/Kings account considerably,[4] he still makes a point of telling us what in each reign was happening to the temple. There is a veiled hint in 36:3; to meet the heavy financial demands made on him by Neco of Egypt, Jehoahaz must have drawn on its treasures. In the reign of Jehoiakim, 'Nebuchadnezzar also carried part of the vessels of the house of the LORD to Babylon' (36:7). With Jehoiachin, himself taken to Babylon, went 'the precious vessels of the house of the LORD' (36:10), and when the fall of Zedekiah ended the era, 'all the vessels of the house of God, great and small, and the treasures of the house of the LORD' were carried away, and the temple itself was burned down (36:18–19).

Alongside that concern of the ·Chronicler's goes his parallel interest in the kingship. Throne and altar have been so clearly the twin centres of Israel's life that it would be strange not to find them linked here also. The events of more than two chapters at the end of 2 Kings are condensed into a narrative hardly more than one-third of the length of the original. With much of the surrounding incident discarded, the royal line figures all the more prominently; the history has been streamlined into a breathless sequence of the rise and fall of kings. Not, curiously, 'sad stories of the *death* of kings';[5] although Samuel/Kings tells us that two of the four did die within our period, the Chronicler mentions no royal death later than that of Josiah, as if for him each of these four portraits simply fades out as the next picture appears on the screen. So wagonload by wagonload the spoils of the temple disappear from Jerusalem, and so son by son the family of Josiah is toppled from the throne.

Now it has been the Chronicler's central message that kingship and priesthood together form the core of the life of God's people. Without the proper representation of God to man and of man to God, it simply cannot exist. This necessary pattern underlies the whole of history, but it is seen at its clearest in the days of the monarchy of ancient Israel, the days the Chronicler describes, where it is embodied in an actual nation with religious and political

[4] See 2 Ki. 23:31 – 25:21. Jehoahaz's 5 verses become 4; Jehoiakim's 9, 4; Jehoiachin's 10, 2; Zedekiah's 24, 11.

[5] Shakespeare, *Richard II*, III.ii.156.

institutions of a particular type. We should try to visualize the buildings of old Jerusalem, and to picture there in our mind's eye the succession of kings and priests, the two great families of David and Aaron; for in them God has set up what is in effect a huge and complex visual aid, an entire educational system to help us grasp this vital truth and its immense range of implications.

But by 600 BC the system has served its turn. God sets about dismantling it, and the armies of Egypt and Babylon are his tools. 'The treasures of the house of the LORD, and the treasures of the king and of his princes' (36:18) are taken away; temple and palace alike are burned to the ground. Put away your lesson books, and let me see what you have learnt.

## 2. The deposing of the leaders

There is however more to the wars by which the monarchy is dismantled than the mere demolition of a structure. We must look more closely at the key component in it, the twin leadership just referred to. At whatever page the annals of Israel might fall open before us, we should find two men standing side by side at the heart of the nation's life, one from the tribe of Judah and the other from the tribe of Levi. The list of 'the descendants of Solomon' (1 Ch. 3:10ff.) and that of 'the sons of Aaron' (1 Ch. 6:3ff.) run parallel through the length of the history of the monarchy. There are few points at which we can link the one to the other with certainty, but we do know that at almost any given point in those four hundred years a representative of each, a king and a high priest, would have been presiding over the welfare of God's people. Every king and every priest was a flesh-and-blood person, a responsible individual. God's way of setting up a right relationship between himself and his people, in both directions, was at any one time literally embodied in two human beings. Law guided the priest in his Godward ministry, and prophets guided the king in his manward ministry, but each was during his own tenure of office the incarnation of one principle or the other.

What then in the last wars of Israel is God doing in this respect? We are looking now not at the broad general picture, but at these two figures at the centre of it. As the Chronicler brings his readers inexorably towards 587 BC, the year of catastrophe, what is he telling us about the kingship, and what about the priesthood?

Unlike the priests, the last of the kings are named, as their forefathers have been. Each in turn represents God to man, and however badly he does it he is still the one person of his time who is made in a special sense in the image of God, invested with the dignity of royalty, to be named and known and respected. But with the sons of Josiah something is missing. The Chronicler has noted the death of every one of their predecessors; it is as if he has wanted to point out the almost unbroken succession from David to Josiah – 'the king is dead, long live the king'. But these four, each in turn, simply disappear from the scene. One by one the last four lamps of kingship fade into darkness.

On the other hand, the last of the priests, like most of their predecessors, are not named. Their ministry has been to represent man to God, as each of them in turn, wearing the breastpiece of twelve precious stones, one for each of the twelve tribes, has carried 'the name of the sons of Israel ... upon his heart ... into the holy place'.[6] In that sense their personal identity is not important. Accordingly, the end of the priesthood is described by the Chronicler in terms of the spoiling of the temple, which we have already noted.

So what happens in 587 to the kingship and the priesthood? It would be tempting to apply to the former (and one might make a parallel judgment on the latter) the lines of James Shirley:

> The glories of our blood and state
> Are shadows, not substantial things;
> There is no armour against Fate;
> Death lays his icy hand on kings:
> Sceptre and crown
> Must tumble down,
> And in the dust be equal made
> With the poor crooked scythe and spade.[7]

But that is almost the opposite of what the Chronicler is saying. It is not that royalty (or priesthood) is a matter of outward trappings, which collapse at the touch of death leaving only the common dust of humanity. It is rather that kingship (like priesthood) is the reality which persists, even when the flesh which has temporarily embodied it lives no more.

[6] Ex. 28:29.
[7] James Shirley, *The Contention of Ajax and Ulysses.*

What happens to these realities after the downfall of Judah may seem to be a temporary eclipse and then after a lapse of time a reappearance. Five hundred years after Zedekiah an Israelite once more took the title of king,[8] and the priesthood was revived a great deal sooner than that, and in a much more genuine form. In the Jerusalem of the time of Jesus we find a fully operational temple and palace. But we must distinguish the senses in which Herod and Caiaphas are, and are not, embodiments of the ideal. Of course such men as these are not true representatives of God to men or of men to God. Yet kingship and priesthood cannot simply be ideals; the very words imply that they are meant to be incarnated, that one is the quality of being a king and the other that of being a priest, and they can only really be grasped and experienced when a living person fulfils them in the flesh.

The double sequence of leaders in Israel was brought to an end, not because the ideal could not be expressed in human form, but because in that age and in those circumstances the incarnation of it had gone as far as it could go. But the Chronicler would have us look forward to something better than a mere concept. He would echo the words of the Psalmist, and say that with the passing of the last king and the last priest of the days of the old Israelite monarchy, he expects God to anoint in due course a king who will live throughout all generations, and one who will be a priest for ever.[9]

## 3. The punishing of the rebels

Again we must remind ourselves that God's intention in subjecting his people to these final years of war was more than the calm, dispassionate removal of last term's teaching materials. The appearance in it of a procession of flesh-and-blood men, the kings and the priests, points us towards a development of the same thought: all the people involved in these events, and not just the leaders, were real, responsible, human beings. True, the whole grand structure had served an educational purpose. It illustrated a series of principles. But the drama which set forth those principles was not played out by a company of puppets. It employed living actors, a whole nation of them, every one not only playing a part but

---

[8] Aristobulus I, first of the Hasmonean kings. His family, that of the Maccabees, was a priestly one, and for a while Israel was ruled by men who were both kings and priests.

[9] Ps. 72:5; 110:4.

also living a life, not only representative but also real. As time went on more and more of them showed themselves to be actually, personally, rebels against the rule of God. The last eleven years of the monarchy exhibit both a king who 'did what was evil in the sight of the LORD his God', and 'all the leading priests and the people likewise ... exceedingly unfaithful' (36:12, 14).

In brief, the system had served its turn, and was now being dismantled; the leaders had embodied, with a sufficient variety of success or failure, its central principles, and were now being deposed; and the entire rebellious nation had mocked, despised, and scoffed at the compassionate word of God, 'till there was no remedy', and it had to be punished (36:15–16).

We may recall once more one of the chief differences between the writers of Samuel/Kings and Chronicles. They seem to find in history two different ways in which God's retribution for sin works. Samuel/Kings repeatedly says that the fate of Judah had been sealed practically a century before it finally fell upon the nation. Manasseh's sins had made it inevitable, Josiah's reforms had been unable to avert it, Jehoiakim's folly had simply sprung the first of a series of traps set long before (2 Ki. 21:10–15; 23:24–27; 24:1–4). The Chronicler, on the other hand, has in mind particularly the evils of Zedekiah's reign, in 36:11–16, when he says that Judah had so incurred God's anger that '*therefore* he brought up against them the king of the Chaldeans' in the final catastrophe which destroyed the monarchy (36:17).

The fact is that both doctrines of retribution are true. There are, as Samuel/Kings says, consequences of sin which affect later generations. That has been known at least since the ancient revelation to Moses of a God who visits 'the iniquity of the fathers upon the children and the children's children'.[10] There are also consequences for the sinner himself, as God says perhaps most clearly through his prophet at the other end of Old Testament history: 'The soul that sins shall die'.[11] Throughout his sermon the Chronicler has been selecting from the vast storehouse of Israel's history such material as will bring out basic spiritual principles. Of these two principles he chooses to illustrate the latter, for it is in a very real sense the more profound of the two. My sin will certainly affect others; but in the last analysis I must be made to understand that it will affect *me*. Of course the Chronicler is perfectly aware of

[10] Ex. 34:7.   [11] Ezk. 18:4, 20.

the complexity of life. He knows that there were many factors, long intertwining sequences of them, many rooted in the distant past, which finally led to the destruction of Judah at the hands of the king of Babylon and his Chaldean armies. It remains true, all the same, that if *I* sin, *I* shall suffer. In the final wars by which the Lord allows his land to be devastated he is directly punishing the rebels who at that time live in it.

But he has one more object in view beyond all those we have so far seen.

## 4. The establishing of the peace

The end, when it does come, is described in an oddly unemotional way. We might have expected a writer who has shown such enthusiasm for the temple and its services, and for the royal line of David, in their heyday, to be correspondingly distressed at their downfall. Instead, apart from his forthright condemnation of the sins which led to it, he speaks of the exile in tones which are quite matter-of-fact, and even optimistic. The wars in which the house of Josiah fell in ruin were a clearing of the ground for the building of a new peace. Of course the Chronicler has reason to speak optimistically, for both he and his first readers know (being themselves a part of it) that there was going to be a restored community. At the same time he wants the renewed life of Israel to be a greater thing than what he and they are experiencing in their own time; otherwise why is he bothering to preach his sermon at all? The specific *aim* of the sermon – the particular results he would like to see flowing from it – is another question. I do not think he is hoping simply for increasing commitment to the worship of the rebuilt temple, or even an increasing commitment to the Lord. I certainly do not think he is hoping for a restoration of the monarchy in the old style. There is nevertheless in his closing verses a note of hope and encouragement for the future, which seems to be saying rather more than merely 'It was worth picking up the pieces and cobbling together some sort of new life'. There are elements in the life of God's people which persist through the disaster of 587 BC, and they are not to be regarded merely as oddments salvaged from the wreck. Rather, they are the keel and the ribs of the vessel, which the storm has stripped of much that once seemed an integral part of it, but which are themselves found still to be intact, a perfectly sound basis for a rebuilding. To return to a word which we used in chapter 9 to express one of the Chronicler's chief ideas, they are the great *continuities*.

There are three of them.

'Those who had escaped from the sword', the remnant of Israel, 'became servants' to the kings of Babylon 'until the establishment of the kingdom of Persia' (36:20). Their enslavement would last only for a limited time, and when the empire of Babylon fell before that of Medo-Persia *God's people* would still be there. The Chronicler's readers may look up from his book, look around at one another, and verify for themselves this first great continuity. They themselves are still, through such earth-shaking changes, the continuing people of God. Though the old-style kingdom and priesthood have vanished, they are being taught by the Chronicler the inner principles which David's throne and Solomon's temple stood for. They know that where the God-to-man and man-to-God relationships are right, there the true Israel will always be, from now till the end of time.

Secondly, *God's word* survives the catastrophe as strong and as true as ever. Not only does it emerge unscathed, it is actually validated and fulfilled by these terrible events (36:21). 'The word of the LORD by the mouth of Jeremiah' may refer to 36:20 (the people enslaved) or to 36:21b (the land left desolate).[12] In either case the point is that nothing of what has happened is outside the plan of God. Indeed, none of it is outside his *declared* plan. He has said, and we have the declarations in Scripture, that all these things are under his control. His word continues to be heard, and continues to prove itself true. It is being heard again by the Chronicler's first readers. It is being heard still by us. The living, daily-fulfilled word of God is the next of the great continuities.

The third is *God's land*. For the years of the exile it 'lay desolate' (36:21). From one point of view this was a dreadful thing; Jeremiah describes the faithlessness of the Lord's people as 'making their land a horror, a thing to be hissed at for ever. Every one who passes by it is horrified and shakes his head.'[13] But from another point of view the desolation was a positive blessing given by God. The principle of the sabbath, of which this verse speaks, meant to Old Testament Israel not simply that the people should rest for one day in every seven, but that the land too should rest – that is, lie fallow – for one

---

[12] The references in Jeremiah are 25:11; 27:7; 29:10.
[13] Je. 18:16.

year in every seven.[14] For as long as that ancient law, like so many others, had been flouted, the land had not 'enjoyed its sabbaths'. By the desolation of the exile it would be possible 'to fulfil seventy years' of sabbath rest, and to catch up on all the time during which the law of the sabbath year had been ignored. (The Chronicler seems to have in mind the whole length of the monarchy.)[15]

On this note the magisterial sermon comes to a close, for 36:22–23 are a borrowing of the first verses of the book of Ezra, added by the Chronicler or by a later writer to link these events with those that followed. Why the strangely muted ending of 36:21? Neither triumph nor disaster; neither blaze of glory nor smoking ruin; nothing about kings or priests, temples or palaces; nothing about politics – nothing, even, about people; only quiet fields and hills silently renewing their strength for the start of the next great 'working week'.

And here we find in a very real sense the last and greatest of the continuities. Every twentieth-century visitor to the Holy Land must find this the most astonishing of his reflections: that *this is where it all happened.* Landmarks and levels may not be the same, and it may be hard to visualize the events of Bible times where later centuries have added and altered so much. But the land is the land. We who can tread its paths today belong to the same continuum as 'the people in the story'. They do not inhabit some fictional never-never land, nor is there any divide, requiring a leap of faith, between the world of Fact which is ours and the supposed world of Truth which is theirs. God was active then in a history which is part and parcel of our history, in a geography which is continuous with our geography. 'Only connect!' Everything connects. Never imagine, says the Chronicler, that the men of the Bible lived in a world disconnected from ours. They were real people in whom the same God was at work in the same ways as he is today. There is one church, one faith, one Lord. Allow for the differences of language and culture, allow for the fulfilment in Christ of the promises of priesthood and kingship, allow for the completing of God's

[14] Lv. 25:1–7.

[15] 420 years of the kings + 70 years of exile (when the land had a rest from the kings!) = 490 years, 'which may be a round figure, or may correspond exactly to the time from Saul's accession – whose precise date is unknown – to the restoration ... The seventy years can be reckoned either from the date of Babylonian ascendancy in Palestine, c. 605 BC, to the release from exile, 537 BC – which is approximate, or from the final sack of Jerusalem, 586 BC, to the dedication of the new Temple, 516 BC, which is exact' (McConville, p. 270).

revelation in Scripture; but the principles have never changed. To know the Chronicler's God is to know the God of all history, who lives and loves today as he always has done, and will do for ever.